Bill and Ju... It is a plea... to have shared p... of our journey throu... Warmest regards, Doug

my life
in stories

Putting Foliage on the Family Tree

Douglas Minge Brown

Printed and bound in Canada

ArtBookbindery.com
Empowering Writers to Self-Publish™

ISBN 978-0-615-23646-9

To Sarah

*My story and my life
begin with you*

Contents

Preface	7
Ken	11
Siblings	21
Mom	27
Dad	35
Gillinghams	45
More Dad	47
My Childhood	59
High School	65
Stanford	73
The Army	81
Business School	85
Judy	89
Wells Fargo	101
Pasadena	111
Women	119
Sarah	121
Los Angeles Friends	125
Sarah's Family	129
Grandparents	143
Together	155
Corporate Development	163
WellService	171
Staff Services	177
Hillsborough	181
Hillsborough Friends	189
San Francisco Main	193
Marketing	201
Quito or Bust	207
WESTNET	213
Crocker	215
Albuquerque	225
Witch Hunt	233

More Albuquerque   239
Talbot   247
The Boys   253
Pets   267
Houses   271
Health   275
Tuition Plan   283
Politics   287
SeniorDiscounts.com   293
Volunteering   295
Parenting   313
New Mexico Friends   315
Sarah's Surprises   321
Party Time   327
Traditions   341
Corruption   345
The Press   349
New York   351
Corporate Board Service   357
Dribs And Drabs   359
Epilogue   361

Preface

For thirty years I have been accumulating notes on various family stories and incidents in the hope that I would someday find time to assemble them into a narrative. Last year's "sabbatical" in Manhattan provided the perfect opportunity.

My intent is to provide a legacy to family and friends, strengthened by a desire to avoid the vacuum of information from my parents' childhoods. Tragedy so dominated Dad's boyhood that he never once spoke of his father. Mom's youth came during the twilight of the Victorian era when information was heavily filtered and frequently re-constituted. These perspectives were among the unexpected revelations from writing this book.

Upon hearing that I was compiling a memoir of family stories, my former classmate Fred Rehmus immediately asked, "Are you including the negatives?" I answered "Yes," as I had concluded that it just wouldn't be real without doing so. How would the kids and others understand how our family developed if I chose to skirt topics such as the alcohol problem of a family member or a business failure of mine? I plead guilty to the tendency to go easy on the subjects of this piece, as they are not in a position to defend themselves, and I accept the risk of disappointing any family or friends who feel treated unfairly. Also, please forgive me if I occasionally mount the soapbox to deliver a rant on some heartfelt topic.

The text that follows is not strictly chronological, and there are just enough dates and genealogy to give context. For the most part, it is a series of stories to "put foliage on the family tree."

Caltech physicist Richard Feynman lamented that scholars frequently claim knowledge when they merely know the name of something. He commented that it is only a beginning to know that a bird is a type of warbler. One does not have useful knowledge of the warbler until one knows its song, what it eats, its nesting and migration habits, and family patterns. It is my hope that these family stories contribute "useful knowledge," dimension and flavor to your understanding of our family.

But for the invaluable assistance of Diane Callahan, these stories would still be locked in my memory. Her competence, encouragement and good cheer are woven into the fabric of this book. Special thanks go also to "editor-in-chief," Elliott Brown.

Compiling these stories has been a source of pleasure for me. A Chinese proverb holds that the reward for a life well-lived is that it can be relived in one's memory in later years.

Mother and Ken – 1936

Ken and Doug – 1938

Ken

All my earliest recollections involved brother Ken. He was just under two years older than I, and it was almost eight years before my younger brother arrived. It was always Mom and Dad in the front seat; Ken and Doug in the rear. We got in trouble together, got sick together, and shared every childhood experience. Our home was somewhat isolated at the end of a long cul-de-sac, and neither of us had classmates who lived within a half-mile. For much of this eight-year period, Dad was away in the Navy which drew Ken and me even closer as we teamed to help Mom.

Ken was born on February 23, 1936 at Peralta Hospital in Oakland, the hospital for Mom's family doctor, Dr. Willis. Ken was the first in our family's history to have been born in a hospital. Ken came home to 701 Harvard Avenue in Menlo Park. It was a two-bedroom rental ($40/month) just a few blocks from the train station, and it remained the family home for the first four years of our parents' marriage. In 1939, our family moved to Hillsborough to shorten Dad's commute to San Francisco and to provide more room for a growing family.

The Menlo Park home was the scene of a memorable incident. One Saturday afternoon, Dad was engaged in a good book, but Mom wanted to talk. Dad put down his book for a bit, then tried to resume his reading. Apparently, Mom was relentless. To escape, Dad finally repaired to a small attic room. Sure enough, shortly thereafter followed the unmistakable patter of feminine feet. Upon her arrival, Dad bolted down the stairs and locked her in the attic. Dad then was able to enjoy his book in glorious solitude.

After a time, Dad concluded that perhaps she had "had enough" and unlocked the attic door. Mom emerged in stony silence. Convinced that he had made his point, Dad once again resumed his reading. Then, he thought he heard something. He turned to see Mom with a wicked expression, approaching slowly with a large tub of water. Dad leaped from his chair and shot out the front door, followed by a cascade. Just then, they saw a prominent local judge and his wife coming up the walk to pay an unannounced social visit. The horrified couple turned and drove off, deaf to Dad's explanation that they were just engaged in playful pranks and not an angry marital spat.

Ken's intellectual gifts quickly became apparent. He began reading at a very early age, and I can recall his devouring books, several per week, when he was only five. Math was an equal passion, which later translated into great skill at bridge, chess, and code-breaking. At the age of eight, Ken broke the challenging "Code of the Dancing Men" from A. Conan Doyle's Sherlock Holmes story.

About age four, our parents noticed that Ken was limping. When our pediatrician, Dr. Ray, thought to measure his legs, he discovered that one had grown longer than the other. Specialists at Shriner's Children's Hospital found that one leg had stopped growing due to Perthes Hip Disease. After an operation by Dr. Booth to scrape off diseased tissue, Ken's good leg's growth was arrested by a brace for a year to allow for the repaired leg to catch up. Then he wore a cumbersome full leg cast for another year.

With Ken immobilized, his darling younger brother decided to take target practice. My parents were aghast to see me launching toys out of my crib in the direction of my defenseless brother. Dad decided to have some fun with me. He tied strings to my toys, tethering them to the crib. He then watched in delight from around the corner my surprise at seeing the toys boomerang back at me.

Ken was a handsome youngster with curly dark hair, and he closely resembled my father. This resemblance plus his great intelligence may have created high expectations that contributed to his later difficulty in following through on tasks.

Ken and I became inseparable. We called ourselves "portable best friends." Most kids like their own bedrooms, but Ken and I enjoyed each other's company so much that we successfully petitioned our parents to room together. My fondest remembrances with Ken were playing in the woods near our home, making trails and building forts. After the winter rains softened the meadows, we would pull up grass with clumps of dirt attached for great grass ball fights with the neighborhood kids, Dave Wisnom, Mike Jones, Bill Seawell, and Freddy Wurlitzer.

Freddy Wurlitzer was bright and energetic. He was also rather spoiled by his mother and much older sisters. Sharing and generosity were not the norm for Freddy. Given this tendency, you can imagine our surprise at his response one day when Ken and I shouted to him at his second story window for him to come out and play. He said he couldn't because he had a cold, but we could visit him if we'd like. He then held a box of chocolates out the window and said we could help him eat them. Puzzled by this uncharacteristic offer, we ran up the stairs to check it out. Freddy then repeated the offer and eagerly held out the large box of chocolates to us. Cautiously, Ken and I opened it, and indeed there was a sea of tempting treats before us. Only they were all glistening. Sick Freddy had licked them all. As I turned away repulsed, my clever brother asked, "Are you sure we can take as many as we would like?" Confident that we would be deterred by the specter of germs, Freddy said, "Sure." Thereupon, Ken lifted off the top layer to reveal an untouched array below. Freddy's howls of protest attracted his mother. Dismayed to learn of Freddy's deceit, she let us march off with our spoils. Perhaps as penance for this act, Frederick P. Wurlitzer, M.D. went on to a distinguished career as a cancer specialist and then spent many years doing voluntary medical missionary work in West Africa.

There were lots of lessons outside the classroom. With an older brother and other older boys in the area, I grew up fairly fast. One day, though, I almost stopped growing up. We had Flexy Flyers that we loved to ride down the steep hills of Hillsborough. Lying just inches off the ground, 20 miles per hour felt like 200. A favorite venue was our steep driveway. We would barrel down, slam onto the level road below, then go airborne over the down slope on the other side. Our landing strip was the soft dirt of the firebreak. Because the driveway was blind to the road, passing cars were a major hazard, and we depended on a scout below to give us the all-clear on traffic. As I waited at the top, the all-clear signal seemed a very long time in coming. What made it especially strange was that I heard no cars go by. Finally, I was cleared to go and let it rip. As my Flyer leapt into the air below the road, I came to realize the reason for the delay. Ken and Dave Wisnom had dragged some gnarly logs to the landing space. Suspended in air, I felt like Wile E. Coyote trying madly to tread in place before plunging down. Fortunately, I was able to bail out into the soft dirt before crash-down, and I got hero points from my brother and his perfidious peer.

Next door neighbor Dave Wisnom was a couple of years older than Ken and was great fun. One time when we were very young, Mom had dressed us in little grey flannel suits for a party when Dave asked if we could come over to play for just a little while. Mom admonished, "OK, just as long as you don't let them play in the dirt!" When she called us home to leave for the party, she was livid to find both of us filthy. Upon confronting Dave, he responded with what became a family classic, "Oh no, Mrs. Brown, that's not dirt; it's manure!" We had been sliding down a great pile of manure that had been brought in for their garden.

Ken and I had a great scouting career together. Our Troop 92 and Cobra Patrol were crack units, and we had fun on our weekend campouts, at scout camp, and at the 1950 Jamboree at Valley Forge. It was an especially proud moment when we got our Eagle Scout awards together. We continued in a vigorous merit badge competition which ended with our garnering 101 badges between us.

One badge was especially memorable. Bird Study was one of the most challenging ones to achieve, as a scout had to record observation of 50 different bird species. Ken and I thought we were well prepared, but then we encountered Mr. Barney Williams. Mr. Williams was a venerable African American gentleman who had a legendary scouting career with 103 badges himself. He was also quite a bird fancier and had a large aviary in his backyard. For Mr. Williams, the standard requirements were only a starting point. He asked us to identify all of his many birds and to describe their habits. We had to return twice before Mr. Williams was willing to sign off on our achievement. Even though we were put to much extra effort, we grew to appreciate someone who demanded more than the ordinary.

I am convinced that lowered expectations are among the root causes of America's lagging performance in education. This mind-set puts a lid on achievement and aspirations, especially among youth from disadvantaged backgrounds. For a stark contrast of the standards of my youth compare to those of today, look at how the *Reader's Digest* feature testing one's "Word Power" has regressed. Two generations ago, this vocabulary test included words such as "didactic" and "eponymous." Today, the words are along the lines of "theory" and "marginal."

Physical Development merit badge was another challenge, especially for me, as I was a bit of a chunky monkey. One of the requirements was to do 20 push-ups. I had seen my dad do them and asked for his advice. He was pleased to demonstrate and then instructed me to lie prone with my hands placed under my shoulders and then to push up. I did so and pushed. And pushed. But there was no "up." Dad turned away somewhat disgusted, saying, "I've never heard of anybody who couldn't do a push-up – you'd better practice!" My dilemma was how to practice something I couldn't do. I then devised a plan. I started by doing standing push-ups off a four foot tall bureau. I found I could do them easily and worked up to 20 of them. Next, I switched to a two foot bench and gradually built to 20. Finally returning to the floor, I found I could do six real push-ups. In a few weeks I finally was able to pass the test.

I felt that our Cobra Patrol of eight scouts had the talent and training to be the top group in the upcoming contest among 100 or so patrols at the county "Camporee." I assigned each boy a specialty and drilled them to perfection in knot tying, first aid, pathfinding, fire-starting, etc. The only weak link was Jimmy. Jimmy seemed bright enough, but was inattentive. I figured we would probably be in a good position to win even if Jimmy had a mediocre score in his assigned area, pathfinding. On the day of the contest, we all scampered off to our assigned areas where our skills would be tested.

Shortly thereafter, I was summoned by Tommy who was in an agitated state. Apparently, our great pathfinder Jimmy was unable to find his station, so he stopped off at knot tying and pre-empted Tommy by signing up as Cobra's representative in that contest. When we tried to get the boys assigned properly, the officials would not allow any changes. Although Jimmy predictably bombed out on knot tying, Tommy actually did fairly well in the pathfinding exercise. Our patrol tied with another for first place in the county.

Scouting taught us a number of life lessons as well as new skills. At Camp Pomponio in the San Mateo redwoods, there was a cohort of scout leaders who wore handsome white neckerchiefs emblazoned with a blue eagle and the letters "KD." They stood for the Knights of Dunamis, an honor society whose entry requirements included being an Eagle Scout. Dad had been celebrated as the first "Knight-Eagle" in the country. When I got my Eagle, I was eager to apply. I then learned that one had to be 15, and I was not even 14 yet. I was greatly disappointed. Several years later, while I was off at boarding school with scouting growing distant in the rearview mirror, I received an unsolicited invitation to join none other than the Knights of Dunamis! I was amazed to realize how burning desire had cooled to the point that I simply declined the invitation.

Ken attended Burlingame High School. Despite being a modest-sized school in a fairly affluent community, its educational offerings were pathetic. A classic example was a semester-long course called Freshman Orientation. The course instructed students in the school's colors, room numbering system, mascot, etc. Never mind that the eager freshmen already knew all this stuff on their own by day two. Quickly running out of gas, the course content then shifted to grainy black and white films on highbrow topics such as teeth brushing. The movies were shown in a darkened room, and most of one's grade depended on the neatness of one's notes. There was a rush for the few window seats where slivers of light helped steady one's hand. When it came my turn to take this course, I simply took a dark seat, wrote my notes any which way and then copied them over later, slightly askew. English class was not much better. Only two books were required for the whole year: *Ivanhoe* and *Bambi*!

Despite these softball offerings, Ken's grades were poor – he even managed to get a "D" in that pitiful Freshman Orientation course.

Frustrated by their inability to coax or coerce better performance out of Ken, my parents packed him off to Cate, a boarding school 300 miles south in Carpinteria. There, under closely supervised study halls, Ken's academic performance recovered. He also did well in football. While his early hip disease limited his foot speed, Ken was pretty well coordinated and was exceptionally strong. All of us were pleased when Ken was accepted by Stanford, partly on the strength of his perfect 800 on the math SAT.

Ken also qualified for a very generous full-ride Navy scholarship if he could pass the physical. The requirements were incredibly detailed, including standards for straight teeth and even a potential disqualification for being "too ugly" (sorry, Abe Lincoln). One of these standards was a height minimum of 5'6". Shortened by the Perthes Hip Disease, Ken measured 5' 5 ½" when he appeared for his physical. The doctor told Ken to revisit early in the morning after hanging from a bar to stretch out. Doing so increased his measurement to 5'5 ¾". The doctor then asked Ken to lean towards him, whereupon he thumped Ken on the crown of his head with one of those little rubber mallets used to test knee reflexes. With the resultant lump, it was mission accomplished.

With newfound momentum and confidence, Ken seemed to be on a good trajectory. We were shocked when he flunked out of Stanford after only two quarters. Old habits of neglect and procrastination had returned.

As was typical for a young man in that era who had an interruption in his academic progress, Ken joined the Army. Ken loved the Army and its structure. When his amazing mathematical aptitude became apparent on tests, he was assigned to cryptography school at Fort Gordon, Georgia. He then was assigned briefly to Germany where he got to know another young trooper by the name of Elvis Presley. Unlike most celebrities, Elvis was every bit the regular soldier, pulling his kitchen duty and sharing beers with the guys. Being a powerful babe magnet, Elvis also shared his coterie of females with his buddies.

Most of Ken's three Army years were spent in Izmir, Turkey, a key listening post for intercepting and decoding Russian messages. Ken loved the Turkish people, and they reciprocated. Wrestling is the national sport there, and Ken was an Army champion. That skill and his willingness to learn some Turkish made Ken very popular. When Ken returned home, Dad had just bought a beautiful antique Turkish rug for our dining room. Ken stared at its beauty and then said he thought he could make out some of the Arabic script in the corner. Captivated, Dad eagerly pressed Ken for a translation. Showing his prankish side, Ken proclaimed that it said "Made in Taiwan."

By the time Ken returned to Stanford, I had leapfrogged ahead of him by a year. I did not want to be my brother's keeper, but I did want to see what I could do to help. He joined my eating club, and I arranged to have Ken room with two friends of mine who were both diligent students. In checking discreetly with my buddies, they reported seeing very little of him and didn't know how he was doing. After just one quarter, the sad results were reported. Ken had rolled out of Stanford again.

Obviously, some toxic psychological factor was at work, drawing Ken to failure. Was it Dad's glorious achievements presenting an impossible standard? Perhaps that was a factor, but Dad was always sensitive about this influence, and he made every effort to conceal his record from us. Many times we learned from others of his stunning accomplishments.

Ken did not return to college. He joined PG&E as a clerk in their San Mateo office. It was a good choice, as the regulated utility provided the structure that Ken needed.

One day, Ken was approached by a customer who said he had just gotten a raise and wanted to switch to full-time service. Puzzled, Ken replied that they had various power plans, but they were all full-time. "Oh no," said the customer. "I'm on the half-day program now." Ken dispatched a crewman to the fellow's house, and indeed power went on at 6 p.m. and then abruptly shut off at 6 a.m. The crewman suspected that the customer was a joker who had installed some timing device in the circuit, but a thorough scan revealed none. Finally, the crewman followed the line all the way to the street and was stunned to learn that the house circuit had mistakenly been tied into the city streetlight system. For two years, the customer had calmly accepted daytime hours without power while his clocks stopped, ice cream melted, etc. The lesson for me is that while some people are quick to complain, others will suffer in silence.

Ken was a little chagrined next to be assigned to be a meter reader. I believe I helped bolster his self-esteem when I printed him some calling cards indicating that he was a "Consumption Analyst." This incident brings to mind my first use of a calling card. As lowly bank trainees were not provided with cards, I printed up a batch on my own. On my maiden call, accompanying a bank officer on a visit to a hardware store owner, I was pleased to be able to participate in the exchange of calling cards. The customer studied my card and then gazed quizzically at me and asked, "Tuesday, May 9th?" Only then did I realize that I had mistakenly presented a dental appointment reminder that I had stashed in my wallet next to my calling cards.

Ken's math skills enabled him to become a highly successful gambler. He was especially good at counting the cards in Blackjack and found himself *persona non grata* at several casinos. For about five years running, he made more money gambling than he did on his job.

On the job front, once again Ken aced a test, this time an exam to test for aptitude to become a PG&E computer programmer. His career took a turn for the better, as did his social life. A fellow computer programmer, Jeanne Dutreaux, became the love of his life.

Although Ken was a heavy smoker, he generally maintained good health. You can imagine our surprise to learn that some discomfort in his chest at age 25 turned out to be a malignant sarcoma. Heroic surgery, chemotherapy, and radiation at Stanford Hospital managed to arrest its development and send the cancer into remission.

The final chapter on Ken is painful to revisit. He married his beloved Jean at a ceremony at our family home on June 9, 1969. I was honored to be his Best Man, and my daughter, Becky, served as a flower girl. We then saw them off to their honeymoon in Pebble Beach. I returned to my bank job in Pasadena where three days later I received a call from a man whose voice was so raspy I could hardly recognize it as Dad's. He called with the news that Ken had just died. With his lungs scarred from radiation and weakened by his smoking habit, he was unable to fight off a respiratory illness that quickly progressed to a fatal pneumonia.

Dad was so generous and supportive of Ken's widow. Immediately, he paid in full the mortgage on her home in Foster City and kept in touch with her through the years. She has kept the name of Jeanne Brown and has never remarried.

Nothing will ever take the place of brother Ken, but I am pleased that my Kenneth Minge Brown memorial funds at the Stanford Business School have grown to seven figures and now support three full fellowships per year.

Siblings

In 1940, on January 16, the day after my second birthday, my sister Barbara Minge Brown was born. She was born with leukemia and did not survive the month. I don't believe she ever left the hospital, as I don't recall ever seeing her.

Early in 1945, my mother again became pregnant. It was a very difficult pregnancy, made more so by Dad's being away in the war in the Pacific. Ken and I did our best to comfort her. Convinced that Mom's poor appetite was due to her not eating the right foods, we would bring her our very favorite sandwich, the "Blisterrust." Dad's college summers had been spent in arduous labor, clearing blisterrust-infested gooseberry bushes from slopes in the Sierra. To replenish their energy, the blisterrust workers would eat sandwiches of peanut butter, honey, and raisins, the thicker the better. And nothing was too thick for our ailing mother. After delivering our monstrous creations to her bedside, we were delighted to return later to see nothing but a few crumbs on the plate. It was not until years later that we learned why Wags, our Springer Spaniel who camped out under Mom's bed, gained about 30 pounds during her pregnancy.

On December 8, 1945, brother Harrison Minge Brown was born. I remember running down Black Mountain Road upon spotting the family car bringing Mom and Harry home from Mills Hospital. Harry was a handsome, lively baby.

From his earliest days, Harry was interested in science and mathematics. He had a series of fascinations, one of them being any kind of valve or water fixture. While other kids took blankets or stuffed toys to bed, Harry's nocturnal companion was a faucet.

Harry was very bright and generally excelled in his studies. A notable exception was in the fifth grade at Hillsborough School when he encountered "dull Miss Hull," a ponderous teacher with few redeeming qualities. Not realizing that Harry was bored stiff, she recommended Harry repeat fifth grade. Our parents yanked him out of that school and enrolled him in Carey School, a small private academy with strong individualized attention. Upon testing and interviewing Harry, they promptly jumped him ahead to the seventh grade. Harry went on to excel both at Carey and later in high school at Menlo School and on to Stanford.

At Stanford Harry studied physics for eleven years. Seemingly always a year away from getting his Ph.D, he finally dropped out, bitter about feeling exploited as cheap labor. Along the way, he became heavily engaged in opposing the Viet Nam War. As Dad was then President of Stanford's Board of Trustees, the protest groups used Harry as a poster child, and he railed to the press about Dad and other university leaders. After leaving Stanford, Harry spent a year or two teaching math at Menlo School, before taking a job at Diffraction Optics for the balance of his career.

The brilliance of the scientist doesn't always translate to brilliance in the field of diplomacy. Several years after college, I returned home to a family gathering. Shortly thereafter, Harry came through the door and pitched his Shell Oil bill in Dad's direction. To which I reacted, "Hey, what goes – Dad never paid my gasoline bills." Harry summed up the situation succinctly, "Dad's richer now."

Some physicians come from the same school of tact. In later years, Dad developed some knee problems. His doctor took X-rays and put them up on the light board to show the source of the problem, pointing out, "See, it's just bone on bone here." Dad looked at the X-ray and then said to the doctor, "That's not the knee that hurts." Thereupon, the doctor responded, "Well, it will!"

Ever since college, Harry has lived in a small rental flat on Cambridge Avenue in Menlo Park, only a few blocks from my parents' first home. There, he enjoys playing his guitar and addressing mathematical puzzles. For years he has worked on trying to solve the classic mathematical conundrum of proving that there can be no limit to the size of prime numbers. Several of his articles and letters on the subject have been published in mathematical journals.

When Sarah entered the picture, she was dismayed to learn that my relations with Harry were distant. After all, he had served as my Best Man at our wedding. She invited Harry to dinner at our Mill Valley home. When Sarah presented a savory frittata she had baked, he shoved his plate across the table, angrily declaring, "I don't eat cheese." We continued to see Harry on family occasions, but Sarah and our boys grew increasingly frightened by his angry outbursts over seemingly trivial matters.

Ken's and my relationship with Harry had been satisfactory in his early childhood years, but our ten and eight year age differential created a mini-generational gap. Harry was only five by the time both Ken and I were away at boarding school. As our interests diverged, Harry increasingly began to identify me as part of "the Establishment," the ones who were responsible for Viet Nam and other evils. One time when Harry accosted Sarah about some societal ill, he prefaced his tirade with "Your generation _ _ _." Sarah had to remind Harry that she was only one year older than he.

When Dad died, it provided an opportunity for Harry and me to reconnect, as we were the two principal beneficiaries of our parents' estate. When it came time to split up the personal property, Harry declared he wanted none. Nonetheless, I got a truckload of things I knew he should want and delivered it to him. Although Dad's will did not specify any reimbursement for unequal division of personal property, I felt honor-bound to write him a large compensatory check.

Shortly after the estate distribution, it came time for Harry's 50th birthday. It had been traditional for such events to be celebrated at the Burlingame Country Club. Sarah and I offered to host a party for whomever he might like to include. In a postcard response, Harry declined and said that the family was over for him when Dad died and that any future celebrations would be done by him alone in the mountains. We have not seen him in the twelve years since. The only news we receive is from his occasional contact with Eva Borak, Dad's longtime secretary with a heart of gold. Despite this estrangement, I do not feel Harry harbors animus towards me or my family. I think he just likes to be alone.

Dad, Ken, Mom, Harry – 1953

Mother and John Gillingham – 1916

Mom

My mother, Gloria Frances Gillingham, was born on October 20, 1912 in the family residence in New York City's Gramercy Park Hotel. Her mother, Frances Nourse Gillingham, was an opera singer, and the family lived among a colony of musicians. Down the hall lived famed violinist Yehudi Menuhin, and on the floor above, pounding away on his piano at all hours was a fellow named Rachmaninoff.

My mother's mother was American-born (Chico, California), but her father, John Rowley Gillingham, was a British subject. Curiously, Gillingham was born in 1873 in Kobe, Japan, one of the very first Europeans ever to have been born in the island kingdom. His father was there as a tea trader. "Tea trader" may have been a bit of a euphemism, as there were persistent rumors that the tea shipments may have included opium. He made a considerable fortune and retired in his early 40's. His robust lifestyle included fathering several children out of wedlock, whose Baptismal records read, "Father: J. R. Gillingham, Mother: Japanese Woman," a telling indicator of British imperial mind-set.

Mother's father joined the Hong Kong Shanghai Bank (now HSBC), and after several tours in Asia, a job transfer took him to New York. Another transfer then assigned him to San Francisco as President of the local HSBC Bank. What a life it must have been for him. John Gillingham was picked up at their Berkeley home at 9 a.m. by a limousine with the two morning papers ready for his reading before driving onto the ferry at the Oakland terminal (the Bay Bridge was not completed until 1937). His workday began at 10 a.m. Lunch was usually at one of the men's clubs, extended up to two hours by dominos and scotch. The workday ended at four when his driver reappeared with the evening papers. On the boat ride home, John usually engaged in pinochle with his friends. Occasionally, the game got so consuming that the players would stay for another round trip. Other than those occasions, he was home by five. Mother said that they frequently went out to various business and social functions where alcohol was a major factor. Both of Mother's parents died in their 60's.

Mother had a generally unsatisfactory relationship with her mother, who she regarded as never having gotten over being a Prima Donna, but she adored her indulgent father and her paternal grandfather, the "tea trader," who lived to be 96. Her brother John, the 13th John Gillingham in the line, was a handsome, bright boy, a year older than my mother. While my mother was often teased unmercifully by her hyperactive brother, she remained fond of him and was ever grateful for his role in meeting my father.

My father was in Army ROTC while at Stanford, as was schoolmate John Gillingham. When John's parents came to visit their son during the ROTC unit's summer encampment in Monterey, the family arrived in the bank limo. Seizing an opportunity for an irreverent prank, Dad and several buddies decided to race motorcycles around the stately black limo, coating it with a layer of dust. When Dad managed to see inside the car, he noticed a very pretty girl. At that point he called off the marauders and decided he should get to know John Gillingham better. While that friendship never fully blossomed, the introduction to his sister certainly did.

Mother was a good, conscientious student at Anna Head's School in Berkeley (now Head-Royce School). In retrospect, though, I wonder if perhaps she had some degree of learning difficulty. I cannot recall her ever reading a book, only magazines, usually scanned back to front. She was an excellent tennis player on a high school team that was doubtless the best in the U.S. Among her teammates were Helen Wills and Helen Jacobs, both of whom went on to become national champions. Mom also played on the Mills College team, but her attendance there was cut short at two years when she left college to tend to her parents who were suffering from terminal illness. Mom was through playing tennis by the time I was a youngster, but she was a very crafty left-handed ping-pong player.

Mother's other great passion was artistic creation. She drew well and had a fine sense of design. Every Christmas she would do a new "peek box," a cardboard box draped in tissue paper with painted cutouts inside and a light source provided by tissue-covered holes worked into the design. When viewed through a dime-sized peephole, a magical three-dimensional scene would unfold. My favorite one depicted our family home from across the canyon, as it would have appeared in a wintry snowfield, which, of course, never came to temperate Hillsborough. Mother engaged in all kinds of whimsical artistic endeavors. One of them was to take plain white tennis shoes and dye them all different pastel colors, like Easter eggs. It would be decades before I ever saw anything like it in the commercial world. I only wish Mom could have enjoyed the kind of creative outlet that today's women have.

Mother's favorite artistic expression was her flower arranging. An entire room in our home was devoted to her craft, filled with all manner of vases, frogs and other paraphernalia. She frequently won the highest awards at local flower shows, and our home was graced with her creations. Mother had a great range of capabilities, from soaring majestic pieces to small intimate nosegays to thematic arrangements of every different kind. She was a mainstay of the Hillsborough Garden Club, which honors her memory with the Gloria Frances Brown Annual Lectureship.

One day she was preparing an entry for the county fair and asked me what I thought of it. As a candid ten year-old without adult diplomatic skills, I began giving it an honest critique – that it was pretty, but maybe needed a few adjustments. She bristled at my comment and suggested that if I was so talented, I should submit an entry. Stung, but determined, I proceeded to the garden and assembled an entry for her to submit. Smugly, she said, "We'll see how this comes out." At week's end, the judging was done, and out of about 100 entries, my mother's was rated 6th best, a high honor. But a blue ribbon in the family trophy case evidences the prize given for first place for a delicate little arrangement of petunias, lilies, nasturtiums, and geraniums by a 6th grader at Hillsborough School. Even Mom was proud.

Mother used to enjoy recounting the visit of a noted Japanese flower arranger to their garden club. The club members wanted to provide him with materials to use in his demonstration. The visitor politely declined and insisted on gathering his own materials from the nearby woods and fields. The group marveled at the beauty of his creation, but on closer inspection saw that his brilliant red foliage was the extremely toxic poison oak. The poor visitor spent an extra several days in the local hospital to recover from his rash.

Mother, with her wide range of artistic interests, was easy to satisfy on gift-giving occasions. For many years I added ceramic and porcelain bird figurines to her extensive collection. We had a sure test as to whether a gift had hit its mark. It was a winner if it remained in Hillsborough, but if we later found it at the Farm, our family's vacation home, we knew it had fallen short.

Once I was convinced I had the perfect gift. When I was at boarding school, Mother would periodically send me packages of cookies and such. I was struck by how many extra stamps festooned these packages. The stamps literally marched up one side and down the other – far more than required. When I asked her about it, I gained a glimpse into her way of thinking. It went something like this, "Let's see, I understand that I should put on a dollar of stamps, but just to be sure, I'll put on two dollars worth. Well, one never knows; I'd better make it three dollars. That may actually not be enough, so ..."

I decided to get Mother a little postal scale for Christmas. She expressed delight and exclaimed how much money she would save. Then weeks later, the first package of the new era arrived – slathered with as many stamps as before. The next one, the same thing. When I next came home, I asked Mom whether she was using the scale. "Oh, yes," she said, "It is wonderful." I then asked why was she still using as many stamps as before. It quickly became apparent that she was using the scale as just a starting point for her rounds of serial anxiety about the adequacy of the postage! I had dealt with the factual aspects but left the behavioral ones unchanged.

Sometimes context can trump all other aspects of a situation. Mother was attending a horticultural program sponsored by Stanford University. She waited through the long line at her alphabetical bracket to register. When she finally got to the front, the registrar said, "Mrs. Brown, you belong over there in the B's." Only then did she realize she had queued up in the "G" line. The school setting had taken her back 45 years to her maiden name of Gillingham.

Mother also had a delightful naive streak. On a family vacation to Hawaii, our departure was delayed by various trucks servicing the plane. Mother saw that one of the trucks extended a large tube to the plane and asked what it was. I responded that it was a sanitation truck offloading from sewage tanks on the plane. Mom looked astonished and said, "So that's what they do with it!" I then asked what had she supposed was done with "it." She responded, "Well, I always felt sorry for those poor people in Kansas."

I don't know just when or how Mother's difficulty with alcohol developed. I remember her being simply angelic when I was very young. She loved to sing and had a great sense of humor. Perhaps contributing to her use of alcohol were the incessant demands of Dad's busy legal career and the stress that he brought home. Motherhood added its burden. I feel there must have been some frustration from her not having more outlets for her creativity. Also, there may have been some psychological baggage from being raised in a family steeped in the Victorian tradition of keeping deep secrets. It seems incomprehensible in today's world of over-disclosure that one could experience what my mother did on her wedding day. A relative from England remarked to Mother that she resembled one of her half-sisters. Dumbfounded, my mother said that she had no half-sisters, that her mother had never been married before. The relative answered, "Why, my child, your mother was married twice before." What a shocking revelation, one likely to shatter her feelings of trust towards her family.

For another glimpse of life during the Victorian era, it was customary for expatriate British families living in Asia to send their boys off to boarding school in England at about age seven. Due to the lengthy steamship voyage required, home visits to Asia were impractical. Sometimes as long as five to seven years would pass before parents would see their children again. Just imagine, after such a prolonged separation, the parents standing by the gangplank, inquiring of the children filing off the ship, "John? John? Are you John?"

I also wonder about the influence on Mom of life changes during the 1940's. First, there was the loss of Barbara, a cherished daughter Mother would loved to have raised. Then, instead of a compact little family of four that enjoyed going to the Farm together, there was an eight year younger baby added to the mix. Meanwhile, Dad returned to his legal practice after the war, probably working extra hard to make up for lost time. Finally, although the wartime years brought special burdens to wives left behind, they also conferred a degree of independence and greater responsibility. The transition back to a more subservient family role must have been difficult.

For the most part, though, current thinking is that alcoholism is a disease. Studies have shown that the pressures and stresses on persons who cannot handle alcohol are no greater than those affecting persons without this affliction. Whatever the cause, it first became manifest about 1948, dramatically so one afternoon when she bounced her car off trees and telephone poles all the way up Hayne Road. In subsequent years, I can remember few family occasions that were not tainted by Mom's drinking to excess.

Dad so loved Mother that her drinking problem was too painful for him to face realistically. Unwittingly, he became a co-conspirator when he bought into her excuses that her condition was due to allergies or diet pills or whatever. On one notable birthday at the Clift Hotel, Mom had passed out at the table, yet Dad kept on as if nothing were amiss. Finally, Sarah and I had to insist that "Dad, it is time for all of us to go home." Mother never enrolled in an Alcoholics Anonymous program or any other kind of counseling. Mom's health went into a gradual decline, exacerbated by the influences of alcohol and of smoking, and she succumbed to lung cancer on January 1, 1990. For all her talents and underlying spirit, the last forty years of her life left me longing for the way she once was and the way I would have loved for my children to have known her.

Dad at Stanford – 1930

Honeymooners at Crater Lake – 1935

Dad

Dad's early years were hidden to us under a shroud of silence. Only a few milestones survive this era: His birth in Mobile, Alabama on October 16, 1911; his father's death by suicide in 1917 – by pistol in the family parlor; his mother's remarriage to a man who subsequently lost his business and then his life to alcoholism shortly thereafter.

Despite these losses and four family moves before he was ten years old, my father emerged remarkably well-adjusted. He had an other-worldly amount of talent – intellectual, athletic, and social. And this package of talent was harnessed to a relentless determination. Few people who have ever lived have been so richly endowed. As a thirteen year-old, his intellectual ability came to the attention of Dr. Lewis Terman, Stanford's pioneer in the field of human intelligence. When Dad's I.Q. tested as high as anyone ever had, Dr. Terman offered him admission to Stanford on the spot. Fortunately, his mother had the good sense to delay his attendance to age 15. In the meantime, Dad became San Francisco high school champion in three track and field events while at Lowell High School. All the while, he became a Boy Scout leader, winning 72 of the 75 merit badges then available. The only ones he missed were due to age ineligibility, such as the automobiling badge. Dad was selected by Admiral Byrd as one of the country's six outstanding young men who were finalists for the Boy Scout to be chosen to join his pioneering expedition to the South Pole. Again, Dad's sensible mother interceded to keep him on a safer course. It is hard to imagine he had time for anything else, but in fact, Dad also had an evening paper delivery route.

At Stanford, it was more of the same. Dad graduated number one in the class of 1931, lettered three years in track, and was elected both class president and student body president. All this by a student three years younger than his peers. Along the way, he also held outside jobs throughout his collegiate career.

Dad started at Stanford Law School, but soon received the news that he had won a Rhodes Scholarship to Oxford. Dad had a shock, though, just as he was leaving for Oxford. He learned that some of the courses were taught in Latin. In response to Dad's protest that he had never studied Latin, an Oxford don replied archly that "Every educated gentleman knows Latin." Fortunately, Dad was working his way to Europe on a freighter and spent every spare moment during the two-month trip teaching himself Latin. By the time he enrolled at Oxford, he found himself being complimented on his command of the language.

In any new situation, there is a learning curve as one comes up to speed on local knowledge. In Dad's case, he was one of the late arrivals to Oxford and found that the only dormitory rooms left were way up on the drafty fourth floor – with one notable exception. A choice ground floor room was unclaimed. Dad seized upon this opportunity and settled in. The first night, though, he awoke startled to find several students in his room. They promptly shushed him to be quiet as they crept out of his room to the hallway. Only then did Dad come to realize that this room was the preferred route for students sneaking back into the dormitory after curfew. Dad quickly relocated to an upper floor room.

As before, Dad was active in athletics, this time winning letters in tennis and rugby in addition to track. An Oxonian tradition provided a powerful incentive to succeed in athletic contests. Winning teams were awarded "first water" for bathing afterwards. Most notable, though, was his mastery of his legal studies. Once again, he was the top graduate in his class, and one of Oxford's noted legal scholars inscribed a book to him with the legend that his was the best legal mind the professor had ever encountered.

Dad's Oxford period was not without its "old school" moment. At Oxford Law, no formal grades were given until the end of the three-year course of study. If one did not pass the week-long final exam, there was no partial credit; it was as if the three years had not happened. As if this all-or-nothing aspect were not enough, there was the added pressure of a grueling four-hour oral exam. For the oral exam, the student was to appear alone in front of a panel of stern bewigged professors seated at a raised dais. Before being ushered into this tribunal, the student was required to don an examination gown with a high starched collar. Some students fainted dead away upon donning the fateful gown.

When it became Dad's turn, one of the professors produced a British five pound note and asked Dad whether it was "property" or merely a "chose in action," which was a claim on property. Dad recognized this question as a classic legal conundrum and responded that currency had aspects of both. The professor replied with the comment that they hadn't requested ambivalence and asked again which one was it. Dad then offered that he leaned toward the view that it was property in that if one lost the note, he was out the five pounds. The professor then said, "That will be all, Mr. Brown." Dad awaited the next question. The professor then repeated in stronger terms, "That will be all, Mr. Brown." Shocked and chastened, Dad slinked out of the room barely five minutes into an exam scheduled to last four hours. Only the next day did he learn that the Oxford dons had already decided to honor him with a coveted "First."

Dad never lacked for courage. When an Oxford professor gave a particular interpretation of an opinion by U.S. Supreme Court Justice Benjamin Cardozo, Dad disagreed with the professor's view and tried in vain to persuade the professor to his position. Finally, Dad wrote Justice Cardozo to check with him directly. The Justice's gracious letter in response, agreeing with my father, is one of our family treasures.

Dad's brilliance in the abstract is one thing, but it was quite another to experience first hand. When I returned home from boarding school on Spring Break, I told him that I had the lead in the school play, *Julius Caesar.* Dad asked me if I knew my lines yet. When I said I did, he then proceeded to recite about twenty lines, almost perfectly. I asked whether he had studied up for this occasion. Dad said "Oh, no, I didn't know you were in that play, and I haven't read it in twenty years." He even seemed a little wounded that I would ask such a question. Before Google became available, I would routinely query Dad as a source of reference on a wide array of topics.

Oxford's schedule had long breaks that afforded students an opportunity to see Europe. Best of all, the Rhodes stipend covered those travel expenses. These trips were wonderful experiences and served to foster lifelong friendships. On shorter vacations, Dad hung around London, fascinated by the shops and craftsmanship. He was especially taken by the little Japanese ivory carvings called "netsukes" which served as fobs at the ends of cords to prevent the "inro" (lacquered boxes) on the other end of the cord from slipping out of the sash of a kimono. The figures were incredibly detailed and usually depicted animals and various subjects of Japanese mythology, often in very whimsical fashion. Remarkably, these objects cost only 40 to 50 cents, a price that even a scholarship student could afford. Thus began a collection that eventually numbered over two hundred pieces, some of which came to be worth in excess of $10,000 each. It seemed fitting that Sarah and I should donate this collection to the Stanford Museum as a memorial to my father. For Stanford, this donation represented not only a tribute to one of their favorite sons, but also a restoration of a collection of netsukes by Jane Stanford that had been lost in the 1906 earthquake.

Cousin Frances Gillingham Herbert related an amazing story from the Oxford era. Recently, Frances had taken her young daughter to the beach in La Jolla. As her daughter was dancing in and out of the shallow surf, the ever-vigilant mom cried out, "Be careful, Gloria." Just then an elderly gentleman was walking by and stopped. He asked Frances, "Is your daughter's name 'Gloria?' I once dated a lovely girl named Gloria." Frances responded that she was named after her aunt, Gloria Gillingham. The old man was stunned and replied, "That's the girl I once dated, Gloria Gillingham." The gentleman then related that while my dad was off in England at Oxford, he started seeing my mother periodically. Then, one day he answered the door to find three large men standing there. They were from the Stanford football team and delivered a message. "We understand that you are seeing Bob Brown's girl, and we're here to ask you to stop." Faced with this menace, the gentleman abruptly ended the relationship. Apparently, Dad didn't learn of the activities of this thuggish squad of benefactors until years later.

Dad and Mom married on May 29, 1935 at Berkeley's St. Clement's Church. The reception was held at Mom's family home at 2820 Claremont in Berkeley, after which the newlyweds embarked on a motor trip to National Parks throughout the West.

Upon graduation from Oxford Law School, Dad joined the venerable San Francisco law firm of McCutchen, Olney, Mannon, and Green. Joining the firm with Dad was an outstanding cohort, including Morris Doyle, Burnham Enersen (my godfather), and Gerald Trautman. Two of them would go on to become presidents of the Stanford Board of Trustees, one as head of the American Bar Association, and another as CEO of a Fortune top 50 corporation. All four of them would in time have their names affixed to the firm.

Loyalties were strong in those days, and partners formed strong bonds. Usually, the only reason lawyers would change firms or firms would recruit other lawyers was due to the loss of a specialist, such as a tax law partner. Lawyers also were paid relatively modest salaries back then. The constant turmoil among today's law partners has been fueled in part by the tremendous escalation in legal fees. Technology has also played a part, as small firms can start up without the extensive law libraries of their predecessors. Until a few years ago, there were strict curbs against legal advertising. Lawyers were strongly discouraged from stimulating lawsuits, lest they be regarded by their peers as engaging in "champerty."

An action of my father's was uncommon then and would be unthinkable today. Dad had become the principal lawyer for the Hewlett Packard Company, a member of their Board, and close personal friends with Bill and Dave. Both of them appointed Dad as executor of their estates. The State of California prescribed a fee schedule for the services of executors. In Dad's view, the state-mandated fee for such services never contemplated that estates could reach multi-billion dollar proportions. Dad's potential compensation would have been in the tens of millions of dollars. He took the initiative to petition the court to reduce the fee to about 20% of the usual schedule, a level he regarded as more reasonable. Dad also insisted that the fee be run through his law firm. Our society's cynical lawyer jokes did not arise out of that era or his kind of law practice.

Mother's father chose my father to be executor of his estate. Dad discovered that Gillingham had been unable to resist the blandishments of a charming securities broker. His portfolio included a trunk, full of worthless mining stock certificates. Dad had to chuckle over the name of one of the defunct holdings, the "Robber's Roost Mining Company." Then Dad got a call from the broker expressing regret at John's bad luck in the market, and as a gesture of ostensible good will, offered to buy back one of the apparently worthless stocks for $1,000. Understandably suspicious, Dad checked out the company and learned that just that week, the company's fortunes had taken a major turn for the better when a court ruled in their favor on a dispute with a neighboring property. Being the thorough lawyer that he was, Dad dug deeper and got a transcript of the case. Convinced that the lower court judge had erred and that the case would be overturned on appeal, Dad accepted the broker's offer with profuse thanks. Sure enough, the decision was overturned, providing the broker with an opportunity to begin his own collection of worthless securities.

The year after my parents began building their Hillsborough home, they bought "the Farm" in the Santa Cruz Mountains, about four miles inland from Soquel. My mother's brother, John Gillingham, had opted to take the Carmel home from their family's estate, and with the equivalent cash amount of $8,000, my parents bought the secluded 33 acre spread with a rambling farmhouse that reliably dated back to 1850. It had two tumbledown barns and a number of outbuildings such as cookhouses, which we took down plank by plank over the years for firewood. The half-mile dirt driveway and the house itself were lifelong projects. Something was always in need of repair, tasks which absorbed most of our time there. Dad's reason for buying such a remote property was in part a move towards potential self-sufficiency should the social unrest of the late 1930's boil over into a change in the social order.

The property had an abundance of fruit trees in fertile, loamy soil. The previous owner, Mr. Dakin, was a noted horticulturist who developed over 100 varieties of fruit on the Farm. One plum tree sprouted seven different kinds of fruit from grafts he had performed.

The crops ranged from tropical guavas to holly, usually found only in the Northwest. There were also a few curiosities such as a cork oak tree, which had a thick bark of spongy cork. One singular avocado tree was dormant most of the time. Then one year in the 1950's, its crop was so abundant that it yielded $7,000 in revenue, enough to sustain the Farm for several years. Generally, we sharecropped to enterprising young Frank Beccaria who harvested the bountiful pear crop. Frank went on to become a successful local real estate operator. Down by the creek, there was a magnificent stand of *sequoia sempervirens*, one of which a surveyor measured to be almost 300 feet tall.

The beach was only five miles from the Farm, and the summer fog generally receded by noon. We especially liked to go to Capitola where Babe's hot dog stand served up split grilled dogs on toasted buns with mustard and a large pickle slice. Best ever! Most of our beach forays, though, were to a deserted stretch remarkable for its seclusion. Privacy was always Dad's goal, but we teenagers much preferred the potential action that busier beaches offered. We coined the derisive name "Drake's Beach" for Dad's favorite, on the theory that Sir Francis Drake had been the only previous visitor. Our other favorite local spots were the wonderfully tacky Mystery Spot and the tawdry Santa Cruz boardwalk. Most of our entertainment was right there on the property – hiking, skipping rocks in the stream, digging forts in the sandstone cliffs, and bounding down the slopes of the soft plowed fields as if we were wearing seven league boots.

Our immediate neighbors were Ray and Margaret Bethel. Margaret had only a fifth grade education, but was extremely well read and could go toe-to-toe with Dad on many topics. It was Ray who one day walked up the road while Dad was working on the roof to announce that Pearl Harbor had just been bombed.

In early 1942, Dad joined the Navy and went to Cornell for officer training. After a brief spell in the San Francisco Office of Naval Intelligence, Dad was sent to Honolulu to join Admiral Nimitz's staff. I remember his leaving San Francisco Bay on a PBY seaplane. Soon headed in the other direction was our dear live-in maid, Mitzi, a Japanese American who spent the duration of the war at the relocation camp at Manzanar. Mitzi loved to gamble pennies with Ken and me on a horse race game. A piece of rice paper had scribed in it eight horses and running lanes. Upon lighting a wick at the end, a smoldering flame would advance down each lane in fits and starts.

Mitzi and her sister returned to San Mateo four years later and appeared to bear no ill will regarding their treatment. In my view the internment of Japanese Americans was regrettable, but not the outrage that some current commentators claim. There was deprivation of liberty and some loss of property, but the treatment was humane by all accounts. One should remember the mood of America in 1942, reeling from the shock of Pearl Harbor and the atrocities of the Bataan Death March and the news from Nanking. There were local incidents of assault against Japanese Americans – to the point where some San Francisco Chinese took to wearing cardboard signs reading, "I am not Japanese."

Our country's treatment of Japanese Americans certainly compared favorably to that of Americans in Asian countries overrun by the Japanese. For living a peaceful life in the Philippines as a missionary, my mother's Aunt Rebecca was incarcerated in Santo Tomas Internment Camp, where she was among those who died from starvation and lack of medical care. Perhaps the most important takeaway from this comparison should be America's willingness to express critical opinion about its actions in contrast to the Japanese government which generally continues in its longstanding denials. On the European front, I admired Dwight Eisenhower's prescience upon his troops' encountering the horror of the Nazi death camps. Anticipating the likely onset of denial by the German people, he insisted that extensive photographic evidence be created and that local townspeople be herded through the camps to assist with the burial of the remains of the victims. These actions undoubtedly served to limit the spread of denial and probably helped the German people come to closure on that most shameful chapter of human history.

Dad's intelligence unit was filled with very bright fellows: top professionals, scientists and mathematicians. But for all their brilliance, there was also much to be learned from the old Navy hands about how to cope with Navy regulations. One day a Chief Petty Officer approached one of the officers and asked him to bring his wastebasket to the corner of the room and empty it there. The Chief then lit the papers on fire and stood by for a few moments while flames shot up. He then doused the blaze with the fire extinguisher he had at hand. To allay the onlookers' concern about his sanity, the Chief said that now he could file a fire report. Then in about three weeks when the Inspector General came for his annual audit of their records, any missing documents would have the ready explanation of "presumed lost in the fire."

Dad's brush with danger came after the war. One of his clients was Anaconda Copper Company. The company's general counsel was nearing retirement, and he tried to recruit Dad as his replacement. The offer would have tripled Dad's salary, but he loved the law and did not want to relocate the family to Montana. A few years later, the company plane crashed in Canada. Aboard were all eight of the top executives of Anaconda. Dad would have been one of them. That tragedy gave rise to today's business practice of limiting the number of top company executives who can ride together on the same plane.

Gillinghams

Also returning from the war was Mom's brother, Captain John R. Gillingham. Uncle John, as we boys knew him, was always very nice to us. His buoyant manner could descend into boorishness when alcohol was involved, but we kids found him delightful. His extroverted demeanor belied a keen intelligence flavored with creativity. He, too, was identified in the Terman study as a "genius."

Ken and I turned out to be the first offspring from a union of parents, both of whose bloodlines included Terman children, or "Termites" as they became known. Our development was of keen interest to Terman's researchers. They arrived with clipboards to test four year-old Ken and were delighted to see him clock in at about 160 I.Q. When they turned to me, I somehow sensed the opportunity for a memorable sight gag. Although I was actively walking and talking at age two, all they saw was a drooling infant crawling around on the floor backwards going "Da-da-da-da." The researchers discreetly filed out of the house without further comment.

John married Ora Thelen, a talented (another Termite) and accomplished woman. The Thelens were a distinguished East Bay family. Ora's brother, Max Thelen, and his family became good friends with my dad and then with me after his daughter Nancy became a colleague at the Wells Fargo Marketing Dept. The Gillinghams had five children – John who became a distinguished "Curator's Professor" at the University of Missouri and widely published author, Paul who became a psychiatrist in Cincinnati, Arthur, a lawyer, who lives in Sacramento, Henry, and Frances, a lawyer and woman of stunning beauty.

A favorite moment of mine was when we were celebrating my seventh birthday with the Gillingham family at their home in

Berkeley. Ora brought out the birthday cake, a rectangular sheet cake about two inches high. Ora asked *sotto voce* to my mother, "Do you think Dougie is old enough to cut the cake?" Rising to the bait, I eagerly sought the role of cake cutter. When I applied the knife, though, I found I could barely penetrate the frosting. I sawed away in mounting frustration. Finally, to the hilarity of all, including myself, I came to the realization that Ora had frosted an inverted metal baking tin.

I always enjoyed the Gillingham kids, but their being five to twenty-three years younger, and as family visits became infrequent, I did not have the opportunity to develop close relationships with them during our youth.

A real joy for me has been to become reacquainted with young John in the last few years. Every summer he and Barbara drive out from Missouri to their beach house in Santa Cruz. When they dropped by New Mexico several years ago, John and I stayed up until 3 a.m. going over family history. I hadn't stayed up like that since college. John has become one of the world's leading experts on the European Union and its economic structures and has won widespread acclaim both in the U.S. and in Europe. It has also been a pleasure to re-kindle my friendship with Dad's nephew, Randy Williams, who has now become a fellow Bohemian

The recent wedding of John and Barbara Gillingham's talented daughter Nicole to Thor Myhrstad, a software entrepreneur, gave us a welcome opportunity to become re-acquainted with the next generation of Gillinghams. Their other daughter, Ann, is pretty and introspective, and John G. IV is a most impressive young man. Paul and Maura Gillingham's genial son, Matt, inherits from his father the mantle as the largest specimen in the extended family. Frances and Eric Herbert's three daughters, Gloria, Natalie, and Claudia are a delight, and we are especially proud of my mother's namesake, Gloria, who is headed to Wharton in the fall.

More Dad

Dad loved golf. His aptitude for the game showed early when he broke 90 in his first full round as a teenager. He loved the competition and the beauty of the pastoral setting. One time when Ken and I were being trucked off to Sunday School as he headed for the country club, we complained about this inequity. Dad alibied that he was exercising his religious belief of pantheism, communing with nature while on the golf course. Usually both weekend days he spent on the course, and Mom often joined him on Sunday afternoons. At home, the living room rug was often used as a putting green. Dad's handicap floated between four and six, and he became club champion with a round of 69. He had three holes-in-one (Mother had one, too), and he was able to shoot his age at 75. As in many other aspects of his life, he was at his best when the pressure was on.

Dad employed his golfing skills in a rather unusual and costly way when a visitor came to the family home on Hayne Road, shortly after we moved in. The visitor was remarking on the dramatic canyon view and expressed the opinion that it was perhaps half a mile to the other side. Dad said it was more like 200 yards across, and a wager ensued. To settle the matter, Dad teed up a golf ball on the front lawn and let fly with his driver, which usually netted him about 250 yards. They watched as the ball gently arched the span, and then not so gently shattered the plate glass window of a house across the canyon. Dad quickly drove over to the house where he confessed to the event and settled up with the astonished neighbor, his wager winnings a mere down payment on glass repair.

Dad loved to make small bets to add zest to his golf matches and to sporting events we watched. He especially enjoyed devising trick bets. A favorite was when early in football season he would propose to an unsuspecting victim that he thought USC or some other powerhouse team would win this year's Rose Bowl game. He would boldly take that team against all others in the field, which presented an enticing prospect for unwitting victims. Once his quarry was hooked, Dad would then gleefully explain that "this year's game" had already been played last January and won by his team.

A rascal like that was obviously fair game for retribution. My favorite time was when Dad and Mom were visiting us shortly after we moved to New Mexico. As we drove towards Santa Fe, Dad was puzzled by a road sign reading "Las Vegas – 84 miles." Dad said, "How can that be? Isn't Arizona between here and Las Vegas?" - not realizing that it referred to Las Vegas, <u>New Mexico</u>. I had the pleasure of stringing him along with a yarn about an obscure back route through the mountains and how the route was shortened by the earth's curvature. Finally, with the mileage signs to "Las Vegas" pared down to impossibly small digits, Dad came to the realization that he had been duped.

In later years, Dad watched TV golf whenever it was on. Whenever it was not on, he watched with great enthusiasm whatever sporting event was on – even bowling. Mother would often join him to watch Sunday's final golf rounds, usually dozing off but insisting on being awakened to see the winner and his wife in a victory embrace.

As I think about Dad's love for watching TV sports, especially golf, I know he would have so enjoyed watching Tiger Woods play. In fact, when I watch Tiger, I carry thoughts of Dad with me.

Among Dad's many superior physical attributes was exceptional eyesight. His vision was 20-10 or better. Only one time in his young life did he meet his equal. A shipmate on one of Dad's voyages to England was reputed to be the most eagle-eyed. They challenged each other to a contest to see who could first identify the names of ships approaching in the sea lanes. To Dad's surprise, the sailor was consistently a little better then he was. Finally, Dad came to realize that his competitor had the advantage being familiar with the ships identified. Just as one can recognize a street sign sooner if one has a name in mind, the seaman had the advantage of preconception. When Dad shifted the contest to objects where there were no such clues, it was a dead heat.

Radar was not widely available until well into World War II, and visual aircraft identification was part of Dad's Navy training. As a plane might appear only briefly between clouds, skills were honed to the point of recognizing craft in the briefest of intervals. At the beginning of Dad's training course, the instructor flashed an aircraft photo for about a tenth of a second. None of the students could identify it as even a plane, and a mood of pessimism prevailed. Then the instructor said, "Let's try again." An image again appeared for the same brief interval, but this time there was widespread recognition of a photo of a nude woman. Confidence was restored and eventual competence achieved.

Brother Ken's eyes were almost as good as Dad's, and our son Elliott had the same acuity. Mine were a different story, but I was unaware of my near-sightedness until the fifth grade. Whenever Dad and Ken would engage in airplane-spotting contests, I would play along, thinking they were faking it. I would join in the assumed fakery with comments like, "It could be a B-26, but the tail assembly doesn't look quite right." I was stunned when a school nurse came to our class to give eye exams, and I could not get much beyond the big "E." When fitted with glasses, a new world unfolded. I could actually see detail in movies. Those dark blobs outside the window at night became distinct trees. For the first time, I experienced the phenomenon of seeing a man on a roof across the canyon and hearing the sound of his hammer trail the image of it. And, yes, Dad and Ken could actually see those planes.

Competitions of all kinds were a big part of our lives while growing up. Routinely, dinner would be interrupted by departure to the encyclopedia or dictionary to resolve a difference. One particular challenge provided a great source of satisfaction for both Ken and me. While at our Farm, Dad was balancing his checkbook, and there was some calculation discrepancy. We boys immediately concluded that it couldn't be a transposition because the difference was not divisible evenly by nine. For all Dad's general brilliance, he did not have a keen intuitive mathematical bent. He was skeptical and challenged us to prove that differences due to transpositions had to be divisible by nine. Ken and I went to separate rooms. We emerged simultaneously after about twenty minutes. We had each solved the problem, but I had done it in algebra while Ken had a geometric solution. It was such a high moment for us as Dad shook his head in amazement.

Another childhood lesson in mathematics was dictated by the father of a boyhood chum of mine. He hosted a 12th birthday party at Bay Meadows race track for his son and 10 of his son's friends. He gave each of us $10 to bet and said for us to note what happened to it during the course of the eight races. Midway through, the father came around to each boy to see how our $10 bankroll was holding up. Only one of the boys was ahead at that point. When he came to me, I cheerfully produced undiminished the $10 bill he had given me. He said I was supposed to bet it to learn what would happen. I responded that I already knew what would happen – with an eight race card on a pari-mutuel format with the track taking 10% on each race, I figured that the average bettor would stand to have only $4.30 to show for his $10 at the end of the day. And that diminution didn't include entry fee, parking fee, gasoline to get there, etc. He stared at me rather blankly and repeated that I was supposed to bet it to "learn my lesson." At the end of the day I fibbed that yes, like most of the other boys, I had lost it all and tossed in the air several ticket stubs that I had gathered from the ground. The father was happy that I had "learned my lesson," and I was happy to still have the $10.

Christmas cards were a major enterprise in our home. Mother and Dad shopped for one with great care, always choosing a landscape scene, often a stark snowy one by Eyvind Earle. Dad sent about 250 to a list that was rigorously maintained. There were no personal notes added and no photographs included. Reciprocal responses were noted, and the lack thereof sometimes led to an adjustment in next year's list. I know the thought behind this exercise was one of genuine friendship, but I always regarded it as a bit mechanical. Sarah's approach brought the holiday card process to life for me. We always include a photo, a brief paragraph on our activities and address them personally, even though the list has grown to over 600. This task gives us a great deal of pleasure, as it provides the opportunity to focus on friends and how much they mean to us.

Dad was a stickler for getting facts right, almost to the point of obsession. At social gatherings, when a guest would be telling a story, Dad would frequently interrupt with a correction along the lines of, "It couldn't have been April; it must have been May." The guest would gamely regroup and proceed until the next interruption. One time in private, I tried diplomatically to suggest to Dad that his habit broke the flow of the conversation and that often the precise facts were not material to the thread of the story. His legalistic response was that everyone knew he had this habit, and if he didn't correct an error it would amount to a verification of that error. I expressed the view that others were not as mindful of details, but to no avail.

Being around Dad was never entirely easy. His insistence on getting the facts right and his sometimes fierce demeanor could keep others off-balance. This style belied a nature that was always thoughtful and kind and caring. Dad didn't know just the first names of staff in the law firm, he knew last names, their family, and things they enjoyed doing. He was a hero to a great many people from all walks of life.

Dad also had a naive streak. He expressed astonishment when it was revealed that one of his law partners was gay. His secretary, Eva, hardly looking up from her typewriter, said, "Robert, there are seven gay lawyers in the firm!"

Dad was honest and ethical and courageous. He never hesitated taking on tough challenges. To support Wendell Willkie in the 1940 Presidential campaign, Dad decided to lobby for his candidate at union halls, which were bastions of Roosevelt support. He enjoyed the lively debate, acquired some new perspective, and felt that he changed a few minds. He also quickly became disenchanted with the morality of politics and politicians. To prepare for an argument in front of Supreme Court Chief Justice Warren, Dad asked a junior colleague to research Warren's position on matters related to the case while Warren was serving as Governor of California. After a week of intensive research, the young lawyer reported that he had no idea as to Warren's position on the matter. He said it depended entirely on the particular audience that Warren was addressing!

Dad's courage was on display on many occasions. Our neighbor at the Farm, Ray Bethel, suffered from a painful disability. Ray had been a Navy diver, and while engaged removing underwater obstacles at Anzio, his ship came under attack. The captain had no choice but to extract the divers immediately. Too quick an ascent forces bubbles of nitrogen out of the bloodstream, causing a painful permanent condition known in lay terms as "the bends." To continue his qualification for disability pay, Ray had to report annually to Oak Knoll Naval Hospital for a check-up. One year, the Navy concluded that his disability status should be changed from 100% to 92%. He still was unable to do any meaningful work, so the only effect of this change was to reduce poor Ray's disability pay by 8%. Enter Bob Brown. In about two weeks, Ray's classification was back to 100%.

Another such incident involved the Wurlitzer family. The Wurlitzers were heirs to the musical fortune, enriched further by Mrs. Wurlitzer's being a Pabst from the brewing family. We kids in the neighborhood often played ball in the rough lot that the Wurlitzers owned across the street from their home. Then one day, bulldozers arrived. Some months later, "Wurlitzer Field" had been created, a several acre park with a cement basketball court and a beautiful fenced and irrigated baseball diamond. Hillsborough had no parks – only the playing field at the one school in town. When the Wurlitzers tried to donate their private park to the town, the town council refused out of concern for the maintenance cost. Raimund Wurlitzer then turned to Dad. Dad called the head of the town council and said he wanted to verify the story so that he could convey it accurately to *Time Magazine*. He thought *Time* would be keenly interested in a story of a wealthy community with no parks for its children turning down the donation of a park. Predictably, the town council caved. I have also found the threat of publicity a useful weapon at times in my career.

In his vocation, Dad's trajectory was straight up (I resist the term "meteoric rise," as all the meteors I've seen have been descending rather rapidly). He soon became a senior partner in the McCutchen firm and joined a number of corporate boards: California Water Service, Greyhound, Hewlett Packard, and San Jose Water. Dad served 20 years on the Stanford Board of Trustees, including two terms as President of the Board. To honor Mom, he also served several terms as a Trustee of Mills College, and he was elected to the American Academy of Arts and Sciences in honor of his extensive service to education.

A low point in his Stanford service was that it included the peak of the Viet Nam War protests wherein the University President's office was torched; Harry was in the news lambasting him and Stanford; and renegade professor Bruce Franklin was inciting disruption. In response to bomb threats, for a while we had 24-hour security at our home.

Most of Dad's legal work involved negotiating contracts or settling matters in dispute. Occasionally, though, he would make court appearances on behalf of clients. On one such occasion, Dad was presenting a case before a judge who was notorious for being inattentive. Dad put together a most compelling argument. When he argued it in front of this judge, he was pleased to see the judge appearing to listen. In fact, the judge began taking notes. Greatly encouraged, Dad reached new heights of oratory. Eventually, Dad did prevail in the case, whereupon he wanted to know which particular points were deemed by the judge to be noteworthy. Dad sidled up to the bench to see. Peering over the rostrum, he could see the page of notes, comprised of the judge's signature being practiced over and over all down the page.

After years as legal counsel for California Water Service, Dad was asked to become its chairman and CEO. Part of the compensation package was a company car. As was typical of his choice of cars, he requested a mid-sized Buick. A few months later Dad was paid a visit by the company's Human Resources Director. His message was that Dad should get a nicer car. Dad declined, saying his Buick was just fine. The HR Director then explained to him that the CEO's choice of cars dictated car choices all down the line and that the field people felt compelled to drive Yugos and such. Dad said they could all have nice cars as far as he was concerned. "No, Mr. Brown," he explained, "they won't do that. You have to buy a nicer car." Relenting to the ethic of hierarchy, Dad upgraded to a Cadillac, thereby setting in motion appropriate upgrades throughout the company.

Dad also got a lesson in labor relations while at Cal Water. The union contract was up for renewal, and the union had made its wage demand. Dad told his Human Resources Director that he thought the union's demand was reasonable and should be accepted. The HR Director responded, "Mr. Brown, management can't just accept the union demand. Union leadership would be discredited." The HR Director then explained that if management didn't show some resistance and didn't engage a negotiation, the union membership would conclude that the union leaders had not asked for enough. A negotiation dynamic was necessary for a proper working relationship.

Speaking of labor relations, it should be noted that while we boys had a regular schedule of household and gardening chores, Dad was majestically exempt from such duty. His explanation was that his responsibility was confined to shoveling snow. You can imagine our delight one day when an unusual cold snap delivered a thin layer of snow to the front walkway of our Hillsborough home. Eagerly, we hustled Dad out for photographic evidence of him with shovel in hand.

As was the custom with members of the San Francisco "Establishment," Dad joined the Bohemian Club and the Pacific Union Club. One of his proudest achievements was taking the initiative to break down the barrier against Jewish members at the Pacific Union Club.

Bohemia provided many years of joy for Dad. Because it is an all-male group and guards its privacy, wild and fanciful rumors rush in to fill the vacuum of information. It is simply a gathering of fellows who enjoy music, entertainment, lectures and stories in a rustic setting far removed from worldly cares. The Club's principal notoriety comes from its exclusion of female members, a practice I generally deplore. However, it is difficult to see how coed camping in the woods with ready access to liquor would not spell trouble.

Dad's favorite Bohemian memories were the stimulating conversations with others who were at the top of their respective fields. Bohemia offers a matchless opportunity to see such leaders when they are "off duty." I remember approaching Mel Lane, *Sunset Magazine* co-CEO and head of their wine and food activity. Seeing him enjoying a glass of wine, I asked this noted oenophile what particular properties he was identifying. He responded, "Oh, I don't know – I'm just drinking to get a buzz."

Accommodations at the encampment in the redwoods known as "the Grove" are organized into "camps" which are similar to fraternities. My Bohemian experience has been greatly enriched by the special bond that has developed at my camp, Sempervirens. There is no more welcoming feeling than to be greeted by beaming co-captains, Jacques Littlefield and Bob Patterson and culinary wizards Dick Borda, Mike Keller, and John Hanna. And campmate David Abernethy with his quiet, intelligent, agreeable manner often reminds me of my brother, Ken. Bohemia has provided me a priceless opportunity to re-kindle Bay Area friendships and gave me precious time to spend with Dad and with Sarah's grandfather, Brick Elliott.

Dad's 65th birthday was an occasion for a special celebration. His favorite San Francisco restaurant was the sumptuous Redwood Room at the old Clift Hotel. He especially appreciated their extensive wine list. On this occasion Dad told the sommelier that he wanted a fine selection and identified a premium vintage. "Excellent choice," said the sommelier who bustled off to fetch it. He returned with a large bottle swaddled in a napkin and said, "Mr. Brown, I believe this is the appropriate choice." Dad looked at the bottle and then looked again before realizing that I had conspired with the sommelier to bring a giant bottle of Geritol.

We knew that the Christmas after Mother died in 1990 would be a morose occasion for Dad. To help dispel the gloom, Sarah and I and our boys took him to the Royal Hawaiian for the holidays. The tropical venue did help a good deal, but as we headed for Christmas

Eve dinner at the Kahala Hilton, Dad's sad visage was noticeable to all. I said I would go get the car. A few minutes later, Dad heard an odd racket approaching, and the "ahoogah" of a Model T horn. I had rented it on the sly and stashed it around the corner for just this purpose, and it was a true joy to see him beam as we bounced down the road in that vintage buggy.

Speaking of Hawaii, I've always enjoyed one of Dad's homilies, "Don't sit in the front row unless you like to do the hula."

Life's passages produce some curious turns. For several years after we lost Mom, Dad did not have much appetite for social life. But the older female cohort is numerous, wily, and persistent. A lovely contemporary of his asked him on a date. Dad wanted companionship, but felt flustered and asked me, as someone more recently experienced in the dating scene, what he should do. At Sarah's canny suggestion, we arranged for a double date, easing his social re-entry and relieving some of the romantic pressure.

Dad came to Albuquerque to be with our family for Thanksgiving, 1994. The weather was perfect, and we had a great time together, including a lovely gathering at the Moise home. As was our custom, we wagered (dimes) on the outcomes of the NFL games. When it came time for Dad to return home, son Joe and I were the advance guard in taking Dad to the Albuquerque airport. We were standing by the gate when I stepped aside to make a phone call. Just then, Joe called out to me. Dad had slumped to the floor and was gone from a massive heart attack. It was comforting that an ER doctor was near and attended to him immediately, as it relieved us of the concern that heroic measures may have saved him. Dad was in good health right to the end of his 83 years and left us during the afterglow of a perfect family weekend together.

Dad's funeral services were held at St. Paul's Church in Burlingame, which was packed with the many lives he had touched. Sarah and I gave the eulogies. To keep proceedings from becoming too maudlin, we had a Dixieland band perform the Stanford Fight Song during the recessional. Well-wishers gathered at the family home. I will be ever grateful to our Albuquerque friends who made the trip to support us – the Hankinsons, Moises, Salazars, and

Talbots. They and others helped greatly to deal with a loss I will never fully get over. Dad's remains are with those of Mom, Ken, and Barbara in a vault in dank Colma. I don't like to visit there. I prefer to visit with him in the nature he so loved, especially the redwoods of Bohemia.

My Childhood

I was born on January 15, 1938 at Peralta Hospital in Oakland, the same place where Ken had been born. By then, the Menlo Park bungalow was getting crowded, as my "bassinet" was a bureau drawer in my parents' room. My parents decided to build the house that would be their home for the rest of their lives.

We moved into the home at 943 Hayne Road, Hillsborough in January, 1939. The date was well fixed because Mom and Dad were still unpacking boxes at about 9 p.m. when Mom suddenly shrieked to Dad, "Oh my God, we forgot, it's Douglas's birthday!" Frantically, they drove to San Mateo to some drugstore just as it was closing and bought a Hostess cupcake, stuck a candle in it, and celebrated the birthday of an oblivious one year-old.

I cannot recall generally being left "home alone," but I do remember one occasion when I must have been. Mom and Dad came in the front door, then looked up horrified to see me sitting halfway up the stairs surrounded by shards of glass. On my lap was a dead hawk which had crashed through the window nearby. Seeing my parents' astonishment, their four year-old war baby explained, "We were bombed."

My parents didn't go out often, but when they did, our usual babysitter was Mrs. Olsen. She was a kindly elderly woman of perhaps 75 years. One time I confronted her with a question, posed as only four year-olds can, "Mrs. Olsen, how old are you?" She answered sweetly, "How old do you think I am?" I then blurted out, "Forty!" Not realizing that forty was the largest number I knew, perhaps the equivalent in my mind to a thousand, she seemed delighted and ever after favored me with all manner of tasty treats.

That year I started kindergarten at Hillsborough School (now South Hillsborough School) where I was to remain through eighth grade graduation. Most of my classmates stayed the entire period also, and we still join for periodic reunions. Our kindergarten teacher, Miss Smith, was a gorgeous 24 year-old blonde. When Dad met her, he immediately said, "She won't last long!" Naive to the meaning of his comment, I replied, "Oh no, Dad, she's real nice."

Schoolwork was not overly demanding and left lots of time for building forts in the woods with Ken and the neighborhood boys. All sports activity was through teams at school. There was no Little League or other outside sports organization. We competed in touch football, basketball, and baseball with nearby schools.

Probably influenced by Dad, I became an avid sports fan. My earliest recollection of spectator sports was during World War II watching armed services teams play football at San Francisco's old Kezar Stadium, which later became the original home of the San Francisco 49ers. Before television became available, we hung on every word of the radio broadcasts. The first World Series broadcast that I can recall was when I was eight, and the Boston Red Sox were playing the St. Louis Cardinals. Several of us had gathered in Assistant Principal Schwartz's office to hear the game during lunch hour. The Red Sox were ahead 3 – 2 when I had to leave for the Boy's Room. I had been vocally rooting for the Cardinals, and upon my return, I asked anxiously for an update on the score. Mr. Schwartz said that I had missed all the excitement and that the Red Sox were now up 43 – 2. When I asked how that could be, he said that Ted Williams had put one over the fence into a parking lot, and in the ten minutes it took the Cardinals players to find the ball among all the parked cars, Williams had circled the bases 40 times!

Dad came home from the Pacific infrequently. One very special time was in early 1944 when the whole family spent a week at Yosemite Lodge. It was the first time I'd seen snow. The icicles, the snow drifts, the icy fringes on the deep green Merced River, the beautiful snow-capped canyon rim above. It was magical.

There are just a few other places I have been whose physical beauty is as breathtaking: Moorea as seen from the water, the view from above at Kalaulau Lookout on Kauai, and the Grand Canyon from the north rim come closest. A place where I believe manmade development achieves a perfect blend with the beauty of nature is the Hotel Llao Llao in Bariloche, Argentina.

With Dad away at war, I followed the war's progress avidly. Each week I would wait eagerly for the war update in *Life Magazine*. At age 6, I remember recoiling at the news of the Battle of the Bulge thwarting our advance against the Germans. The war was all-consuming. Goods were rationed; we grew a victory garden; savings stamps filled pages until we could buy war bonds. There were frequent air raid drills where we observed blackouts with all the lights in the town turned off. Nearly all the dads were in the service. Wartime themes dominated music, art, literature, and social discourse.

I remember "VJ Day," the end of the war, especially well. I was at Dr. Ray's office in the middle of a physical exam when suddenly there were sirens and horns everywhere. Nurses, doctors, patients, my mother – all ran out and shouted and hugged and danced in the streets. All except me, in the examining room, shivering in my skivvies.

We kids were full of bravado in our own war games, and we took an enormous toll on imaginary enemies. Our hubris was shattered one day when Jerry Gritsch came home. Jerry was our hero, a strapping 6'4" Adonis who was an All-League football player for San Mateo High School. When he went off to the Korean War in 1950, we were confident Jerry would quickly mop up the North Koreans. When Jerry came limping home with his knee shot up, we were stunned. It was a true epiphany as to the random ways of war.

Ken and I were on that Boy Scout Jamboree trip, staying in the Willard Hotel in Washington D.C. when the Korean War broke out. The papers on the street blared in six-inch headlines "WAR." And there we were, three thousand miles from home in the nation's capital. We felt that we were at Ground Zero, and we gazed up anxiously for the sight of enemy planes.

Nonetheless, the 1950 Jamboree was a great experience for us. It was Ken's and my first trip out of state, and we traveled via the Northwest, stopping in Yellowstone, Minneapolis, Chicago, and New York on the way to the encampment in Valley Forge, Pennsylvania. The trip home was more of a straight shot across the middle of the country, but we did make a memorable stop in Salt Lake City where we heard the inspiring Mormon Tabernacle Choir.

There were many "firsts" for us on that trip. As the train proceeded through the muggy Midwest, we were complaining that the air conditioning wasn't working. Then we got out on the platform in Minneapolis and learned what high humidity really was. I felt as though I had been draped in a warm wet blanket.

Generally, we slept on the train in sleeping bags on seats which folded flat. Occasional hotel accommodations were modest. Lest one get the wrong impression about our staying in the now elegantly restored Willard, it had fallen into great disrepair at that time. In New York we stayed in a smelly Times Square hotel where we enjoyed launching paper helicopters that rose on thermal currents from the streets below.

When Dad later asked us how we had spent our precious three nights in New York City, he nodded with approval when we said that we visited Hayden Planetarium on the first night. His response was a little different when we admitted to our choices on the next two nights, the movies "Rocket to the Moon" and "Rocket Ship X-L 9."

The Jamboree encampment was another great experience, especially the opportunity to meet scouts from around the country and around the world. An instant flea market ensued with kids trading artifacts from their regions for those from elsewhere. Horned toads from Texas were among the most popular items. Alerted in advance to this phenomenon, we brought little chunks of lava rock from Mt. Lassen. Before Alaska and Hawaii became states and Mt. St. Helens re-awakened, Lassen was the only officially active volcano in the U.S. It's the sort of thing that scouts go for, and we quickly ran out of lava rocks. A few resourceful but less scrupulous members of our troop found an abundant source of re-supply. The ballast rocks from the nearby Pennsylvania Railroad tracks, well seasoned with effluent from travelers, looked very much the same as lava rocks. So much for the Boy Scout oath.

In the fall of my eighth grade year I won the San Mateo County Spelling Bee. This achievement was regarded as a big deal by my English teacher who then announced to the class that I would be exempted from English class for the rest of the year as a reward. After a brief rush over my newfound free time, I came to feel like an exile. While others were in class, I had to hang around outside, all alone, shooting hoops or hitting tennis balls. How much better it would have been had they assigned me some special reading or other enriching exercise.

Along with most of my chums, I had a crush on cute little Betsy Bingham. As she was the only girl short enough for Billy Seawell, we all thought it was fair that they pair up. Lucky Billy! When Vicky Laughton organized a 40th reunion for our class in Monterey, I was delighted to see that Betsy looked as cute as ever. About a dozen classmates attending, including favorite chum Bill Knorp, made it a very heart-warming event. The highlight was that our eighth grade teachers, Miss Hinton and Mr. Glover, attended. Both were in their 90's and both looked terrific. I guess we didn't wear them out, after all.

Other memory flashes of childhood:

- Winter storms would sweep into the Bay Area, and rain would pour in sheets for days. Gutters would swell; creeks would rise; the clay hillsides would slump. It was exciting.

- I can recall only one real tragedy during grade school years. Heidi Holmes, a beautiful blonde girl in Ken's class, died of leukemia.

- No one we knew got divorced.

- There were traditions at Hillsborough School. Fourth graders did the Maypole Dance in the outdoor Woodland Theatre, the colored streamers forming a beautiful weave and the girls looking so pretty. Every year there was a Christmas pageant with beautiful Christmas carols sung.

- In the days before freeways, vacation trips along the highways were punctuated by stops at the Giant Orange or The Snake Pit and the reading of Burma Shave ditties.

- After war time rationing ended, food was plentiful and nutritious, but very unsophisticated and bland by today's standards. A major breakthrough in cuisine for me came in college when I had my first pizza.

- Growing up, neither Sarah nor I can remember the doors to our houses being locked. The only home in our neighborhood with an alarm system belonged to a reputed mobster. These days even church doors are locked.

High School

My freshman year at Burlingame High was an easy, pleasant one. I fell in with a great group of guys, most of whom were leaders from other scout troops. My tennis game was improving, and I was the top student in a class of 300. I did miss Ken, who had been packed off to Cate School to get his studies on track, and there was a lot of stress at home, but on balance it was a good year.

One day there was a break from the usual school routine. It was Vocational Day, when adults from various professions came to address small groups of students. That evening Dad asked what groups I had selected – perhaps law or medicine? I replied that I had selected forestry, firefighting, and the Marines. Incredulous, he asked me why I had wasted the day. I said that from him and family friends, I felt I knew a good deal about law and medicine, but that this was a unique opportunity to learn about other fields. Later in life, one of my favorite books became Stud Terkel's *Working* which chronicles the daily lives of people in various callings, such as bellhops and jockeys.

While Dad never pushed his profession on us, he did ask when I was fifteen whether I might consider the law as a career. At the time I had a summer job in San Francisco, and I suggested that I break away one afternoon and just hang out at his office to see what it was like. He thought it was a splendid idea, and I followed through a few days later.

Dad's office was a very busy scene, filled with urgency. For some reason, we went our separate ways at the end of the afternoon and then reunited at dinner. Dad asked pointedly what I had thought of my experience. I related that I had been very impressed by all the importance. Dad joined in to cite some of the day's accomplishments, deals brokered, matters settled, etc. He then said, "So maybe you want to be a lawyer, then?" I repeated how impressed I was, but said, "No, I don't think so." He said, "Well, didn't you see that today we settled this and filed that?" Again, I agreed that it was an exciting, productive day, but I said that most of his time was spent arguing. He said, "Of course, that's what lawyers do!" I agreed that it was vital work, but I just didn't enjoy arguing and would rather lean towards medicine or business. It proved to be an illuminating exercise.

That summer job was also illuminating. Uncle Bob Williams arranged for my job at a San Francisco print shop run by a neighbor of his. It consisted of all sorts of miscellaneous duties including counting, wrapping, and delivering print orders, usually menus for local restaurants. The shop routinely shorted its customers by a significant amount – apparently, customers usually didn't check the delivery count. Then one day, a local seafood restaurant owner came in, bellowing that he had been cheated. A bit of theater ensued. Our boss asked how many packages had been received. "Only two short-changed packages!" was the reply. Our boss then said there were supposed to have been three, and he sent me and another worker to go look for the "missing package." While in the back room, I confided to my colleague that I had pulled the job from the press and that there were only two packages. He said, "I know – just make noise." When we emerged empty-handed, our boss said, "We'll turn this place upside down to find it!" Once the visitor was out of range, the boss yelled out, "Let's go – run 500 more seafood menus!"

That job also provided a colorful moment of comeuppance for me. My supervisor was a gangly character from the Texas hill country. One day he sent me to the storeroom to fetch another can of black ink. The closest match I could find was a can of ink that looked to me to be a dark iridescent navy blue. Finally, the super stalked back to the storeroom himself and grabbed the can. When I said I thought it looked blue, his response was pretty convincing, "Son, that ink is as black as the inside of a bruised crow!"

When it was time to go back to school, there was to be a change. Dad was concerned about how little homework I was doing at Burlingame High. I would show him the one or two math problems or the couple of pages of reading, all of which I usually did on the way home on the bus. One day he asked if I would like to see how I might fare at Cate School. He brought out their entrance exam, which consisted of their freshman final exams in the subjects I had just been taking and acing with a straight "A" average. I was shocked at the exam, seeing all manner of material that was way beyond me. With 70 a passing grade, I got a 66 in algebra, my best subject, a 58 in English, and a pathetic 25 in Latin. I was both overcome with panic that other kids were vaulting that far ahead of me and enthused about reuniting with Ken.

I approached Cate with a great deal of apprehension about my academic deficiency. Wake-up time was 6:30 a.m., but I set my alarm daily for 4:30 to get a head start. I was obsessively conscientious, double-checking everything and working on various skills, even my handwriting. By the end of the year, I had not only caught up, I won the Scholarship Cup for the highest average in the entire school. Often in life, I have found that fear of failure is a more powerful motivator than the desire for success.

Superficially, the Cate years were a success. I was captain of the tennis team, quarterback on the football team, the lead in the school play, and I had a flawless record of citizenship. Upon graduation, my grades and test scores got me into Stanford. But my years at Cate were not happy years. Many of the kids were from what we then called "broken homes." Three of my twenty-five classmates subsequently committed suicide. One rather effeminate boy in another class was bullied and hounded unmercifully. And there was always deference by school administration to the kids from families of wealth – decidedly, not our family. I had a fabulous education, kindled my first romance, learned to smoke and love jazz, and formed some fond friendships, but on balance I left with a melancholy feeling.

Among Cate School's traditions was an annual school-wide treasure hunt. Early in the spring, the school took the day off to send students running all over the 100-acre campus. The student body was organized into pairs who were sent in search of 20 successive clues. The record for the fastest completion of the hunt was something like four hours. My partner Bob Curry and I stood with the other students, but just as the mass of students bolted down the hill to the announced site of the first clue, I suggested to Bob that we wait and reconnoiter. Puzzled, he asked what I had in mind. My hunch was that there were only so many intriguing places where clues might be hidden. I immediately thought of the tower, a distinctive school landmark. Perhaps it harbored a clue that was well down the list. Sure enough, taped inside was clue number 17. We then proceeded in a very orderly, measured manner to solve the next two clues, and then, barely 45 minutes into the daylong hunt, we had the prize in hand. Usually the Headmaster was hovering nearby the finish line once four or five hours had elapsed. But this time, we had to seek him at his home.

Headmaster Miller was at first astounded by our feat, then apoplectic that we had taken such a shortcut. He decided to invalidate our approach and let the scramble continue in the customary fashion. To this day I don't know what the proper ethical course should have been, although I'm inclined to think what we did was all right. In later years I've come to realize that the problem was that the rules did not specify that all clues must be solved in sequence.

Another memorable event involved a visit to Caltech. Annually, General Electric held a contest for the top science students from about 400 Southern California high schools. Five students would win full-ride college scholarships. We were ushered into a large auditorium and given a bluebook and an exam with just three questions, the most obscure questions imaginable. The one I remember concerned a hypothetical new element just discovered with a certain density and other properties. We were to figure out what some other properties might be, such as the freezing point. I didn't know where to start on any of the three questions. My near neighbors appeared equally stumped, but here and there throughout the room were about a dozen students eagerly engaged in filling out their blue books. In a whispered aside to my neighbor, I said, "I think that's who they're looking for." I then got a small measure of satisfaction when barely 20 minutes into the two-hour test, I walked dramatically down the ramp to the table at the front and slapped down my (empty) blue book, saying, "Piece of cake!" – to the great consternation of the nerd herd.

We often hear of the "good old days" without realizing the degree of tolerance and understanding that has developed in subsequent years. While growing up, none of us recognized "learning disabilities," much less differences in learning styles. Accepted wisdom was that there was a simple continuum from smartest to dumbest, and everyone had a spot along that line. If a child showed signs of being bright but still had trouble with schoolwork, he or she was accused of not concentrating or being lazy. In retrospect, one of my favorite classmates may well have suffered from a learning disability. He was such a nice fellow, and I worked many hours with him tutoring him on his studies. I was pleased to see his grades improve quite a bit. I was unaware that his family knew of my involvement, but he must have told them because one day I got a very unusual message from the Headmaster. I was to be given a special leave and to be picked up by a limo. It was to be a dream date that his parents arranged, a date with a Tournament of Roses Princess to the Brown Derby Restaurant in Los Angeles. We both felt a little awkward, but she was a real head-turner, and the trophy photograph of us later created quite a buzz on the monastic campus.

The L.A. crowd at Cate was great fun. Robert Niven, George Ellis and Eddie Gregson loved to party and listen to jazz. A favorite spot was Howard Rumsey's Lighthouse at Hermosa Beach where Bud Shank played a mellow sax. San Francisco had some great spots, too, featuring Dave Brubeck, Cal Tjader, George Shearing, Oscar Peterson and many others who I enjoyed with Cheever Tyler and later with college chums. I still want to light up a cigarette when listening to jazz. Thanks to Bill Haines, I finally managed to stay upright on a surfboard which qualified me for admission to the SOM Club – South of Malibu. On warm evenings in L.A., cruising in Eddie's Mercury convertible, all seemed right with the world. I've always loved L.A., although I know San Franciscans aren't supposed to.

A memorable social event from my L.A. days came when I started dating a girl named Connie. When I called her house, her mother answered. Upon identifying myself, she snarled, "Well, you have a nerve!" and hung up. Was my reputation that bad, or had I just encountered the Doberman of gatekeepers? After a suitable delay, I called back and this time got Connie. When I told her of the incident, she broke out laughing. She then explained that she had recently had a rather messy break-up with *another* "Doug Brown." Further, she said she was having a challenge explaining to her friends that she was dating "a new Doug Brown." Responses were generally along the lines of, "Honey, don't fall for it – they never change." Fortunately, this sitcom did not have a long run.

Part of the adventure of going off to boarding school was the journey itself. The ride from San Francisco to Santa Barbara on the Southern Pacific Daylight was a beautiful trip. Much of the time was spent playing bridge and swapping stories. One time, though, I had to take the plane home – my very first flight! With six stops along the way it wasn't much faster than the train, but it would get me to San Francisco in time to accept a girl's invitation to a dance at Burke's School. It was to be the longest trip of my life. Just as I was marveling at the receding landscape below, I began sweating profusely. I asked the flight attendant if I might have a cold towel. She brought one, along with several bags. I had never heard of airsickness, but I soon learned. By the time we landed, I was so ill that when Mom rushed up to greet me, I had to shield my face with a tennis racket. No, I didn't make it to the dance.

A very special feature of Cate is its beautiful location on a mesa overlooking lemon groves and the ocean two miles distant. Behind are three ridges of mountains, stretching up to 5,000 feet. From the top, the Channel Islands stand in relief. The ocean becomes about 10 degrees warmer south of Point Conception, which is just above Santa Barbara. In addition to board and body surfing, we would take large paddleboards out to the kelp beds that lie offshore. Some of the thickest kelp beds in the world are found off Carpinteria where they are harvested for iodine. The kelp was so dense at the surface that it supported nesting seabirds. Escapes to the beauty of nature helped me to deal with the problems at home and the melancholy of boarding school.

During late high school and early college years, Christmas vacations were consumed by wall-to-wall debutante parties. These events all led up to the climactic Cotillion at San Francisco's

Palace Hotel where twenty to thirty debutantes were "presented" to society. It was all very elitist, but they were lavish parties. Freed from our sheltered boarding school lives, we eagerly embraced this indulgence. One season I attended 26 parties. It was a chance to re-engage with kids from other schools and a wonderful opportunity to get to know their families.

Occasionally, adult supervision was lax. At one Hillsborough party where the parents took an early leave, things went way over the top and well down the other side. Around midnight, a rumor started that the party was running low on alcohol. A hoarding frenzy ensued with kids stashing drinks in hiding places all over the house and in the extensive gardens. The next wave of panic came as some began discovering the stashed drinks of others. The drill then became a mad dash to consume any drinks one could find. With revelers climbing and falling from trees, I made a hasty exit. I later heard that drinks and the carcasses of drinkers were being found well into the next day.

Stanford

What a difference there was from the college admissions scene of those days to now. Legacy counted more heavily then, and with good grades and test scores, I didn't bother applying anywhere but Stanford, a decision that would be foolhardy today.

Leaving Cate for Stanford was exhilarating. The freedom, the choices, the scale of the place, and its traditions ushered in an exciting new period. There was the obvious thrill of having girls around. In addition to collegiate binge drinking, many former boarding school boys engaged in binge dating, resulting in over half of our Cate class having their college careers interrupted until they refocused their energies. I stayed afloat, but I had a pronounced sophomore slump before regaining academic momentum.

In 1955, I began college as a premed student and got off to a good academic start, thanks in large part to superior secondary school training. That first summer I immersed myself in the field as an orderly at Palo Alto Hospital. While I continued to find medicine fascinating, I became discouraged about the long gestation period. A Dr. Brown in X-ray befriended me and urged me not to pursue the profession unless I was masochistic. He was 36 (twice my age), balding, and still had a ways to go on his residency. He said his wife was nagging him; all his non-medical friends were buying houses; and he wished he had chosen another course in life. His influence played a part in my realizing that I didn't have the dedication for that degree of deferral. And my subsequent interval of academic decline may have made the decision for me, anyway.

A steady relationship with a studious girlfriend helped to salvage my GPA midway through college. Also, roommate Steve Tallent, a brilliant student as well as great company, convinced me that the challenging upper division courses would hold my interest better than the easier but bland survey courses I had been taking. Following his sage advice, I plunged into an array of advanced courses with great relish.

Many of my friends joined fraternities, but I was not entirely comfortable with the elite aspects, and I was a little concerned that their hyper-social atmosphere would destroy any hope of my academic recovery. Instead, I found a great group in the El Tigre Eating Club. Among the ten pledges were Steve, our class president, Dick Coffing, and future Supreme Court Justice, Steve Breyer.

My active social life took a toll on my budget, and I found myself scrambling to make ends meet. For several years I dug myself out by hashing (waiting tables) for my food bill and by becoming the campus representative for the *San Francisco Examiner*. The *Examiner* paid a fee for each paper delivered, but the real money was in getting $5 bonuses for selling new subscriptions. Our paper's market penetration on campus was excellent with one glaring exception - women. Men were not allowed past the front door of the women's dorms, and few women wanted the inconvenience of traipsing down to the front door for the morning paper. I decided to recruit a network of women to deliver the papers to the rooms for a cut of my fee and bonuses. Circulation increased 30%.

It almost increased a great deal more. The paper ran a contest during football season. They listed 20 college games for the upcoming weekend and invited readers to compete for a $1,000 prize for 20 correct picks. The vagaries of college athletics would often produce no winners all season. One day a student approached me to subscribe to 400 copies of the *Examiner*. He figured that with 20 x 20 papers he would cover all the possibilities and waltz off with the prize. This proposal produced a real dilemma for me. My bonus from the paper for 400 new subscriptions would be $2,000, over a year's living expenses for me at that time. However, I knew that to cover all the possibilities was an exponential calculation that produced a number that was in the billions. In good faith I could not let this (English major) student proceed on a false premise. I told him that his buying 400 papers would increase his chances 400-fold but would hardly make a dent in his overall probability. He was very pleased with this enlightenment and decided to order 20 papers anyway, which produced a very welcome extra $100 for me as well as a clear conscience.

My other jobs at Stanford were cleaning a pool at an Atherton estate in exchange for a room over the garage and providing cakes for the grad schools. Stanford's Business and Law Schools were adjoining, and every morning my girlfriend and I would bring to the school lounges four cakes that we baked the night before. We learned quickly that only chocolate cakes would sell reliably. Both chocolate cake with white frosting and yellow cake topped with chocolate were called "chocolate cake" by the students. We operated on an honor system in those innocent days. A decorated coffee can would receive payment of 15 cents for a pre-marked $1/16^{th}$ slice and 30 cents for a $1/8^{th}$ slice. As a lark, I decided to label the sizes "medium" and "large" instead of "small" and "large." Darned if the customers didn't refer to the small slices as "medium." Our sign depicted one of the two cake types on the front and the other on the back. Whichever variety was depicted would invariably sell faster. We would then flip the sign if we wanted the other type to move. It was a graphic lesson in the power of advertising.

College afforded me leadership opportunities that tiny Cate could not, and I enjoyed becoming dorm president and serving on the student council. The most satisfying activity, though, was being appointed Chair of the 1957 Big Game Bonfire.

Big Game Bonfire was a cherished tradition at Stanford. On the eve of the Cal/Stanford football game, the Stanford student body would attend a giant rally in the dry lakebed of Lake Lagunita. A highlight of the rally was the ignition of a bonfire that was about 50 feet tall. Atop the pyre was a paper maché "Oskie," an effigy of the Cal mascot. As popular as this event was, school administration was threatening to drop the tradition due to a rash of injuries in the construction process. For several years, between ten and fifteen students had suffered injuries during the month-long assembly process. Some of the wounds came from fights with bands of Cal students who came to raid the bonfire and ignite it prematurely. Twice in recent years, they had succeeded. I was serving on the student Executive Committee, and our president asked whether I could accomplish the job safely. I accepted the challenge and then set about thinking it through. It occurred to me that the main problem was that the extended assembly period made construction discipline difficult to enforce and left the project vulnerable to raids. I gathered together a task force of buddies and challenged them to devise a plan to build the bonfire in one day. Quickly, key parts of the plan fell into place. Instead of hiring a truck to haul in debris for three weeks, we'd hire twenty trucks for one day. The only advance construction was getting PG&E to install the triangular grid of six tall telephone poles that framed the structure. We also dug shallow trenches beneath the site to enhance the draft. On C-Day (construction day), over a hundred volunteer workers met the trucks. As one squad nailed on side cribbing, another dropped in brush and junk wood. Stationary ladders were affixed to the structure; all on the ladders wore hard hats; and the workers formed a bucket brigade to hand up the tinder. The whole thing got built in about five hours, compared to about a month previously. As to safety, we had no accidents whatsoever in the construction. One foolish boy was poked in the face with a stick while "sword fighting," but we didn't think that should count.

Then the real challenge began – guarding the structure. By this time it was dark, and additional reinforcements brought the guard complement to about 200. They took their job very seriously by establishing outposts, then an inner ring of defense, and finally, a "death squad" who sat against the actual structure. To our delight, there appeared at the edge of the field a yelping little band of Cal students running towards us with torches in hand. We had anticipated this possibility and had planned a strategy. Our defenders kept their silence until the raiders were well inside the perimeter. Then 200 Stanford worthies arose with a shout and surrounded the astonished little band. The Cal guys quickly dropped their torches in fear of their lives. We then sent them on their way intact, except for their heads which we shaved with electric razors we had stowed for just such an occasion. It turned out that several of the raiders were Cal football players. Their humiliation may have contributed to our victory on the gridiron that Saturday. A write-up of this event served as my essay in my successful application to Stanford Business School.

A key Bonfire Committee colleague was Jim Robertson. Sometimes, another person will connect with your life, time after time. Jim and I were classmates and teammates on various activities while at Stanford, then in raising funds for the Exploratorium, followed by joining the Bohemian Club together. Later, Judge Jim enlisted our son, Elliott, as his law clerk and then presided over Elliott's admission to the California Bar. Another classmate whose serial connections continue to amaze me is John Bohn. He keeps popping up in the most surprising places, most notably, out of the subway in St. Petersburg when I was visiting there.

Captain Doug and Coach Stanley Durrant

Specialist 6 Brown at Award Ceremony

The Army

In my junior year I joined the Army Reserve. There was a seven-person unit at Stanford, a Strategic Intelligence Research and Analysis team. About 40 such SIRA units were attached to universities around the country. They worked on assessing the resources and infrastructure of various nations that were regarded as potential threats to our security. Our unit was headed by Colonel Walter Peterson, the delightful pipe-smoking head of Stanford's News and Publications. Because there was a waiting list of some 80 students who wanted to get in on this interesting and cushy duty, I almost didn't apply. Then during my interview, Walt dropped a hint, saying he regarded the list as a candidate pool, not a waiting list. I was accepted, and it turned out to be fascinating work with six great guys. Our two weeks of annual summer duty were at the Pentagon where we coordinated with our Regular Army counterparts.

Early on, I got a lesson in military acronyms. I came to Walt to ask about an unusual first name that kept appearing in intelligence reports, "Fnu." To my embarrassment I learned that it stood for "first name unknown." My favorite acronym was "Unk Unk." That was the term used when a particular fact was so unknown, we didn't even know what we were looking for; hence, "unknown unknowns."

Walt Peterson was a font of homey wisdom. One of the fellows in our unit was a bright civil engineering student who one time went on at great length about how modern flexible building techniques would minimize earthquake damage. Walt nodded, but then smiled and said, "I sure hope that the 'Big Fella' who makes the earthquakes knows about all that."

I took an extra course load my junior and senior years so I could graduate in March, slip in my 6 months active duty requirement, and start grad school in September without missing a beat. Basic training was at Fort Ord in Monterey. I got such a kick out of Army life. It was a chance to associate with guys from all walks of life. My bunkmate was Pancho Bonilla, who was trying to help his citizenship chances by serving in the Army (not a bad policy, by the way). He played the guitar and had a smoky, melodious voice. You'd want to go clubbing with Pancho.

There were many life lessons from my time in the Army. Issuance of Army uniforms took place in a huge warehouse where recruits were handed large duffel bags and then sent from station to station picking up gear. A sergeant came by and barked at me, "Trooper, where's your duffel bag?" I pointed at the one by my side. He said, "Keep your eye on it – after a while, they all turn green." Another time I was on "Kitchen Patrol" at 2 a.m. scrubbing pots. The mess sergeant saw that I was not doing it with great enthusiasm. He came to me and said, "Son, this here Army can take away your pay, and they can take away your liberty. There's just one thing they can't take away. And that's your pride. Why don't you put a little more effort into the job?" After that inspiration, my pots started gleaming.

The Army frequently asked for volunteers in a way that left the respondent in peril. Usually, they were "lady or the tiger" type of questions where one had to choose blindly. A request for artists led to whitewashing rocks. The guy who volunteered as a "musician" had to carry and beat the big bass drum on marches. But volunteering to try out for the drill team did turn out to be a good deal, as we trained in cool Monterey while the rest of the troops went on bivouac at sweltering Camp Roberts.

There were the inevitable surprises, such as a time on Kitchen Patrol when my wrist was growing sore from opening up scores of large cans of tomatoes. The mess sergeant took away my can opener and said, "Not like that – like this!" With that he turned the cans on their sides and began chopping them apart with a meat cleaver. Bits of label and metal flew everywhere, especially into the tomatoes.

My favorite Army "snafu" was when we practiced a nuclear response drill by scattering in the hills and digging shallow trenches with our entrenching tools (they're not shovels, trooper!) and then crawling in and covering up with a tarp. After an hour or so, the all-clear siren blew, and we regrouped. Well, some of us regrouped. About half the troops, greatly sleep-deprived, had fallen into deep sleep in their little burrows in the warm summer morning. Some didn't return until that evening.

Another life lesson has stood me in good stead in civilian life. An old hand alerted me that inspectors and auditors are always going to find something wrong, so give them something that's easy to fix. That advice proved helpful in barracks inspections, which one needed to pass before weekend leave would be granted. It's easy to remake a bed tighter, but it can take hours away from weekend time if one needs to re-clean a rifle. The best diversion was to leave a *Playboy* magazine in the laundry bag for them to find. They wouldn't even bother to look at your rifle after bagging that prize.

Advanced intelligence training at Fort Meade, Maryland was highly professional. I enjoyed the subjects and enjoyed the soldiering. I was amazed at the competence and thoroughness of Army Intelligence. One of the projects we worked on was the invasion of Baltimore – not as a mock exercise, but to be ready to re-take the city should an enemy capture it. I was pleased at the end of my tour there to be given awards as both "Outstanding Student" and "Outstanding Soldier," the first time both honors were awarded to one person.

The Army tried to interest me in becoming an officer. I didn't want to make that commitment, but I was curious to see how I would do on the Officer Candidate School test. The test involved solving 20 problems. They were not too difficult, and I was steaming along. Until question eleven. Question eleven had trains departing from several British stations at various times in various directions. Then the Royal Mail Train was to come through the middle of all this. As it had priority, numerous sidings came into play. I started sweating bullets. After a few minutes, I abandoned the question, hoping that it was not the harbinger of more difficult questions to come. However, the rest of the questions were routine, and the answers came easily. After re-checking my work, I had about 20 minutes to devote to question eleven again. I got nowhere. After collecting the papers, the officer in charge asked, "How'd you guys like question eleven?" The group answered with a collective groan. Then, "How many of you got stuck there and didn't get any further?" A few hands went up. The officer said that answering that question correctly would require a powerful computer. It was planted there to weed out candidates who might get mired down in a battlefield situation and not look for ways to get their unit around the obstacle.

Upon exiting the Army, a sergeant made one last try at getting us to re-enlist. He spoke of the security, the retirement benefits, the challenges and the camaraderie. Finally, he had some advice for those of us who were determined to return to civilian life. He said that we should go to the dictionary and pick out two of the biggest words we could find, string them together, and then apply for such a job at the unemployment office. His suggestion was "lithographic analyst." He said the clerk will look it up and find no such positions available, which would then qualify us for unemployment benefits.

The pay for reserve duty was only about $90 per quarter, but that pay provided vital discretionary money to buy birthday gifts and the like. Especially welcome was the travel pay. The Army provided $360 for round-trip travel from San Francisco to Washington, D.C. for summer duty. That amount approximated airfare at that time. I rode the bus for $120 round-trip. This odyssey required a 69 hour straight-through trip each way. During one trip I devoured all seven of Ian Fleming's James Bond novels.

While my Army service was during peacetime and was not the stuff of heroism, I do bristle when I hear a politician try to disparage the military service of a rival by citing that the service was "only in the Reserves". When you put your right hand in the air and take the oath, they own you for the next six years. They can send you in harm's way whenever and wherever they need you. Reservists and National Guard troops have paid a heavy price for us in many of our nation's conflicts.

Business School

I was relieved to be accepted into Stanford Business School in the fall of 1959. My undergraduate GPA was barely 3.0 (pre-GPA inflation, however, that was well above average), but they liked my essay about the Big Game Bonfire, and my test scores were excellent. Back then there were no test prep courses, as the College Board stoutly maintained that it was useless to try. I note with some irony that the College Board is now among the entities offering test prep courses. Anyway, I decided to buck conventional wisdom and spent about three weeks in intensive self-study. How could it not help to refresh oneself on the quadratic equation and on obscure vocabulary words such as "halcyon" and "nadir?" That decision probably made the difference for me.

The two years at Stanford GSB were intense. The workload was very demanding, and fellow students were highly motivated. There was good camaraderie, most associations coming from working together on group assignments. In our class of about 225, there were only two women and a sprinkling of minority students. The quality of instruction was superb, and the class discussions were stimulating.

Business School was great for imparting instruction on the skills of business, such as accounting, financial analysis, and statistics. It also helped hone writing skills, as we were required to write short focused papers daily in nearly every subject. All classes employed the case study method, which provided me with insights as to how to be effective in advancing a point. I noted that often someone would make a telling comment early in a discussion that would be generally ignored. Then, midway through the discussion, someone else would raise that same point and be accepted with general acclaim. I concluded that many in the audience simply weren't disposed to listen carefully until they had their say. Also, it seemed to me that there was an unseen rhythm to discussions that made certain timings more propitious. In addition, it always helped to gain consensus if one referred to the previous remarks of others in presenting one's views. The position in the room, or around a board table, appeared to me to have an influence, too. Optimal placement in theater seating was somewhat off to the side about 2/3 of the way up. Around a table it was down the table from the person chairing the meeting.

For all the advantages that a good MBA program confers, I am continually impressed by executives who hit on all cylinders without this advantage – college drop-out Bill Gates heading the parade. Alexander Hamilton succeeded brilliantly without formal financial training (but a few lessons in marksmanship could have helped).

The much-vaunted benefits of networking are indeed valid. It cannot just be a superficial exercise practiced during school, though. The best networking comes from later active social participation, such as in alumni groups or fundraising.

When it came time to look for a job, I interviewed with California firms only, mostly from Northern California. The Business School's Placement Office was nice, but not much help. As I was in the top 5% of my class, they insisted on trying to recruit me into a Ph.D program. It was flattering, but I had had enough of academia and wanted to try the "real world." Banking seemed to present the ideal outlet for my financial and sales interests as well as guaranteeing California geography in the days before interstate banking. B of A struck me as too big; Crocker and Wells seemed big enough and well-positioned for growth.

I had a good interview at Crocker, but it didn't end well. The executive said, "We like you, but we don't hire for our training program until the trainees are at least 28 years old." Being barely 23, I asked what might he suggest I do for five years? He said they liked candidates who had "gotten their feet wet" in the marketplace. I then commented that I had every expectation that I would work hard and be successful. If so, why would I want to step back to an entry-level position five years from now? He merely shrugged in reply.

As a postscript, five years from that time, I was on the cusp of being appointed a branch manager at Wells Fargo, and ten years after that, Crocker had to sell to Midland Bank after its talent pool ran dry. And that Midland takeover later provided me the opportunity to join Crocker at a level quite removed from entry level.

Judy

My first wife was the former Judith Ann Svibergson. Her father was Swedish, although the family came from the Finnish-controlled Åland Islands. Life in the Åland Islands was hard. The terrain was rocky and the climate harsh. The chief utility of this little archipelago was its strategic location amid the principal shipping lanes of the Baltic Sea. During World War I, six different armies occupied the territory. As each new wave of soldiers came, the women would dress in the shabbiest of garments and smear dirt on their faces to discourage romantic overtures.

Judy's father, Nils Svibergson, spoke little English when he arrived in the U.S. as a young teenager, which led to his being assigned to a third grade class. He related his embarrassment at sitting in a little desk with his lanky knees up by his ears. Nils taught himself English by repetitive comparisons of the English and Swedish versions of the dictionary and the Bible. Nils Svibergson's wife, Margaret Rogers, came from a large Boston Irish family. They met while he was in Tufts Medical School and raised their daughter Judy in Tewksbury, Massachusetts until migrating to Castro Valley, California in 1955.

Nils was a true family doctor. He served entire families and was an extremely skilled diagnostician. His office staff consisted of his wife Margaret as nurse and his sister Linnea as nurse/receptionist. Nils was so focused and conscientious that his office was constantly prodding him to get on with patients. Most local doctors tried to avoid taking on Boy Scout physicals, which were required before departing for camp, because the Council paid only $3 per physical. Not Nils. Not only did he do most of the local scout physicals, he did them with painstaking thoroughness. In the process he discovered abscessed teeth, kidney problems, heart problems etc. Several young lives may have been saved. He also continued to make house calls long after other doctors had stopped. At social gatherings it was obvious that local surgeons, other specialists, and pharmacists had nothing but the highest regard for Nils Emil Svibergson.

Nils Svibergson's three siblings also went into medicine: Linnea, his nurse and medical assistant, Agnes as a nurse, and Ruth as a pediatrician and child psychiatrist. Linnea and Agnes never married, moved out West together with Nils, and lived nearby in Castro Valley. Linnea and Agnes were steadfast keepers of the Swedish Christmas tradition. Mired in long, dark cold winters, the Swedes celebrate this tradition with great festivity. It begins when a young girl dressed in white enters a darkened room with a crown of lighted candles as Saint Lucia, the saint of light. Our daughter, Becky, was angelic as Saint Lucia. The Christmas dinner is a formidable feast. Most of the traditional dishes are savory – with the notable exception of the *lutfisk*, which is a white fish marinated in lye. If marinated too long, the fish disappears, eaten by the lye.

Ruth Svibergson married Dr. C. Henry Kempe, an eminent pediatrician and virologist. He served as Dean at the University of Denver Medical School and is generally credited with two important medical/social advances. Henry was the first physician to recognize formally the problem of battered children, and he vigorously promoted the problem's recognition in the medical community. The national center for study of this condition is named in his honor. He was also the chief advocate to persuade the international medical community that smallpox had been eradicated and that the risk of further vaccination outweighed the potential benefits. Little did any of us realize the perverse unintended consequence – that an unvaccinated generation would be vulnerable to smallpox virus becoming a bio-terrorist threat, resulting in the recent restoration of large stockpiles of smallpox vaccine.

The Kempe family taught me another lesson. Visiting their home in Denver was an exercise in chaos. The five Kempe girls ruled a scene of uncontrolled frenzy – constant screaming, running, jumping. No apparent limits. Henry and Ruth, the psychiatrist, would endure this turmoil with complete equanimity. Coming from a tightly controlled family, I felt sure the whole clan was destined for eventual incarceration. It was a shock to see all five develop into successful, productive citizens, including three doctors, an author, and a lawyer. Maybe some permissiveness with love can be as effective as a more controlled environment.

Judy's mother was a rock of strength. Margaret was conscientious almost to a fault. Every vacation trip was preceded by all-night housecleaning lest she not survive the trip, whereupon others might judge her to be an inadequate housekeeper. Her strong Catholic ties led to frequent invocations to the Saints, especially St. Jude. Barely five feet tall, she was a bundle of energy. Although Margaret had driven in Massachusetts, she was worried about the perils of California driving and did not get behind the wheel for a number of years. When I came on the scene, I saw what an inconvenience her immobility presented, and I was determined to teach her to drive again. It was a testament to the excellent quality of our relationship that I was able to get her back on the road.

While Nils was sparing in his conversation, Margaret talked nonstop. This situation led to the "migration of the chaise." Nils constantly read medical journals, which required great concentration. Margaret's need for conversation drove Nils and his favorite chaise to the far corner of the family room. Then Nils and the chaise moved out to the patio – then out to the garden. The migrating chaise finally found its resting place in a far corner of the garden.

One might expect the Svibergson family to be reasonably comfortable financially, given their thrifty habits with old cars, old house, only child, and both spouses working. Yet year after year, Nils complained that he was making no financial progress. The problem was speculative investments peddled by telephone salesmen. Nils asked me what investments I would recommend. I suggested a portfolio of blue chip equities, such as Standard Oil, Hewlett Packard, and Wells Fargo Bank. Nils would acknowledge the wisdom of this course, but each time we visited, Nils would again complain about being victimized by the overblown promises of boiler house pitchmen. Finally, I realized that Nils had an insatiable appetite for claims that were too good to be true. I then presented my advice differently. I told Nils he could double his money in no time – just invest in Standard Oil, Hewlett Packard, Wells Fargo, etc. I had pangs of guilt over my ploy, but I thought that the end justified the means. I then lined up Nils with a stockbroker friend, and I instructed him never to buy or sell any of Nils' positions without checking with me. The result of this benign chicanery was that Nils eventually enjoyed a comfortable retirement and left a seven figure estate.

Bernard Baruch was once approached by an investor who asked him for investment advice. Mr. Baruch responded, "Well, it all depends – do you want to eat well or do you want to sleep well?"

When Doug met Judy. It was at Stanford in 1957 in a speech class. She was a freshman, and I was a junior working on restoring a GPA depleted from too many forays to the beach. I recognized Judy's name as the roommate of my then-girlfriend, Liz Cooper. Over the next year, I saw a good deal of Judy as a by-product of dating Liz. When my relationship with Liz cooled, the relationship with cute, bright Judy kindled quickly.

She was so bright that she had skipped two grades in school and entered Stanford when she was 16. According to family legend, Judy learned to read at age three and enjoyed scanning her father's medical books. When a visiting adult poked her in the tummy and asked playfully if that was her belly button, she said, "No, that's my umbilicus!"

Over the next three years of college and graduate school, Judy was a constant and beloved companion, and we got married in June, 1961, shortly after my graduation from Stanford Business School. We were married at St. Clement's Church in Berkeley, the same church where my parents were married. Ken was Best Man and Liz Cooper Vickers was Judy's Matron of Honor.

Signs of problems to come were there, but went unrecognized. Judy was so young that it was easy to dismiss her difficulty handling alcohol at parties as naiveté, and for the most part, somewhat charming.

The dark side of alcohol first became apparent during our honeymoon. We took advantage of my two-week Army Reserve duty at the Pentagon to schedule a six-week cross-country trip. As our workdays at the Pentagon wound up around 4 p.m., I looked forward to long summer evenings with my Army buddies and their wives – softball games, movies, and concerts. But to my dismay, when I came home, night after night my young bride was clearly not herself – sometimes to the point of being passed out. Back on the road, together all day on the return trip, normalcy resumed along with the hope of better times to come. A highlight of the trip was a visit to a charming waterfront retreat in Cape Porpoise, Maine, owned by Margaret Svibergson's chums, Loie, a physician and Eleanor, a medical administrator. These wonderful women were ever-attentive to Judy and later to our daughter, Becky. A favorite childhood toy of Becky's was a whimsical stuffed lobster doll, hand-crafted by Loie. Becky still has that doll.

Better times did come, but only intermittently. Our first home was a flat at 34 Marie Street, a block above Bridgeway in Sausalito. Jogging up those steep hills got me back on the road to fitness. (During grad school my "six pack" abs were verging on becoming a keg.)

We were blessed with a lovely daughter, Rebecca Margaret Brown, born April 14, 1963. As it was Easter Sunday, Becky was and always will be our Easter bunny. I was in the operating room at Stanford Hospital at the moment of birth. As we had not known the gender of the baby beforehand, we were understandably anxious to learn. Upon the baby's emergence, the obstetrician snatched the baby out of view and then announced that it had "the father's features and the mother's fixtures."

A most unusual romantic incident came one evening in Sausalito when we were awakened from a sound sleep about eleven by a phone call. It was old friend Don who wanted to come by and have us meet his new girlfriend, "Heather." We quickly dressed and shortly thereafter, Don and Heather arrived for a brief visit. As anticipated, the next day Don called again, asking, "Well, what did you think of Heather?" We shared our impression that she seemed nice, as indeed she had. About a month later, a wedding invitation arrived, announcing Don's plan to marry. Only it was to marry "Sharon." Evidently, Heather didn't make it past the semi-finals of the Don Derby.

Seeking more room, we moved to Palo Alto's Amarillo Apts. and then to San Leandro to a full floor flat at 357 West Estudillo. When Judy became pregnant with our second child, we decided to buy a house. As I was then Assistant Manager of Wells Fargo Bank's Burlingame Office, we began looking in that vicinity. Based on my income, I felt we could afford to pay up to $25,000. I was delighted to learn that my "dream house" was for sale, a pretty little cottage on Burlingame's Ralston Avenue which I had admired since growing up nearby. Delight turned to dismay when I learned that it was listed for $48,000! Checking the area, I learned that the rattiest little houses next to the freeway cost more than I could afford. Remembering a recent trip to Wells Fargo's Fremont Office in the more affordable East Bay, we decided to look at a very attractive development called Glenmoor Gardens. Like most enlightened young adults, we had sworn we would never surrender to suburban conformity. But then we had to deal with the reality of finding a 3 bedroom, 2 bath home with a nice backyard, one block from school and park, all for $23,500. With a 5% mortgage, our payments were $100/month. Even though it was known as model 1316, and neighbors could find our medicine cabinet with their eyes closed, it was perfect for our needs.

The real price to pay for that house was a hellacious commute to frequent meetings in San Francisco. BART did not yet reach to Fremont, so my route was to drive to South Hayward where I would pick up the A/C Transit bus to the City. The entire trip was 1 ½ to 1 ¾ hours each way. Evening banking courses and Army Reserve meetings made for many late nights.

Partly for financial reasons and partly out of pride, I determined to handle all household repairs and improvements myself. Although it required countless repeat visits to the hardware store and constant reference to do-it-yourself books, I was able to keep to my promise through installation of appliances, pouring of patios, re-wiring, etc. An especially satisfying interlude occurred when the bank agreed to let several of us pull salvage from a branch office they were abandoning. My garage was lined with cabinets from the teller cages.

When I accepted the bank's offer to move to Pasadena to head up our operation there, I was pleased to find that we could sell our

Fremont home for $26,000 (never mind that it's probably worth over $600,000 now). I am reminded of my favorite definition of inflation; it's "when your money isn't worth as much as it used to be, back when you didn't have any."

I was fortunate that some social worker was not witness to the following incident: Becky was acting cranky and squirming as three year-olds do when they've stayed up a little too late. I was trying with limited success to get her into a "trundle-bundle," one of those little fuzzy bodysuits. Her non-stop fussing finally led me to bark, "That's the last I want to hear from you!" (Dad may have been a little cranky himself.) The project proceeded better, but then she started whimpering again. To my question/comment, "What now!?" she replied, "You're standing on my foot," which, it turned out, I was. Ah, the perils of parenting.

Becky was excited about the arrival of a baby brother on September 26, 1965. When newborn Kenny came home from Doctors Hospital in San Leandro, she looked admiringly at him in his bassinet. She then turned to us with a look of disappointment and lamented that, "Kenny can't talk, or anything." It was apparent that Becky did not expect to have to wait a few years for a full-fledged playmate to develop.

Actually, Becky would have to wait longer than that. Kenny was a handsome, healthy boy who regularly exceeded the baby norms for physical development. Socially, though, he was very distant. Another troubling trait was that Kenny never seemed to engage in imitative behavior. Whereas most babies would emulate adult behavior, such as fiddling with a doorknob, Kenny did not. When Kenny reached his second birthday without talking, we sought guidance from his pediatrician. We weren't satisfied with his palliatives, encouraging us, "Not to worry, he'll be fine," as we felt something was definitely wrong. We were then in the midst of the move to Pasadena, and we got a referral to Children's Hospital of LA for a battery of diagnostic tests. They ran a number of hearing tests, motor tests, and such. When the doctors concluded that no physical anomalies were present, the tentative conclusion became childhood autism. This mysterious condition is characterized by the subject's lack of reaction and communication, often accompanied by obsessive "self-stimulating" behavior, such as tapping or gesturing. They often act bewildered and are easily upset, especially if a routine varies.

A poignant incident occurred when Judy and I were at the kitchen table puzzling over baby Kenny's condition. Unbeknownst to us, four year-old Becky was nearby and had overheard us. Suddenly, she was standing at the table with a very determined look on her face. She said to us, "Kenny can't talk, but I still love him!" That spirit is with Becky to this day.

Becky Brown has always been such a sensitive, caring person that it was not surprising to see her pick up on a message about charity when she was five. At church, Becky had heard a sermon about helping the poor. Later, we saw her load a bunch of her very favorite toys and dolls into her little red wagon. She began to proceed out the door to the gate in our back fence. When asked, Becky said she was taking them "to the poor children." On the other side of the fence was the family of Fred Poor, an engineer who probably made twice as much as I did.

For conclusive diagnosis of Kenny's condition, Children's referred us to UCLA's Neuropsychiatric Institute. There, they performed a test that not only confirmed his autism, but I thought gave insight as to the nature of the condition. The doctors gave Kenny a mild sedative to induce sleep and then wired him for an electro-encephalogram to measure brain activity. They proceeded to introduce a stimulus, a bell that rang faintly every 30 seconds for about ten minutes. The normal brain reacts to the stimulus, and after a few iterations begins to anticipate the ringing at about the 25 second mark. After the bells cease, the brain waves show a few flurries of anticipation at intervals and then become quiet. With Kenny, a very different pattern emerged. There was no reaction whatever to the first ten or so bell ringings. Then, out of the blue, there was a great flurry of reaction, as if to say, "There are bells going off all over the place!" Then no reaction for the balance of the period, followed minutes later by another flurry, which I interpreted as, "Hey, what happened to all the bells?"

To my mind, this pattern was very revealing of the nature of the condition. It was neurological – Kenny in effect had a "wiring problem." Drs. Lovaas and Ritvo agreed that they thought so, too. However, the prevailing wisdom was a theory proposed by University of Chicago's Dr. Bruno Bettelheim. Based solely on conjecture, Psychiatrist Bettelheim spread the gospel that autism was caused by defects in parenting. Parenting classes were formed to coach these errant "refrigerator parents." I can only guess at the unnecessary pain and suffering his shoddy work caused families already burdened with the weight of developmentally disabled children. I know this pressure contributed to the dissolution of many marriages, including mine.

My failure in this marriage haunts me as the biggest disappointment of my life. Judy tried valiantly to get herself under control and had spells of sobriety that were encouraging. But the relapses grew more serious, and she ended up being hospitalized. Visiting my wife on one floor of UCLA-NPI where she was undergoing treatment and my son on another became an overwhelming burden while trying to pursue my career in Pasadena, an hour away.

For a year after the divorce, I did not date out of a feeling that to do so would be disloyal. There was also the burden of guilt over how my intensity might have contributed to the problem and how I had failed to solve it. The most painful part of divorce is the inevitable effect upon the children. I remember Becky being asked by a family friend whether she would be a "Mrs." or a "Ms." when she grew up. Becky responded that she would be a "Miss" until she married, then a "Mrs.," and then when she divorced, she would be a "Ms." Ouch!

Although custody of the children was joint, I assumed initial physical custody. My friend and Wells Fargo colleague, John Muir, offered his downstairs apartment in their home in La Crescenta. For a year I raised my family with the Muir family, a wonderful Mormon family whose stability provided a needed anchor for our lives. By the end of the year, Judy had moved back with her parents in Castro Valley, and with the support of her mother, she was ready to assume physical custody of the children. Three years later, I was pleased to see Judy remarry to a fine fellow, Douglas Schliebus, who has become a caring stepfather to Becky and Kenny.

As an epilogue, I am so pleased to see that life has taken a decided turn for the better for Judy. This marriage has been strong, and they have happily relocated to Orcas Island outside Seattle. There, Judy has become certified as one of the Island's few Emergency Medical Technicians where she has been involved in numerous life-saving incidents, and she and Doug Schliebus have become pillars of their community.

Becky Brown – 1974

Kenny and Becky –1988

Wells Fargo

I really liked the people I met at Wells Fargo, especially long-time family friend, Bill Barkan. The bank was fairly new to hiring college graduates, much less MBA's. My reward for having an MBA was to be hired at $425 per month instead of $400. It did bother me to learn that the toll taker on my commute across the Golden Gate Bridge was making 50% more than I was. Clearly, he belonged to a stronger union!

My first stop on the 18-month training program was an assignment to the Matson Building Office on lower Market Street. The manager there was Dick Cooley, the most charismatic person I've ever known. He was widely recognized as a rising star in the bank, and within five years was destined to become the bank's CEO. He showed a deep personal caring; he was bright and intuitive; he was very comfortable in the top ranks of society; and he had been a genuine war hero. A flight accident in England had taken his right arm, and he wore a prosthetic arm with a steel hook. His spirit was inspiring. From being a champion right-handed squash player at Yale, he later was Olympic Club champ left-handed. Playing one-handed, he played golf in the 80's. I was startled one day to see Dick briskly tie a bow tie one-handed, using his teeth to secure one end. He even had a great sense of humor about his disability and enjoyed laying cold steel on the back of your neck while passing behind your desk. I had not heard about Dick's missing arm before we met, and I was surprised to see him extend a hook in greeting. I then asked, "Am I supposed to grasp the hook, or should I shake your other hand with my left or what?" He said, "I admire your poise in asking – I do this for shock effect."

Here's another incident. One Monday morning Dick said, "I saw you in Burlingame over the weekend." I responded that I was embarrassed if I had passed him without saying hello. He then said, "No, it was I who was embarrassed, as I was in my gardening clothes, and I ducked into a doorway so I wouldn't be seen by you!" Just how many CEO's would behave that way, much less admit to it? I had the pleasure of working for Dick Cooley on three occasions and have treasured our continuing friendship.

Wells Fargo was just beginning to emerge from "old school" ways when I joined in 1961. Everybody worked to age 65 and then retired. It was lifetime employment. One never switched banks. In fact, it was off-limits to recruit other bankers while they were still employed elsewhere. These days, if someone shows a resume with only one long-term employment, it looks hopelessly sluggish. In my case, I had 23 years with Wells Fargo, but never as long as three years in any one position and with a wide variety of assignments. Only staff specialists tended to stay in the same post for many years, which contributed to a shift of power in their direction. The constant churn of assignments of line officers also produced a reluctance to take on projects that were risky or had a long-term payback.

Old school Wells Fargo produced some unusual moments. I came back to the office in San Francisco late one evening and heard quite a clamor coming from a back room. A peek around the corner revealed two tipsy bank vice presidents pounding away on full keyboard adding machines to prove who was still the fastest machine operator. I don't know whether the scotch helped or hindered.

Then there was Snuffy, Wells Fargo's intrepid loan collector. He was a master of guile in re-acquiring collateral on delinquent loans. One afternoon, Snuffy was sent to pick up a TV set from an apartment in Oakland. He was greeted by a full-dress crime scene with yellow tape everywhere and a chalked body outline on the floor. He poked his head in, showed his credentials, and asked the police if he couldn't just have the TV over there in the corner. He was told that nothing could be moved without the written consent of the owner, who was being held in the county jail on a murder charge. Undaunted, Snuffy went to the jail and was escorted to the cell. Snuffy presented the paper for the required signature. A sullen voice responded, "Yeah, well why should I sign it?" Snuffy put on his most menacing look and said, "If you don't sign it, you're going to be in big trouble!" With an "I don't need no more trouble," the paper was signed.

Women were very new to management ranks, and I was appalled to learn that women officers were required to sign letters using only their initials before their surnames. The clear message was that their correspondence would be taken more seriously if their female gender was concealed. Not only was this policy demeaning to women, it exposed both parties to embarrassment when a caller expected "Mr. Smith," and Jane Smith answered. I am pleased to have taken the initiative to change this policy to allow full name signatures for females.

Another example of business practices in that era came from Charlie. Charlie was a grizzled veteran officer at my first office. He asked me to take some item over to "the girl in the blue dress." "You mean Sandra?" I responded. He then said, "I don't know – I don't bother learning their names until they've been here two years." I conjured up the ludicrous specter of Charlie's diarizing these events, noting two years later that the day had come to learn a particular employee's name.

Another early career experience was my being deputized as a stock transfer agent. This exalted status enabled me to sign my name on stock certificates for ten hours a day for 16 straight days, including weekends. Imagine today's MBA's enduring such duty.

An especially poignant reminder of "the good old days" came when I was a very junior officer at Wells Fargo. One of the bank's top officers, Jack Elmer, announced his retirement. As I had come to know him a little and admire him a lot, I dropped by his office on his last day to pay my respects. Instead of a quick pleasantry, he asked me if I could stay so he could relate a story. Jack then told of when he was a young man at the American Trust Company, a predecessor of Wells Fargo, working in the auditing department. In those days, when one was elected a junior officer in the bank, it was mandated that one buy $10,000 in bank stock. This obligation was welcomed, as all during the 1920's the bank's stock had doubled every several years. Because the young officers had few financial resources, the bank extended them almost 100% margined loans.

With a booming market, several hundred dollars down would become $50,000 or more in no time. Then the Depression hit. The bank's stock had been highly leveraged through an elaborate layering of holding companies. In a little over one year, the bank's share price plummeted from a high of $129 to a low of $2! The resultant margin calls on the bank officers caused financial ruin. Jack and his fellow auditors were assigned to investigate a rash of bank officer embezzlements. With tears in his eyes, Jack said there were two suicides of officers he was investigating. It was clear that Jack had passed a torch to me as one who might be able to see that such heinous corporate practices would never be repeated.

My management training was an 18-month rotation among all the jobs in a branch office. By today's standards, the pace was painstakingly slow. A good deal of it was of dubious effectiveness. Neil, a fellow trainee, was a Harvard graduate. Like the rest of us, he began teller training by spending three weeks sitting on a stool behind a teller, watching the transactions. Finally, the big day arrived, and the two switched positions. Neil dutifully accepted a check to cash, verified that the date was current and the endorsement correct. He stamped the front. Then he froze. In a panic, he turned to his mentor and whispered, "Where do you keep the cash?" For three weeks, he had seen her fish the cash out of the drawer about 100 times a day, but his passive role had lulled him into a trance.

It is easy to deride the ways of old, but with a slow pace of change, employees did learn to be expert in their jobs. Perfection was the goal, not just good enough. Old timers told me that if a teller made two mistakes in a month, he or she was banished to bookkeeping for a month. Different times call for different skills. In earlier days, the best job for an agile seven-footer might have been as a look-out on Columbus's ship.

Then there was Rex Andrews, my first boss after the training program. He had been the head of the training program, and he recruited me to take his place as he moved up a notch. Rex was very approachable and helpful to me, but I had a pang of anxiety when after about a month on the job, Rex asked me if I would meet with him at the end of the day. Was I not performing well? When the appointed hour arrived, he suggested we go across the street to a bar – which only served to heighten my concern. Finally, beers in hand, he told me what he wanted. It turned out that he just wanted my reaction to a situation regarding his family. Specifically, Rex expressed dismay over an unusual name that his wife was advocating for the baby they were expecting shortly. Nan was lobbying to name the baby, boy or girl, "America Andrews." For context, this was before the beat generation and well before any post-9/11 patriotic surge. Rex was clearly looking for my support, which became obvious from my amused reaction. Finally, I offered a suggestion – that Rex reply to Nan that they should consider naming the child "West Virginia" in the hope that it might attract Federal aid dollars. Rex loved the suggestion, and I heard no more about the matter until several weeks later when we celebrated the birth of "John Chapman Andrews."

My next boss was Ray, the personnel officer for the Bay Area branch offices. I had the 48 East Bay offices assigned to me while a colleague did the West Bay. Two weeks into my job, Ray announced he was leaving on a long-delayed three-month sabbatical. Before he left, he revealed to us his work pattern. Behind his desk were three stacks of mail, one for each of the last three days. Each day he would deal with the three day-old pile. Invariably, others had already taken care of most of the matters by the time he finally looked at them. Before Ray returned, we had easily absorbed his job, which was probably his goal all along.

Another example of old time management was Bill in Emeryville. This crusty old bird called me to counsel Warren, his operations officer. Actually, his words were, "I want you to chew him out." As we at headquarters had tagged Warren as a promising young man, I was anxious to hear Warren's view. He was very proud of a whole string of accomplishments and thought he was doing a superior job. It quickly became apparent, though, that his boss hadn't let him know what goals he had for Warren. I suggested that Warren check in with Bill to make sure they were in alignment. Warren did so, and a few months later Bill called me to thank me for my role in Warren's strong improvement. Bill's concluding remark was, "You must have chewed him out real good!"

Transition to a "new school" approach came abruptly at one Oakland office. Edna was a gruff, crabby older supervisor who was known for making her tellers' lives miserable. Even her manager was intimidated. Then one day, the manager called me gleefully with startling news. New hires in the 1970's were a bolder, brasher breed than their predecessors. Latisha, a rather volatile young woman, had arrived at the branch recently. As usual, Edna quickly got on her case. Thereupon, Latisha literally got in Edna's face and snarled, "Don't f _ _ _ with me or I'll cut you good!" Latisha didn't last long, but her influence endured, as an ashen Edna was a changed person thereafter.

As a young shaver in my mid-twenties, I was pleased to be able to establish warm relationships with the cohort of veteran managers. Arlen in the Alameda Office was one such manager, who surprised me one day by asking me if I would like to join the Alameda Elks Club. Knowing that Arlen treasured his membership there, I was gentle in my declination. He then said "That's too bad, because I could probably get you in. If you're from here, it's often difficult, thanks to someone remembering that you shot their dog with a BB gun 40 years ago. They don't know whose dog you might have shot with a BB gun."

Wells was sincere in its efforts to increase diversity in the workforce. But an impediment was that a disproportionate share of minority applicants did not do well on the Wunderlic test required of all teller applicants. This test presents 50 brief problems, most of them involving mathematical calculation. The NFL still uses it to test for mental acuity among their recruits. One might suppose that facility at such a test would translate into success as a teller. However, no one had tried to validate this correlation, and I was concerned that in the absence of such validation, we were open to criticism that we were employing the test for the purpose of screening out minorities. I then did a crude bit of research. I asked my branch managers to rank their tellers on the attributes of accuracy and speed. Over 200 tellers were so ranked by their managers (on a confidential basis). I then plotted those rankings against their Wunderlic scores. There was absolutely no correlation. Just as many top-ranked tellers had low test scores as bottom-ranked ones. As I suspected, work ethic, concentration, and learning on the job trumped initial aptitude. Based on these findings, the bank summarily dropped the Wunderlic test.

After three years as a personnel specialist, I finally worked my way back to "line banking," the basic lending, deposit, and general management side. Early on, I learned the hard way that one cannot manage "by the book." As assistant manager of a Wells Fargo branch in Hayward, it was my first time supervising employees. One of my first duties was to arrange the employee vacation schedule. Bank policy dictated that preference as to when vacations might be scheduled was according to seniority. My dilemma concerned how to regard interrupted service in calculating seniority. Fernell had twelve years of continuous service while Julie had fifteen years of service, but Julie's was broken into segments of five years and then ten years. The policy manual was silent on the issue, but I noted that for the purpose of determining the length of vacation, one was to add the segments to arrive at seniority. It made sense to me that vacation schedule priority should be figured in the same manner. I posted the schedule with Julie first and Fernell second among the eighteen employees. Shortly thereafter, I felt someone's presence, and I looked up to see a glowering Fernell. Normally, Fernell was a sweet older woman, but this was a different Fernell. Apparently, my predecessor had gone on continuous service only, and Fernell had been listed number one for many years – perhaps the only area in life where she was "number one." No amount of logic such as, "You could both take your vacations at the same time, so there's no real difference" had any effect. Fortunately, Julie came to my rescue. When I approached her about her willingness to switch back to the old order, she readily agreed, saying, "Why not, we could both go on vacation at the same time." I replied, "I know, I know. Thank you, thank you." Later, Fernell saw the revised schedule and harrumphed, "That's better." The next day and thereafter, Fernell transformed back into sweet, old Fernell. Meanwhile, I took a big step towards learning about management – it always pays to ask how things were done previously, no matter what "the book" says or logic may suggest.

I was then transferred to Burlingame Office, a large and historic branch that had become a disaster with a failing audit, a failing loan review, bad morale, and no growth. I was asked to go in as #2 to fix it, but I had to serve under the incompetent fellow who created the mess. The untold story was three raging love affairs involving several senior staffers. After some personnel transfers and two years of intensive repair, the ship was righted in all respects. To my surprise, the manager then got promoted to full Vice President. I soon got a good new opportunity myself, but left with head shaking.

At Burlingame I had my first experience with truly abusive customers, ones who would shout obscenities and such. I learned quickly that after giving a warning, banning those folks from the branch was received as a very welcome indication of respect by employees and customers alike. Several years later, in Pasadena, I had given warning to a shouter who subsequently behaved acceptably for the next few months. Then one day, he again blew up. Sheepishly, he came to me and said, "I've done it, haven't I?" I agreed, and we parted company. Or so I thought. As luck would have it, when I found my way to my seat for the symphony season, who was my next seat neighbor but the shouter! Surprisingly, rather than harboring resentment about being booted from the bank, he seemed grateful that it had happened. Chalk up another life lesson.

Transferring among branch offices exposed me to the influence of office design upon the social dynamic. Burlingame had a lobby all the way through the middle, separating the two work areas. Such a configuration can produce a polarized work force. At Burlingame this division had gone so far as to result in two separate holiday parties. Through focused efforts such as rescheduling lunch breaks, a manager can encourage a more integrated team.

A great untapped source of tellers was the retired military. Lots of men and women retired from the service while in their 40's. They were experienced, stable, and could live on a teller's salary due to their supplemental retirement pay. The men were especially welcome as vault tellers, as most female tellers struggled with the weight of bulk coin. However, one particular ex-military vault teller had great difficulty balancing his books. As I had hired this guy, the gruff, old area operations officer was all over me. The difficult part was this teller's specialty while in the Army. He had been a bugle player. I really didn't have a ready answer for, "Why did you hire a bugler?" There's no reason to think that a bugler wouldn't make as good a teller as anyone else, but it sure was hard to explain!

Pasadena

I eagerly accepted the opportunity to move to Pasadena in 1968 to take over the Bank of Pasadena, which Wells had acquired, and to integrate it into the Wells system. After about two months of working in the downtown L.A. office while awaiting regulatory approval, the Executive Vice President for Southern California for Wells took me to Pasadena to meet with the outgoing bank President. This fellow was astounded to learn then and there that I was to take over and said he had promised the manager job to a member of his staff. Here I was, having come 400 miles, bought a house, moved my family, and no one had told him that Wells was bringing in their guy to take over (and he hadn't thought to ask). I then sought out the other candidate and told him that I would feel betrayed if I were he, but that I would look forward to working with him and helping him become a manager of one of the many branches that Wells was to open in the next few years. Unfortunately, he couldn't get over his disappointment and soon left for a banking job in Florida.

As I was taking over as the manager, I was exposed to a stark contrast in management styles. The former bank president hung around the office for a month or two until a new assignment in the San Fernando Valley opened up. He was a burr-headed ex-Marine, and his management style could not have been more different from mine. While I tried to be collegial and collaborative, his style was pure intimidation.

I instituted staff meetings where we covered routine matters, but I also often gave brief lessons on larger bank and economic issues. We had recently discussed the role of the Federal Reserve Bank and the creation and control of the money supply. I had seen in the local newspaper that in a few weeks the Vice Chair of the Federal Reserve Board, Sherman Maisel, was scheduled to speak at the

Caltech evening lecture series. I encouraged the staff to attend and suggested that we could all go out for pizza beforehand. Just then, the outgoing president's voice behind me boomed, supposedly in support of my suggestion, "And I'd like the names of anyone who doesn't want to go!" Instantly, a "want to" was transformed into an ugly "have to" obligation.

A surprising event resulted from my relationship with the City of Pasadena. I enjoyed playing tennis with the City Manager, Don Pollard. One time I asked him if he could help me with a problem. I was president of the local merchants association, and my group was upset with the spread of porn shops in the nearby Old Town area. Don said that the First Amendment limited the City's ability to control such activity, but to keep him posted if it got any worse. It did continue to spread which I passed on to Don. Poof! In just one month the whole porn operation – movie houses, magazines, etc. just disappeared. I was a hero to my group, but I had no idea how it happened. Don then shared with me that suddenly all manner of city rules were more strictly enforced, from building codes to fire codes to loitering restrictions to zoning regulations. In subsequent years, Old Town Pasadena has become the centerpiece of the area's urban renewal.

When I first came to Pasadena, I got a lesson in the ways of journalism. A reporter from the *Pasadena Star News* called to interview me. Towards the end he probed whether I had any interesting or unique hobbies. I responded, "You mean like riding a unicycle?" "Yes!" gushed the interviewer. I had to admit that I didn't have any hobbies or habits that were that unique or interesting. "Are you sure you don't ride a unicycle," he persisted. "No," I replied, "I can barely stay aboard a bike." Darned if two days later when the article came out, it included "in his spare time Brown enjoys riding his unicycle." I guess this thought was just too juicy for him to ignore, and for years afterward, journalistic sketches on me mentioned my phantom unicycling. I resolved to restrain myself in the future from offering overly colorful expressions.

I've always enjoyed calling on bank customers. Visits that afford a glimpse into various businesses are fascinating and instructive.

They help greatly to understand the viewpoint of the customer and to build the relationship.

The biggest new account I was able to lure to the Pasadena branch was the evangelical Worldwide Church of God, which was a great cash machine. My entré was the church officials' love of L.A. Dodgers games. One evening after a game, several of us stayed behind at the Stadium Club to have a few beers. When we exited the stadium, the only gate still open was the same one the players used after they showered and changed. Clustered at the bottom of the ramp was a group of young autograph hounds. They all had programs, which they riffled through to identify each approaching player. Flushed with pride at presumably being mistaken for ballplayers, we young studs in our 30's put extra swagger into our step. When the boys accosted us, one stepped up to me and inquired, "Are you—(maybe Koufax?, perhaps Drysale?)—umpires?"

Another memorable customer call was on a businessman who had been assigned a half-dozen different contact officers over the previous few years. Upon meeting me, he was cordial and asked for my card so he could update his address book. He then turned to me and asked with a twinkle, "I hope you don't mind if I write your name in pencil."

In dealing with bank customers, one learns a lot about their lives. Customer George and his wife came into the office for a home loan. They were excited to finally be "buying their last house." When I asked what that meant, he explained that in his 34 years with the Sears Company, he had made 32 moves. None of them were small moves, just to another part of town. They had moved from Jacksonville to Honolulu to Poughkeepsie and on and on. I asked whether they plunged into each new community or kept their distance, knowing it wouldn't last. They said that they had tried it both ways and had found that plunging in was better, even if it added to the pain of separation later. Fortunately, the era when IBM was said to stand for "I've Been Moved" has subsided, the difficulty of arranging satisfactory employment for two working spouses being the chief reason.

Being a bit of an eager beaver usually produces good results. But not always. I made every effort to get to know our current customers, as well as courting new ones. One good customer I had never met. It was a chemical company with a Connecticut address which kept $100,000 in an account with no activity. Upon phoning the CFO to thank him for the business and to inquire how else we might help, the response was, "Really?" Apparently, these funds were intended as a temporary thank-you to the former president for getting them Rose Bowl tickets some years ago, and the account had been overlooked since. Two days later it was gone. Let sleeping accounts lie? I still like to know my customers and would do it again.

An amusing customer interplay occurred during this period. Francis Moseley was a brilliant engineer who lived just north of Pasadena in an estate ringed by a quarter-scale train layout that he had built himself. Francis created a measuring device company that he sold to Hewlett Packard for a substantial position in HP stock. He had enjoyed serving on the HP Board, but began to feel restless for the action of the entrepreneur again. With dozens of patents to his name, he dug a few out of the drawer, called a couple of his old colleagues, and decided to start all over again. By this time, though, he had come to realize the value of having a board of directors for guidance and to act as a sounding board. Francis then called me, his banker, to ask if I could serve as his outside director. As I had never been on a corporate board, I was delighted. I could see no potential conflict of interest, as his Servo Products Company was so well bankrolled that it would be unlikely ever to borrow from the bank. Nevertheless, I felt it would be prudent to get the bank's OK. Back thundered the reply, "Under no circumstances will we permit a branch manager to be on a corporate board." When the news was relayed to Francis, he then confronted Ernie Arbuckle, who was also on the HP Board, and argued, "How come as Chairman of Wells Fargo, you can be on the HP Board, yet Brown can't be on mine?" Soon thereafter came a call from my boss saying, "I don't know what the hell happened, but get on that board."

My eight years on the Servo Products board gave me a ringside seat on the explosion of a five person company to one employing over 500. Francis did it all over again. He had such an affinity for all things electrical and mechanical. One time he stepped out for a moment from a board meeting to find a pencil sharpener. After about twenty-five minutes had passed without his return, I went to see what had happened. I found him at a workbench with the pencil sharpener in pieces. He declared that he could hear that the gearing and worming ratios were all wrong, and he was fixing it. Francis was so engrossed that he had utterly forgotten that a board meeting was still in progress.

Francis had an original way of thinking about a great many issues. I remember his take on that classic question as to whether the glass is half-full or half-empty. "As an engineer," he said, "I am of the opinion that the glass is twice as big as it needed to be."

My principal contribution to this company was to help them with their marketing, which was primitive. I soon discovered a mind-set that afflicts many executives from the technology sector. It's not just that they are naive about marketing; they have an active aversion to it. Many of them think that a worthy product should sell itself. I constantly had to remind them that the world doesn't beat a path to the door of the better mousetrap. They need to be told how it's better, where to find it, and to generate confidence in the mousetrap company.

Once released from the burdens of my troubled marriage, I redoubled my efforts at work and in the community. One time my assistant alerted me to the fact that I had attended community events for 17 straight evenings. One activity I especially enjoyed was being on the Tournament of Roses Committee. With only a few exceptions, that beautiful pageant is performed in the same manner every year. Seldom in today's world of accelerating change do we have the luxury of doing the same thing over and over and truly getting it right. It was an especially heady time for me, as Stanford made consecutive Rose Bowl appearances, winning both times.

Our branch office's location was right on the parade route. Every year we erected bleachers in our lobby to entertain customers with a perfect view of the parade. One day just before New Year's, an NBC official came by to ask whether they could place a camera on a parapet of our building. I had no objection as long as they took full responsibility for falling objects. He then said, "And we'll pay you the usual fee." Naive me – usual fee? "Yes," he said, "$2,500." That amount was about three months business development budget for my office, and it enabled us to host a party for 75 guests with mimosas, tickets to the game, etc. I marveled at how TV and movie people squander money and how I might have been able to negotiate even more.

In taking over the Pasadena operation, I inherited Al. Al was an African American gentleman who was elderly, but I wasn't sure how old, as he was cagey about his age. He had been used as a courier by my predecessor, a service we didn't need. However, Al was so conscientious and such a staff favorite that we found ways of keeping him busy and keeping him on. Al was a man of integrity, one who was well-grounded. In the aftermath of the Watts riots, a small uprising occurred down the street from us. Al said he deplored the actions of the young blacks who were participating. Then he looked over to the adjacent upscale El Rancho Market and said, "But if they start looting that market, I'm going to get me some of those Cornish game hens." I told him to pick me up some cashews while he was there.

My secretary left to have a family, and I had several acceptable applications for replacement, but none stood out. Then into my office came Pilar. Pilar Valentin was a woman of transcendent beauty and charm with a delightful, lilting Spanish accent. She had come to the States when her husband was transferred from JPL's Madrid tracking station to Pasadena. I thought to myself, "I hope you can type – or something." Indeed she could, but her personal skills were so magical that customers would routinely bypass me to deal with Pilar. Her sophistication sometimes gave me a jolt. During her orientation I was talking about the importance of keeping bank business confidential. She then said, "Oh, don't worry, Mr. Brown, when I was a secretary at the Saudi embassy in Madrid, I was told to be sure to be nice to a particular fellow at the party, for tomorrow he is to be assassinated." OK, I think we have confidentiality covered!

We built a great team in Pasadena and led the city in market share gain. I was also pleased to see that we had made good progress in diversity. At that time, the bank embarked on a program to accelerate the progress of minority officers by hiring above entry level. I agreed to mentor Mel, a handsome bright African American fellow. The plan was to launch him into an assistant manager's job in two years. Just six months later when my assistant manager was promoted elsewhere, I cut short the replacement process by saying that I would be pleased to take on Mel right then. Headquarters was delighted, as was I. My delight turned to dismay when I got his personnel file and learned that he was being paid more than I was. Here I was, with ten years of success in the bank and a Stanford MBA being paid less than a young rookie who was reporting to me. I made a formal protest to boost my pay and got an adjustment to vault me just ahead of him. There is a value to speaking up.

One of the things I've enjoyed doing when taking over a unit is to be sure we recognize staff birthdays. It is a bright moment for all, especially for those on whom the spotlight seldom falls. Shortly after arriving in Pasadena, I orchestrated the first of these birthday celebrations, for Claudine, a single woman in her mid-fifties. When we sprung a cake on her at coffee break, she burst into tears. Finally, she blubbered, "No one has remembered my birthday for thirty years."

Perhaps my most satisfying community activity in Pasadena was when a group of us young business and professional types from the All Saints Church congregation decided to reach out to the local black community to mentor some budding entrepreneurs. My team took on Zawadie, a woman with a flair for spectacular folkloric dresses, and Clifford Makins, a piano teacher, mover, and tuner. We were in the midst of giving Zawadie the marketing muscle she needed when her jealous boyfriend took off, absconding with her car and all her inventory. It was a painful reminder of the impediments to success in that community. Clifford's situation was more stable. With just a few actions, his business boomed. I gave him the trade style, "Makins of Music" in bright red. He was delighted and ran out to buy a red blazer and fashioned a crest bearing his new trade style. We got him calling cards, a phone listing, and most importantly, a way to keep track of his customers and a program to send them semi-annual reminders.

During that era, my friend Steve Tallent provided some very helpful advice. Rather than staying gloomy over one's marital failure after a divorce, it is a time to try some new things. I rekindled my tennis game, even doing well in some local recreation tournaments. I joined a hiking club for a memorable trek around the Big Island of Hawaii, and my roommate and I had a great time at Club Med in Tahiti. For a brief period before a transfer took me back north, I joined the Sierra Madre Mountain Rescue Team and served on the local draft board. I even did some modeling stints for travel and cigarette ads.

Women

At that time, we were seeing the first real breakthroughs in professional and executive opportunities for women. In nearby Duarte, a woman became head of the local phone company for the first time. The holder of this position had always been invited to join the local Rotary Club chapter, but Rotary was a men-only outfit at that time. When the Duarte Rotary went ahead and invited her to join, the national organization ex-communicated them. Without missing a beat, the group maintained its program, meeting in the traditional place every other Wednesday, but now calling themselves the "Ex Rotary Club of Duarte." After *Time Magazine* picked up the story, the national Rotary caved in, and another victory for fairness was achieved.

When one is in the midst of social change, it is hard to appreciate fully its historical significance. In my view, the changing status of women is one of the most important events in the history of humankind. In a matter of a few decades, half of the human race is progressing from limited opportunities to a full range of possibilities. The third world is actively resisting this change but will in time see their barriers fall. In my view, the animus borne by the Arab world against modern Western ways is influenced strongly by the desire of Arab men to keep their women in near-slavery.

We are just beginning to realize the benefits of the opening of opportunities for women. It is exhilarating to see the enthusiasm of women as they cross frontiers. I view the energy and commitment of women in our society as similar to that of new arrivals from foreign shores. The percentage of women in college student bodies grows every year and is currently a decisive majority at 58%. Now, many colleges are beginning to make special efforts to attract male students. When recruiting efforts switch from recruiting women to recruiting men, it is a true sea change. [Query: As women come to dominate college enrollment, will men become the new "co-eds"? – just asking.]

The ascendance of women has a broader significance. It contributes to the destruction of gender stereotypes. Just as it is now OK for women to take on traditional male jobs, it is now OK for men to become nurses. In its greater dimension, the women's liberation movement is a movement of liberation for all.

A few years ago, I witnessed a very revealing exercise at a Stanford Business School alumni luncheon in San Francisco. There were about 100 of us in the room who were asked to participate in a case study provided by the school. The set-up was that an executive in your company was being offered a promotion that required a move to another city. His wife was an accountant who wanted to continue her career. The question was how much effort did we think our company should make to help the wife find a new position? The choices were: a) hire a search firm for her and actively assist; b) offer to pay for a trip or two to search and a classified newspaper ad; c) do nothing. After the answers were gathered and tallied, we learned that half of the room had been given the version I just described, but the other half had been told it was the wife being offered the transfer with the accountant husband being the trailing spouse. To our dismay, we supposedly enlightened executives showed a skew towards doing more for the trailing spouse when it was the husband. Our results were more evenly balanced than most, but clearly we had a little further to go.

Here's a suggestion for removal of yet another barrier to opportunity for women. In the trades and crafts, many tools, packages, and standard sizes are calibrated to the upper body strength of men. Cases of beverages that come in 24-can lots are but one example. Why couldn't women assert that such measures are discriminatory and demand re-setting these measures? A side benefit would be greater access to a range of jobs for smaller and older men, too, and perhaps fewer job related injuries. Think it can't happen? When gas stations switched from full service to self service, stations lightened their hoses and nozzles almost overnight to accommodate female users.

Sarah

After Becky and Kenny relocated to Northern California in 1970, I moved from the Muirs' home to an apartment in Pasadena and began the process of re-establishing my social life. I was suddenly thrust into the role of "eligible bachelor." Friends were kind to make introductions for me, but the most aggressive matchmakers were bank customers. They would trot out their daughters, nieces, and acquaintances to meet me. Twice, I returned from lunch to find prospective female companions in my office awaiting my arrival, and the office staff developed a consuming interest in my social affiliations. A few relationships flourished briefly, but then I was asked by Wells Fargo to return to San Francisco in late 1971.

Just at that time, my friend and former Stanford classmate, Dick Miller, insisted that I meet "Sallie Elliott," the former Sausalito roommate of his wife, Susie. I tried to beg off, as I was preoccupied with trying to disentangle myself from several other relationships. I will be eternally grateful to Dick Miller for his persistence. Actually, it took persistence on my part, too, as Sallie* had a lingering flu and didn't want to meet. However, I was on a deadline to be transferred back to San Francisco in three weeks. For her, the breakthrough came when I finally said, "Anyone this hard to meet must really be worth it."

As she was still not feeling her best, I agreed to bring an "urban picnic" from Jurgensen's, a high end grocery/deli. The first challenge in wooing the princess was to climb the 66 steps to her castle on Kelton Avenue near UCLA. I was delighted to be greeted by a pretty, trim brunette. She was shocked by my appearance – not just my ghastly lavender shirt, but the way I looked. Later, when I

---

*   A name change from Sallie Elliott to Sarah Belle Brown is covered below.

saw a photograph of her late father, I understood the source of her reaction to me. We were near-identical in appearance.

My reaction upon meeting Sarah was less nuanced. I was thunderstruck. She was absolutely fetching in her brown mini-skirt and patent leather boots. As a thirty-three year-old who had been out in the world a while, I was stunned to be so bowled-over. Unable to sleep that night, I wrote her a poem, something I'd never done before.

Sarah's and my relationship flourished on a number of fronts. In addition to being attractive and purposeful, she was fun. After our first dinner that she prepared at her place, she picked up a little dinner bell from the table, rang it, and called out, "Ophelia." Incredulous, I asked if she had a maid. "No," she said, "but maybe someday it will happen if I keep doing this." Little did I realize that someday that would be <u>my</u> role!

When I met Sarah, I was struck by the fact that she was not tall. When I asked about her height, she said she was 5' 2 ½". I replied that people who added "and a half" are usually self-conscious about their height. Thereupon, Sarah said, "Actually, I'm 5' 2 ¾"!

I married Sallie Elliott. She promptly announced she wanted henceforth to be known as "Sarah Belle Brown." Sarah Belle was her given name, and there was a history of "Sarah's" and "Sarah Belle's" down both the Goodwin and Glines families. She figured that the geographic relocation to Northern California would give her a golden chance to make it stick. New friends picked up on "Sarah," oblivious to the change. However, when an old acquaintance entered the mix and called her "Sallie," the new friends figured that must be her familiar name and began using it. Sarah had to be insistent for several years to convert her old friends and to keep them from corrupting her newer ones. Now only a few family members are hold-outs who still use "Sallie."

Our courtship soon became a long distance one after my transfer back to Northern California in January, 1972. I became such a frequent flyer and frequent phone caller that I was sure that our wedding service would be interrupted by objections from the airlines and phone company, protesting that they couldn't afford to lose the business if we married.

When Sarah visited her parents after my weekend visits, her mother would ask where I had stayed. Sarah fibbed that I stayed with my friend Steve Tallent in Altadena. This question and this answer were repeated week after week. Finally, in exasperation, Sarah said, "Mom, he's staying with me." Her mother's response has become a family classic – "In that little bed?"

Sarah was adventurous which was a good influence for me. As a young workaholic, I needed the influence of someone who traveled, ate spicy foods, drove a red sports car, skied and partied, and spoke Spanish. Her college years included terms in both Madrid and Mexico City.

When Sarah speaks Spanish, it transforms her. She not only speaks it beautifully, but she captures perfectly the lilting cadence and gestures. It is as if she has suddenly donned a Spanish costume. It is hard to imagine a higher compliment about one's language skill than what I heard at a banquet in Quito. After hearing Sarah across the table speaking Spanish, my Ecuadorian dinner partner asked, "Your wife's accent, I can't quite place it. Is she Chilean?"

I was never destined to be mistaken for a Chilean. Sarah and I made a trip to Spain to join son Joseph when he was a student there for a term during high school. During our splendid ten day visit, both Sarah and Joseph made good use of their excellent command of Spanish. As my Spanish is halting at best, I deferred to them in matters of communication with the locals. However, when it came time to make an adjustment in our flight home, I felt confident I could handle that task. I dialed the number for American Airlines and with great confidence proclaimed, "*Yo quiero cambiar mi vuelta a Los Estados Unidos.*" A voice responded, "*Que?*" After a repeat request failed to generate any comprehension, I finally capitulated and asked whether anyone there spoke English. When a husky voice asked, "May I help you?", I repeated my request in English. The respondent then said, "I do not think I can help you. This is the hotel laundry room." It then dawned on me that I had forgotten to dial "9" for an outside line. My little misadventure probably provided for lots of merriment among the laundry crew.

None of her fun-loving should suggest that Sarah is frivolous.

In fact, her solid values and her commitment to helping others are crowning glories. While other classmates from her graduate education program at USC sought safe suburban assignments, Sarah opted for assignment to an inner city school teaching English to newly-arrived Spanish speaking children. That commitment has continued all during our marriage – as a Court Appointed Special Advocate for children (or "CASA"), to work with newly-arrived Chinese children, to board service on a number of social agencies and educational institutions. Sarah became Board Chair of The Children's Home Society, California's largest private social agency. She was also a trustee of her initial college, Mount Vernon College in Washington D.C. She continued her record of volunteer service while in Albuquerque, including chairing the development effort for leading charter school, Amy Biehl High School. It is indeed fitting that the University of New Mexico has designated its annual community service award as the "Sarah Belle Brown Award."

Los Angeles Friends

Among the many bonuses in marrying Sarah has been her wonderful collection of friends, whose friendship has remained undiminished through the years. Five of Sarah's six bridesmaids came to Elliott and Deborah's wedding thirty-four years later.

Alison Chaffee Kuehn, Sarah's Matron of Honor, was a classmate of Sarah's at Marlborough. The Goodwin and Chaffee families had been close friends for four generations. After graduating from UOP, Alison married longtime beau Bill Kuehn after he graduated from Stanford and Harvard Business School. While Bill pursued a career in consulting, Alison taught school and raised three wonderful children in a "Hansel and Gretel" house in Pasadena. Several years after having son Pier, Alison endured an extremely difficult pregnancy. For her courage, the Kuehns were rewarded with beautiful twin daughters, Sarah and Katrina.

Upon departure from our Hillsborough home, Bill and Alison Kuehn favored us with a most thoughtful going-away gift. Bill videotaped our home, room by room, using ten year-old Elliott as his narrator.

Penny Gill was in the same graduate teaching program as Sarah at USC. She is a spark of positive energy and is so committed to family and friends. Mike Gill is a lawyer with a successful estate planning practice in downtown Los Angeles. Mike is an excellent athlete, having played on the Redlands golf team, and Penny can do anything athletically. Predictably, their children, Becky and Joe, were both fine athletes and students, and I am blessed to be Joey's godfather. We enjoy our special trips with the Gills – to the point where it isn't a proper significant birthday occasion unless it involves going with the Gills to Greece or the Yucatan or Argentina or other wonderful spots.

Mike Gill is a superb chef. He can visit your refrigerator, and out of the most mundane leftovers produce a gourmet delicacy. Our New Mexico friend, Hal Hankinson, is a kindred spirit, an excellent chef in his own right, and someone who can direct you to several fine restaurants in almost any city in the world. When the Gills visited our new home in Albuquerque, Mike and Sarah devised a delightful contest. Mike and Hal agreed to act as "dueling chefs," producing competing risotto dishes. The chefs rose eagerly to the challenge, even posing for a photo, resplendent in their toques with spatulas in thrust and parry positions.

It was a pleasant summer evening, and the Moises had joined us and the contestants to enjoy their efforts in our new gazebo. Both risottos were superb, and the contest was declared a draw. Then all conversation ceased as ravenous guests ravaged the dishes. So intent were all of us on consumption that a remarkable event occurred. The permanent gazebo table had not yet arrived, so we had created a makeshift table out of a large round of plywood perched tenuously on a rickety card table. Right in mid-fork, the table collapsed. The plywood top fell evenly upon our laps about four inches below. After a momentary pause to reflect on the new situation, the feeding frenzy resumed with the table top still perched on our laps.

Susie Miller was the roommate of Sarah's in Sausalito who married my Stanford classmate, Dick Miller. They were the ones who introduced Sarah and me. A few years later when we moved to San Marino, we moved just a block away from the Millers. Our son Elliott was a contemporary of their son Sumner, and together they made much neighborhood mischief. On the occasion of our 25th wedding anniversary, Dick Miller called us to give his congratulations and to announce that after 25 years, the Miller Warranty had expired and that we were now on our own.

The Gills in turn introduced us to Bill and Joan Dietrick and their three lively sons. Bill is a quiet, affable surgeon, and Joan is beautiful (former Miss Vermont runner-up) and so full of life. They have included us in their delightful annual pilgrimage to La Grulla, a picturesque Mexican beachside club. The club commissioned a local sign painter to create a "No Trespassing" sign by the entrance. The resulting sign has become a club motto, inspiring tee shirts and hats emblazoned with "Notre Spassing."

Sarah's Family

Sarah's father, John Fischer Elliott, was truly a member of the "Greatest Generation." Immediately upon graduation from Stanford in 1942, he became an officer in the Army Air Corps. In late 1943, he married his sweetheart, Sarah Belle "Sary" Goodwin, who lived nearby in the Hancock Park area of Los Angeles. Apparently, she conceived my future wife while they were vacationing in Santa Fe, New Mexico, which took on later significance. When Sarah Belle Elliott was born in Los Angeles at Good Samaritan Hospital on September 7, 1944, her father was involved in missions over the "Burma Hump" and could not get leave. What a tragedy it must have been for the young bride, just two months later, to learn that her husband's plane had gone down in India. He never even met his daughter.

The young widow then moved back to her parents' home on McCadden Street in Hancock Park with her baby daughter. Then just one month later, in December 1944, Sary's sister, Maryly, lost her husband, Sam Wagner, when his plane went down in the Pacific. She, too, moved back home, accompanied by her six-month old son, Sam. For the next three years, the two widowed sisters raised their children together, aided greatly by their third sister, Ann, who dropped out of college for a term to help the family through this crisis. Sarah and Sam remain especially close to this day, more as sister and brother than cousins.

Maryly was the first to move out when she became remarried, to William "Brud" Darsie in 1947. Maryly and Brud grew pears, tomatoes, and corn on their farm in Walnut Grove. For the Darsie kids and visiting Sarah, it was an idyllic, rural, small town setting filled with games in the orchards, 4th of July parades, and all manner of outdoorsy fun. Walnut Grove is located on one of the many islands protected by levees in the Sacramento River delta. Life there moves in rhythm with the seasons of the river. Life sometimes ends there, too, as late night revelers periodically plunge off the levee roads into the river. It was on a boat dock that Sarah's cousin, Jennie Darsie, met tall, handsome husband-to-be Jimmy White. Lots of summertime romances flourished there, about which Sarah maintains a discreet silence. Oft-spoken, though, was Sarah's devotion to Maryly, her beloved "Aunt Minnie," who was ever attentive, ever supportive, and always fun.

Sarah Belle Goodwin Elliott then met James Joseph Shelton in 1949. As he had been married before, they waited three years before getting married. They were married in her parents' home and then moved into the Park La Brea towers. "Joe" Shelton is every bit the self-made man. He was one of eight children from a family of modest means in Mayfield, Kentucky. Although his father held the office of sheriff, which must have conferred respectability, there was never much money, alcohol was a factor, and family life was harsh. It was an era when childhood bore greater risks, and two of Joe's brothers died in their teens, one from drowning and one from a lightning strike – before Joe's very eyes.

Joe was a good athlete, bright, and filled with a burning determination. During the summer after high school, he took a job ferrying cars from a Kentucky car dealer to West Coast buyers. Once exposed to the prospect of a better life in California, Joe made a one-way trip there and enrolled in Glendale Community College. At Glendale, Joe blossomed, becoming a top scholar and student body president. From there, he went on to graduate from Occidental College before joining the Navy in 1942 as an officer in the Quartermaster Corps. Joe was deployed to the Pacific Theatre where he helped supply goods needed for the Allied campaign up the island chains. Immediately after the war, Joe took advantage of his G.I. Bill entitlements to enroll in the Harvard Business School Class of 1947, a class that would later develop into one of the school's highest achieving.

The post-war years were a heady time for many young men in America. The long Depression, followed by years consumed with the war effort left a great talent gap in corporate America. The post-war family formation boom and accompanying consumer goods boom fueled a skyrocketing economy. Into the breach stepped a group of young men (only men in those days) confident in spirit from America's great victory and confident in their battle-tested skills of leadership. Many firms reached down a whole generation to draft this new talent. When Ransom Cook retired as CEO of Wells Fargo Bank at the then-customary age of 65, his successor was 42 year-old Dick Cooley. My father's law firm underwent a similar change when he and three young colleagues took the helm at the venerable McCutchen firm.   In a similar manner, Joe Shelton's career took off. After early success at Ducommon Metals and Suburban Gas, he landed an executive position at Baker Oil Tool (now Baker Hughes). Baker had a great run in the 1970's and 1980's. In fact, for the decade of the 1970's their stock had the greatest percentage gain of any security listed on the New York Stock Exchange.

A unique set of circumstances combined to produce this spectacular result. As oil prices climbed, demand surged for oil service companies, which help extract more oil and gas from existing wells. Under Hubie Clark's and Joe Shelton's leadership, Baker sought to acquire companies in related specialties, such as "down hole fishing tools." A favorable factor was the buoyant Baker stock, which became an appealing currency to prospective acquisition targets. Baker also tended to leave current management in place in acquired companies as long as results continued to be favorable, a practice that helped them gain favor with future prospects. But perhaps Baker's secret weapon in this strategy was Joe Shelton.

Joe adopted the practice of regular visits to the 70 or so acquisition prospects that Baker had targeted. Seldom would a prospect leap into their arms. Over time, though, strong bonds of familiarity and trust would develop from Joe's regular visits. Many of the specialty companies Baker sought were located in rural areas, and Joe was a master at creating good rapport with such company owners. Often it took a precipitating event to trigger a sale – perhaps a health problem of the owner. Under such circumstances, it became an easy choice to turn to Baker and Joe Shelton. Truly, it was a classic acquisition strategy.

Joe Shelton found social acceptance in Los Angeles, aided by Sarah Belle Shelton and her old-Los Angeles ties. Joe joined the California Club downtown, the elite Los Angeles Country Club and the top hat men's golfing groups within LACC, the LK's and the GP's. In time he served as president of both of these groups, whose principal activities were golf and ribald good fun.

Regarding social circles, we were reminded of how small our world is when Sarah and I became engaged. To tell my parents the news, I started to call the Mauna Kea resort in Hawaii where they were vacationing. Sarah then said, "Why, my parents are staying there, too." We had the delightful experience of telling my parents that they might enjoy meeting the couple in room 302, as they were due to become in-laws.

I also learned that there is a high degree of competitiveness that can come from having bootstrapped one's way to success. One of Joe's favorite stories is that when Sarah invited her beaus to the beach to join a family outing, Joe would suggest a "friendly" jog down the beach. Joe jogged every day and was understandably proud of being in very good physical condition in his mid-fifties. Invariably, Joe would leave the young studs panting with exhaustion (I am grateful that he probably drove off a number of rivals). Inevitably, it became my turn. However, I was an active jogger and logged in over 20 miles per week at a brisk pace. As we started down the beach, Joe pointed out a landmark about a mile away and suggested that we go for it. When we got there, he then suggested we continue on to the Santa Monica Pier, about another mile farther. I concurred and we did the prescribed four-mile circuit. As we returned to our start point, I still had lots of gas left. Doubtless, I should have been more respectful, but as he had obviously been goading me, I suggested we run on to another point a mile or two further on. Abruptly he said, "No, we've done enough" and turned to the beach house. To this day Joe maintains that he "ran all of Sarah's boyfriends into the ground." As a 91 year-old, Joe is entitled to his personal legends, but as a 70 year-old, I feel entitled to an occasional roll of the eyes.

I continue to admire what Joe Shelton accomplished, how far he has come from modest beginnings in Kentucky to corporate leadership in Los Angeles. Above all, he has been an attentive parent to Sarah. I will also remain forever grateful for the reception that he, and especially Sary, gave me when I moved back to Southern California to take over Crocker's branch operation there. As Sarah and the boys wanted to complete the remaining nine months of the school year in Hillsborough, I was resigned to "batching it" during the week. Upon learning that I was intending to hole up in a modest hotel for this period, the Sheltons insisted that I live with them in their lovely home on June Street, now emptied of children. I enjoyed a pleasant stay, even though it felt slightly kinky to be sleeping in Sarah's old bedroom amongst her stuffed animals. The only rub was Sarah's complaint to her mother that I was being spoiled by her darning my socks and ironing my tee shirts. Much as I applaud the opening of a world of opportunity for modern women, the old ways did have their benefits for the male gender.

Sary Shelton has been unfailingly kind to me. She is petite, pretty, and vivacious. Sary danced, sang, and loved the symphony and her garden. She is widely admired by a staunch cohort of friends. She is also conscientious and very loyal to her family. For years and years, Sary tended daily to the needs of her widowed mother and her divorced mother-in-law. These elderly women became very demanding, and her mother complained if Sary did not see or call her every day by 9 a.m.

Sary was born on February 8, 1920 in Santa Maria, California, then a small ranching community, located about 150 miles north of Los Angeles. Sary's grandfather was a banker in Santa Maria who acquired several large ranches in the area when they went into foreclosure during an economic slump in the early 1900's. His son, Guy L. Goodwin, managed those ranches, first while in Santa Maria and then later from Los Angeles where the family moved in the early 1920's. Guy married a local Santa Maria girl, one of eight children, Sarah Lavinia Glines.

Sary was one of the three "Goodwin girls" who grew up on McCadden Street in the Hancock Park section of Los Angeles. All three went to nearby Marlborough School. Sary was the oldest and went on to UCLA, then Maryly who attended Cal, followed by

Annie who went to Stanford.

That generation followed a strong "Greek" tradition with Sary pledging Theta and Maryly, Pi Phi. Guy L. Goodwin belonged to the Phi Psi's and Joe Shelton was an SAE. Jack Elliott became a Deke at Stanford, to be followed there two generations later by our son, Elliott. Aunt Bessie Goodwin was a founding member of the Delta Gamma house at Berkeley.

After college, Sary taught nursery school for several years before staying home to raise the family. Her world in Hancock Park was remarkably self-contained. Nearly all their activities – school, shopping, social, work – were within a very small radius. A high percentage of children recycled to live in the area as adults. This cohort was a hard-working, community-minded group. It was as if a small town existed in an enclave within the great Los Angeles metropolitan area. A family story recounts the first time young Sarah Belle Goodwin ever saw a black person. On a train trip when she was four years old, she boldly asked the black porter, "Why is your skin so dark?" – to her mother's undying embarrassment. With the greatest of understanding and composure, the man replied, "I guess my mama left me in the oven too long."

My Sarah's world was a little different from that of her mother. By the time she went to the local Third Street School, there were a substantial number of kids from Jewish families. Sarah was particularly drawn to several of them and felt frustrated when pressures from both sides did not allow the friendships to flourish. Among the friends she made there was a cute African American classmate, "Cookie." One day after school Sarah saw a Cadillac sedan arrive, driven by an African American man. She asked the gentleman if he was one of her classmates' family drivers. He replied, "No, I'm here to pick up my daughter, Cookie." The gentleman was Nat King Cole.

My first memorable dealing with a black man came as a twelve year-old while on that Boy Scout Jamboree. We had taken the train to Chicago where we stepped out into sweltering July heat. Our bus was far across the platform, and my duffel bag was heavy. Just then a large black man wearing a red cap came up and asked, "Can

I help you with that bag, son?" What luck, I thought – this fellow must have been a Boy Scout himself and was still doing good deeds. Effortlessly, he swung the bag to his shoulder, and we proceeded to the bus. I thanked him. When he continued to stand there, I again thanked him. Finally, he bent down and said "Son, I'd appreciate it if you'd say it in silver." At last, I picked up the clue and fished out a tip for him.

The centerpiece of Sarah's family was "Pozo." Pozo was the familiar name for the Guy L. Goodwin ranch, the principal Goodwin ranch holding. The other ranch holdings were sold off over the years, except for Carizzo Plains. Carizzo is a 7,000 acre tract in the California Valley. There was no mineral or agricultural potential, but it was a valuable wildlife sanctuary, especially for migrating birds. Joe Shelton arranged for a bargain sale to the Nature Conservancy who have been wonderful stewards of that land. Native grasses have been restored and natural animal species re-introduced, including pronghorn antelope and tule elk. In recognition of the family's contribution, the property hosts a "Guy L. Goodwin Education Center." Joe Shelton prudently retained the proceeds from that sale as a small endowment to absorb the losses that the Pozo ranch usually generates and to avoid periodic assessments to the family members.

Pozo (Spanish for "well") takes its name from the tiny settlement that is about 16 miles inland from Santa Margarita, a town between San Luis Obispo and Atascadero on Highway 101. It is hilly, grassy terrain studded with oak trees and affords beautiful views of the Coast Range. The village of Pozo is little more than a Ranger station and a great saloon. Many a local tree has been grazed by patrons of the Pozo Saloon, leaving under "Pozo Power."

My favorite story about a small hamlet was when Mickey Mantle was asked by a reporter just where his hometown of Spavinaw, Oklahoma was located. Mantle answered that it was "about five miles past Resume Speed."

Nearly all holidays were celebrated at Pozo by the extended family, presided over by Sarah Glines Goodwin, the family matriarch. The three Goodwin girls had a good relationship, as did their three husbands Joe, Jack Ditz, and Brud Darsie.

While at Pozo for Thanksgiving, we often enjoyed watching some of the great football on TV. One year it was that classic USC/Notre Dame rivalry. Only this year it was far from classic, as Notre Dame was running away with the game – 24 to 7 at the half. It was a beautiful fall day, and a couple of us decided to give up on SC and go for a hike in the hills. Upon our return, I asked how bad the carnage on the field had become. Brud Darsie said the final score was 55 – 24, about what I expected. He then said it was USC on top. I, of course, was sure he was joking, but Brud insisted it was true. I started to propose a wager, but then thought that it was unlikely he would lose a bet when he knew the result. It was in fact the greatest collegiate comeback of all time. USC had scored 55 points during a span of only 17 minutes.

A few years earlier in that rivalry, Notre Dame had thumped USC 51 – 0. In the locker room after the game, SC coach McKay wondered what he could possibly say to boost the spirits of his boys. Finally, he said, "Just remember, guys, across the sea in China are a billion people who will never know about this."

The warmth of Pozo was especially welcome to me. My family had its merry moments, but none of the uninhibited joy that Pozo represented. Our family retreat, the Farm, was a place of happy boyhood memories with brother Ken, but we seldom hosted other family members or family friends. The Farm was my dad's refuge from the incessant demands of his law practice. We had no phone, and the place was very difficult to find. Dad was so sought-after that his colleagues would sometimes search the area in hopes of finding him. Frequently, Dad would cock a wary ear at the sound of a car approaching in dread that he would be found. The pressures of his law practice were relentless.

Pozo remained the hub of the Goodwin family, but family activity gradually decreased as the kids grew up, married and became drawn in different directions. When Sam Darsie moved to Colorado, he decided to sell his interest in Pozo, and some of the ownership interest has been gifted to the next generation.

The next generation of Goodwin family is a delightful gaggle. Sam Darsie is a clever, cheerful fellow, devoted to my Sarah. His half-sisters, Jennie and Caroline, loved to entertain us with their music and were great company. Jennie retains all the energy she displayed as an athlete at Stanford as she approaches her 60th birthday – among her achievements was last year's victory while playing on the national championship senior women's water polo team. Caroline stayed on at her alma mater, UOP, where she has been a highly productive development officer. In her free time she enjoys making costumes and is a great fisherwoman. Mellow Bill Darsie took over management of the Darsie family ranches and is now developing retirement properties in Costa Rica.

After Stanford and raising two children, Liz Ditz rekindled her passion for horses. The youngest Ditz sister is Janet Sarah Tarr, a tireless cross-country runner and later masseuse and dancer.

Nancy Ditz is a bundle of talent. She has been a leader in all her enterprises, notably athletics. She married Stanford schoolmate Bruce Mosbacher, who had been a rugby star there. Bruce was committed to continuing his fitness routine, which included marathon training. Upset about Bruce's long absences on training runs, Nancy finally agreed to join him. While Nancy had been a competitive diver and had served as coxswain on the Stanford crew, she had never tried long distance running. When it quickly became apparent that she could more than keep up with Bruce, on a bet she decided to enter some races. A string of racing successes culminated in Nancy's making the U.S. Olympic team and being the top American finisher in the Women's Marathon in the 1988 Olympics in Seoul. She went on to a successful broadcast career while raising adorable children, Jack and Emily. The family athletic tradition continues with Jack who will attend Stanford on a baseball scholarship, while Emily is a rising soccer star.

Sarah never had a sister and envied the Ditz's, Darsies, and friend Peggy Kappler for the sisterly camaraderie they enjoyed. But Suzie Ditz has become all one could ask of a sister. She has been such a caring, consistent confidant. She and Fred have embarked on many interesting adventures, and her son Jesse is continuing in the family tradition. It is a pleasure to see Suzie's journalistic/literary/public relations successes, but we especially enjoy her companionship.

Jim Shelton, Sarah's half-brother, came into my life as a handsome teenager who Sarah adored. After graduating from Harvard Westlake School (which our daughter-in-law Deborah Kelson was later to attend), Jim went on to get an engineering degree at SMU. Returning to Los Angeles, he learned the construction business at C. L. Peck & Co. He then ventured out on his own as a successful consultant on hotel and office projects all over the U.S., including the Beverly Hills Hotel, Century Plaza, several movie studios, Jon Bon Jovi's residence, plus the splendid job he and Ginny did remodeling their Brentwood home. Jim is a treasured brother-in-law who shares the same birthday with me.

Ginny Shelton was the former Ginny Hodge from Fresno, a USC graduate and real estate appraiser. Together they have raised two beautiful and accomplished daughters, Katie and Coco, both students at Marlborough School, representing the third generation to attend. Jim and Ginny are both very active in social and community groups and seem to know everybody we encounter in Los Angeles.

A favorite Jim Shelton remembrance was when he was project manager of the tower addition to the Century Plaza Hotel. As the project neared completion, a key deadline loomed. To qualify investors for favorable tax treatment for that year, there had to be proof of occupancy by December 31. Just in time, the first guests checked into the Presidential Suite for New Year's Eve, none other than President and Mrs. Reagan. Jim and his team celebrated with a well-earned brew down at the bar. Then came an urgent call from the front desk. Nancy was threatening to leave, as her bath was not hot enough. One of Jim's guys was able to fix the problem quickly, and the day was saved.

Richard Shelton, Joe Shelton's middle son from his previous marriage, is a hero to us. A difficult childhood was followed by an equally difficult period as a struggling artist in New York City. There were several unsuccessful marriages and even a bout of malnutrition. Returning to California, his life settled down. He located in Morro Bay, becoming a sign painter to support his creative work. In time he met Laurie MacDonald, a Cal Poly grad who was working as a nutritionist at nearby Atascadero State Hospital for the criminally insane. This facility is home to some of our society's scariest –

murderers, arsonists, etc. Attendants never wear name tags, lest an escapee track them down. In the midst of this hellish sea, Laurie presented an island of calm. Her great good sense and equanimity have been the perfect complement to Richard's towering talents. Her demeanor and her own considerable talents have sent her vaulting up the corporate ladder at Carnation and later at their acquirer, Nestle, where Laurie is Vice President in charge of communications.

Upon relocation to Los Angeles, Richard was able to devote more time to his creative work. His portraits are superb, and his allegorical work is powerful. A flattering portrait of me is perhaps my most prized possession and stands in the hall that we endowed at the Albuquerque Academy. My only stipulation to Richard was "no horns and no hooves." Richard is one of the best read persons I know, and his art is full of sophisticated literary and biblical allusions. Both Richard and Laurie have been especially kind and attentive to our sons.

Richard and Laurie, flanked by Jim
and Ginny's daughters, Katie and Coco - 2007

Brick Elliott and Grammie Goodwin with baby Elliott – 1977

Grandparents

Longevity is a hallmark of the Goodwin/Shelton family. Sarah's grandfathers lived to 86 and 93, and her grandmothers to 85 and 86. As mentioned before, Sarah's biological father was lost in the war in his 20's, but as of this writing, her mother is 88. While not in Sarah's bloodline, her step-grandmother, Ruth Elliott, lived to 103, and stepfather Joe is still going at age 91.

On the Brown side, three of my four grandparents were gone before I was born. My mother's parents both died in their 60's, and my father's father took his own life when he was in his thirties. However, Grandmother Brown made up for the others by making it to 104! In fact, dying at age 83, Dad survived his mother by only 2 years. My mother's life was doubtless shortened by her smoking habit, as she succumbed to lung cancer at age 77. Sister Barbara died in infancy of leukemia shortly after birth. Brother Ken was age 33 when he lost a battle with pneumonia due to lungs weakened by cancer and by smoking. My brother Harry is now 62 and in good health – as far as I know. Margaret Svibergson lost her battle to breast cancer at age 72, and Nils led a healthy and productive life until age 93. At his services, Judy and Becky gave brave and moving eulogies.

Quality of life among these long-livers has generally been excellent, too. Most of them enjoyed reasonably good physical and mental health until their final days. Joe Shelton has had a series of knee and hip operations, including four replacement surgeries, and currently spends most of his time in a wheelchair. His general mental capacity remains good. Sarah Belle Shelton has an opposite profile. She remains physically active, but Alzheimer's disease is eroding her memory at an increasing rate.

Grandmother Madie Brown was born Madie Francis Diggett in 1888 in Anniston, Alabama. The family then moved to a home in the Ravinia Park area of Chicago. I don't know much about her family or what brought them back to the South, but there she met Collier Harrison Minge, Jr. He was in his family's cotton brokerage business and lived in Mobile, Alabama before moving to Atlanta in 1916. That family included several Confederate Civil War heroes and both Harrison presidents. They bore a son, my father, Robert Collier Minge, born in 1911 and Colleen Minge born in 1914. It was in 1917 when Collier Minge committed suicide. Newspaper reports said that he became "mentally unbalanced" over the events of World War I. I believe that there also may have been economic reverses. It must have been so traumatic for my dad who was only six at the time.

My mother liked to say that there is but a thin line between genius and madness. More than a few of our extended family crossed over that line. Alcoholism, schizophrenia, severe anti-social behaviors, and mental disabilities popped up frequently in both my father's and mother's families. In contrast, Sarah's family members are bright and able, but remain well within the bounds of normality, an influence which I welcome in our family line.

Madie then moved her family to Macon, Georgia in 1920, perhaps in the company of Edmund Brown, who she married. To honor his new stepfather, Dad changed his name to Robert Minge Brown. Edmund and Madie bore a child, Natalie Brown, in 1921. Edmund Brown was Jewish and was a top executive of the Majestic Electric Company, an important manufacturing firm at that time. A corporate transfer brought the family to San Francisco around 1923.

Madie also wanted to be closer to her sister, Betty Diggett, who lived in Oakland. "Aunt Betty" was a pretty woman who had an early career as a singer and chorus girl and later worked at Capwell's Department Store in Oakland. I remember her as a very sweet, gentle lady.

During the Depression, Majestic Electric went out of business, and Edmund Brown reportedly had alcohol problems. He died sometime in the early 1930's, and my father found himself working several jobs while at Stanford in order to send money home.

Madie became active in various women's and political activities in San Francisco. She was a vigorous supporter of James Rolph, long-time Mayor of San Francisco, but a long-shot candidate for Governor of California. Coincidentally, Rolph was a previous owner of Pony Tracks Ranch in Portola Valley, now owned by my friend and Bohemian campmate, Jacques Littlefield. When Rolph won in an upset, he appointed Madie to the State Park and Recreation Commission, where she served for some 20 years. Among Madie's initiatives was the dedication of the park atop Mt. Davidson in San Francisco. Upon mandatory retirement at age 65, she requested assignment as a museum curator. She turned down a spot at Hearst Castle as being too demanding in favor of the Vallejo home in Sonoma. General Mariano Vallejo was the last Mexican governor of California before the territory went to U.S. hands in 1848 at the conclusion of the Mexican-American War.

With typical zeal and energy, Madie plunged into her new career and embarked on research about the Vallejos. She learned Spanish, traveled throughout Mexico, and conducted extensive interviews with historians familiar with the Vallejo family. Her product, a 442-page book titled *The Vallejos of California*, is the authoritative work on that aspect of California history. Another result was Madie's friendship with Mariano Vallejo's grandson and the last remaining descendant of Vallejos, Richard Raoul Emparan. To our surprise and delight, the two decided to get married, he at 83 and she at 82. Madie and Raoul made a wonderful couple and enjoyed ten years together until he passed away in 1980. Madie loved the Spanish culture and often enjoyed wearing period Spanish dress and mantillas. She and "Papa Raoul" are buried at Lacryma Montis (Latin for "Mountain Tear"), the site of a spring on the former Vallejo Ranch, now a cemetery.

Madie's energy and intelligence were applied to a number of worthwhile causes. When Wells Fargo Bank unveiled a plan for a new branch office in Sonoma that was to be in a Japanese style, Madie organized a successful community-wide protest to insist on a Mission style befitting the community's heritage. Madie evidently had little time for home and family, and a streak of vanity caused some distorted behavior. My father said that when she visited him at Stanford, she wanted to be introduced as his sister, which he understandably refused to do.

Madie did not make it to our wedding in July of 1972, so shortly after settling in nearby Marin County, we went to Sonoma for Sarah to meet her and Papa Raoul. Sarah's grandmothers were strong women, but they were traditional ladies who generally wore conservative dress, and I had advised Sarah not to wear a pantsuit for this occasion. Imagine our surprise to see Madie step out in a red pantsuit trimmed in *faux* leopard-skin. When we left for a restaurant, Sarah held open the passenger side front door and readied to help Madie enter. Instead, she bounded into the back seat unaided.

Sarah was appalled to learn that we did not exchange Christmas gifts with Madie. We explained that Madie tended to send odd, cheap second-hand goods and did not seem to welcome gifts. Sarah persisted and sent her a nice gift, whereupon we got one in return. It was a years-old box of thrift store chocolate-covered cherries whose contents had been fused into a solid block by the heat of some previous summer. We resumed our practice of avoiding gift exchanges.

The Emparans, and later Madie in widowhood, lived at 405 Claudia Drive, Sonoma. It was a small yellow wood-frame house a few blocks from the Vallejo home. Years later, long after Madie was gone, we were stunned to receive a Christmas card bearing the 405 Claudia Drive address. Sarah's cousin, Sam Darsie's daughter Belle, had moved into the very same house. When I mentioned this coincidence to Belle, I was delighted to learn that she knew all about Madie and her community contributions but had not known that Madie was my grandmother.

One final sequel involving Madie came several years after she passed away. My father had been the executor of Madie's estate and had done a final closing and tax report in early 1994. In November, 1994 we lost Dad, and I became executor of Dad's estate. Then, in March of 1995, an income tax refund check in the amount of $7,000 wandered in from the State of California. It was in the name of Madie's estate. Now what? I learned that to reopen her estate would cost more than $7,000 in legal and accounting fees. The seven heirs to Madie's modest estate concurred with my decision simply to endorse the check over to the Vallejo home in her memory.

Dad never once spoke of either his father or his stepfather. His family home at 15 Montalvo in San Francisco was in the picturesque area known as Forest Hills. Despite its being only fifteen miles from our family home in Hillsborough, Dad never once drove us by the place to point it out. That home was foreclosed by the bank in 1935, requiring the family to relocate to an apartment. There must have been so much scar tissue from his early life.

The Brown extended family was not especially close. We tended to see cousins mostly on holiday occasions and then even less frequently over time. None of my extended family members attended Sarah's and my wedding. At our rehearsal dinner, we were surrounded by dozens of Sarah's family. My father rose to give a toast which included this remark, "Tonight we came to celebrate what in corporate terms would be regarded as a merger. Now it is apparent that we have been taken over by a conglomerate!"

The same rehearsal dinner and the wedding the next day presented a major diplomatic challenge for Sarah. For years, her grandmother, Lillian Elliott, and Brick's second wife, Ruth Elliott, had not been on speaking terms. Apparently, the relationship with wife number two flourished before the first marriage terminated. On key family occasions, such as Sarah's high school graduation, the family took great pains to make sure there was wide separation between the two grande dames. At our wedding rehearsal dinner, I was in charge of escorting Lillian to her table at one corner of the room while Jim Shelton was escorting Ruth to the opposite corner. Our timing was fateful. As I steered Lillian around a table in the middle of the room, she came face to face with Ruth. Half expecting fisticuffs, I was astonished to hear Lillian say, "So nice to see you, Ruth." Ruth responded, "So nice to see you, too, Lillian." As the two women continued their journeys to their respective tables, I wondered whether the warmth of Sarah's and my wedding occasion had melted the glacier of animus that had separated them for so long. My fantasy was short-lived. As I was seating Lillian, she turned to me and snarled, "He got exactly what he deserved!"

Sorting out Sarah's grandparents was a challenge for me, as she often referred to them by nicknames: Sarah Goodwin was "Grammy," Lillian Elliott was "Nano;" Ruth Elliott was "Nanny," and Brick Elliott was "Nap." Throw in assorted Sarahs, Sarah Belles, and Sadies, and it was like working through a Russian novel.

I regret that Guy L. "Poppy" Goodwin died before I got a chance to know him. Guy was an engineering graduate of U.C. Berkeley, a rancher and a business executive – for a time he was in the frozen food business with partner Clarence Birdseye. At only age 50, Guy was largely incapacitated by a stroke. He is remembered fondly by Sarah and others as a gallant man on horseback, a true gentleman.

Sarah's paternal grandfather, John Elbert "Brick" Elliott, was born on May 31, 1887 in Bozeman, Montana. Now a trendy town of urban refuge, Bozeman then was a dusty frontier village, a dropping off spot for this Scottish immigrant family. Seeing little local opportunity, Brick's father walked to California to check out opportunities there. Encouraged by what he found, he moved his family to Pacific Grove, California in the late 1800's. Brick was an energetic and able young man, short of stature but feisty and determined. His nickname came from his brick-colored hair.

One of Brick's high school jobs was working in a plant that packed saltine crackers into their cellophane sleeves. It was forbidden for workers on the line to eat the crackers. The line was patrolled by a stern German supervisor. His method of enforcing the cracker consumption ban was to grab a worker at random, wheel him around, and command him to "whistle!" Many a sputtering young man was shown the gate.

Another boyhood experience for Brick was the great San Francisco earthquake in 1906. Pacific Grove was well south of San Francisco. They felt a severe jolt, but relatively little damage to the small frame buildings of the town. Although communication lines to the north were severed, Brick said they knew that San Francisco was on fire because the night sky glowed orange for three full days – as seen from 80 miles away and over the 2,000 foot coastal range.

Brick entered Stanford University in 1907 where he majored in geology and was student manager of the football team. Stanford would remain one of his lifelong passions, "my religion," he called it.

Years later, I was witness to what Brick regarded as a potential threat to his religion. Sarah and I were called to a lawyer's office in San Francisco for the completion of documents that would result in an eventual substantial gift to Stanford. The lawyer reviewed the various provisions with us. All went well until the lawyer touched on a provision that addressed what would happen "if Stanford ceases to exist." Eighty year- old Brick's reaction was eminently predictable. "What do you mean – if Stanford ceases to exist? How would that be possible?" The lawyer explained, equally predictably, "Well, sir, it certainly is unlikely, but we have to provide for that contingency." Seeing Brick growing apoplectic, I pulled the lawyer into the hallway and told him the chance Stanford would expire during Brick's remaining lifespan was near zero and that the lawyer was about to blow the deal. I pointed out that in the absence of this provision if Stanford did in fact disappear, the courts would doubtless allocate the funds to some other worthy educational enterprise. The lawyer finally relented and the deal was saved.

Brick Elliott was hired by Shell Oil right out of college to be their first geologist. Today it is hard to imagine, but until that time oil companies relied mainly on intuition to find oil and gas reserves. The old hands looked with skepticism upon this rookie who talked of synclines and anticlines. Of course, it wasn't long before the value of his geology training became evident. Brick Elliott is said to be the first person to explore for oil by flying over terrain to note the geological formations.

In the early 1920's, Brick devised a significant invention that became known as the "Elliott Core Drill." Drillers commonly examined the nature of the rock that was extruded as they drilled down, but the rock came out jumbled – like granola. Brick figured a way to extract intact plugs of rock by creating a drill that lifted out sections. Geologists got a much better reading on the strata below. This invention won Brick the Lucas Medal, the petroleum industry's highest honor.

Rather than merely licensing the technology, Brick created the Elliott Core Drilling Company. His trucks roamed the oil patch, giving valuable service to others. Brick found that the Cadillac chassis was the most durable one to deal with rough terrain; hence the whimsical company motto: "Work for Elliott; drive a Cadillac."

Brick's company thrived and so did he. By the late 1920's he had a private airplane and fully staffed 90-foot yacht. There were rumors of very high living aboard the yacht. It was during this time that Brick's marriage to the former Lillian Fischer fell apart, and his relationship with Ruth Plummer began. Lillian was from a prominent family from San Francisco where they had a printing company. I knew Lillian as a gruff, but dignified elderly woman. Whenever I got together with Brick, he would rant about what a difficult person she was. Finally, I asked one day if he found her so troublesome, what motivated him to marry her. Without hesitation this shrunken 85 year-old man blurted out, "hot pants!"

Then came the Depression. When business slackened, Brick could have exited early and preserved his personal wealth, but he refused to do so out of loyalty to his employees. Brick finally closed down the business in the late 1930's, his capital shrunk to a small fraction of his earlier holdings.

Shortly thereafter, at the beginning of World War II, Brick joined the U. S. Army as a relatively elder statesman (age 55) and was accorded the rank of Major. He had avoided service in World War I when his career was just getting underway, and ever since he had been troubled by guilt over this lapse. He eagerly accepted the opportunity to redress this perceived deficiency. A favorite family picture shows father and only child Jack, both in uniform, shortly before Jack's tragic loss.

Brick and Ruth moved to Austin, Texas in the late 1940's. When I first visited them, they occupied a spacious 10th floor flat with a wraparound balcony overlooking the Texas State Capitol and grounds. Brick plunged into Republican Party activities, a rather lonely calling in a state then heavily Democratic. But Brick persisted, and eventually Texas took a turn to the right. When Texas re-elected Nixon in 1972, Brick Elliott was selected to be chair of the Texas Board of Electors. In the Texas statehouse, we got to witness the unique American ceremony where Brick, resplendent in his Elliott tartan coat, cast the state's actual ballots for President and Vice President of the United States.

Ruth Plummer Elliott was a free spirit from Portland, Oregon. She was an avid sportswoman and was said to be the first woman in Oregon to get a driver's license. Among Ruth's talents was a good command of French. She worked hard to maintain her language skill, subscribing to *Paris Match* magazine until she was in her 90's. As key contributors to Republican success in Texas, Brick and Ruth were invited to a dinner at the White House, hosted by President Nixon. The honored guest was the President of Romania. It developed that neither he nor the First Lady of Romania spoke English, and no one else at the table spoke a word of Romanian. Suddenly, Ruth thought to ask if they spoke French. Indeed, the Romanians were fluent in the *lingua franca*, and for the entire dinner, Ruth Elliott carried the conversation for the two world leaders.

Brick remained a staunch supporter of Nixon, despite mounting evidence of his misdeeds. I can still hear him railing that Watergate was all nonsense, that Nixon would be exonerated. Then, one day while driving in California, we heard the radio report of Nixon's resignation. Thinking that this news might be devastating to Brick, we stopped to phone him to break the news gently. He responded that he had already heard the news and proclaimed that "Jerry Ford's going to be the best one yet!" It occurred to me that an optimistic attitude might be one of the keys to healthy living well into one's 90's.

Brick had been a frequent guest at the Bohemian Grove and submitted an application for Bohemian Club membership when he was in his early 50's. The waiting list continued to lengthen, especially for non-residents of the Bay Area, and his name finally came up for admission when Brick was 71. Brick's sponsor tactfully suggested that Brick shouldn't feel obligated to join at that point and pay a substantial initiation fee – that he could continue as the sponsor's periodic guest. "Nothing doing," Brick replied. "I've waited this long, and I'd love to join". He did, and he then attended every Grove encampment for the entire 2 ½ week duration for 20 years. He probably logged in more time in the Grove than 90% of the membership.

While at the Grove, I encountered more of the insouciance that doubtless contributed to his long lifespan. He explained that when he arose in the morning, he'd try one leg. If that didn't work, he'd try the other. If that didn't work, he would stay in bed a while longer and try again. Once upright, he was a little unsteady, but as he explained, "I'm a little like a bicycle; I'm fine once I get going." Brick also explained how he knew if he had brushed his teeth – "If the brush is wet, it means I've already brushed."

A notable health incident occurred at the Grove when Brick awoke with tightness in his chest. We hustled him down to the Grove Infirmary, which was always well-staffed with physicians – in this case, my former Stanford classmate and Kansas City cardiologist, John Snyder. John quickly determined that Brick, who thirty years before had suffered a heart attack, had just suffered another minor one. During the course of his work-up, Dr. Snyder inquired about Brick's current medications. Proudly, Brick answered, "None – except for these." He produced a small plastic bottle of little red tablets. When the doctor asked that they were, Brick replied "salt tablets." Knowing, of course, that salt elevates blood pressure, the doctor asked why ever was he taking salt? Brick said that all the oil field workers took them. As it had been over 50 years since Brick was sweating in the oil fields, the doctor prescribed a regimen of more appropriate medications.

A love of his life was granddaughter Sarah. Not only was she his only surviving direct descendant, but she was devoted to him with many visits to Texas, cards, letters, and weekly phone calls (although Brick could never seem to get the hang of time zones and would invariably call at five in the morning Pacific Time). Sarah would often spar with Brick about political matters to their mutual delight.

When Brick finally succumbed at age 93 to a kidney ailment, we were so touched by his wish that our five year-old Elliott take the flag that draped his casket and deliver it to his widow.

Bride and Groom – July 15, 1972

Sheltons and Browns at our wedding

Together

Our wedding on July 15, 1972 was delightful. The ceremony and reception were held in the garden of the Shelton family home at 305 South June Street in Los Angeles. Vows were exchanged under the limbs of a majestic ti tree. The minister was Rev. Brandy Lovely from Pasadena's Congregational Church, as my Episcopal minister, George Regas, said that church doctrine would not permit him to marry a divorced man. We continue to admire George and were relieved to learn that his church has since relented on its restrictive policy. Our wedding night was at the nearby Bel-Air Hotel, after which we departed for our honeymoon, split between the Mauna Kea Hotel in Hawaii and the Ahwahnee in Yosemite.

It was on the flight to Hawaii for our honeymoon that Sarah announced to me that this was the day she was stopping smoking. As desirable as that outcome might be, the last thing I wanted to face during our time of newly married bliss was a growling bear, cranky from smoking withdrawal. I promptly got up and bought her a mini-pack of cigarettes that they used to sell on flights. I asked her to pick any other milestone to stop smoking. A few years later, she did – with the help of the "Smoke Enders" program.

Acquiring a home was quite an undertaking. Sarah and I had both spent time in Sausalito and loved its beauty and proximity to the City where I worked. During the months before our marriage, we found that Sausalito was out of our price range, and we began looking in Mill Valley. It was a hot market, and when I found a cozy hillside retreat for $62,500, I committed, pending Sarah's approval. Each of us chipped in $7,000 towards the down payment. As Sarah was still winding up her teaching job in L.A., she couldn't come see it until the weekend. Eagerly, I picked her up at the airport and drove her to see the house. And drove and drove. Mill Valley is a warren of twisty little roads, and I couldn't find the damn house. My bride-to-be acidly commented on my spending her money on a house I couldn't find. Finally, I got my bearings and did manage to locate it. I decided that one of life's important maxims should be, "Never buy a house you can't find again!"

Upon examining the purchase documents for our Mill Valley home, we were dismayed to see that the original grant deed dating from the 1800's had a clause that restricted the property from ever being sold to persons of Asian ancestry. While subsequent statutes have invalidated such restrictions, it was troubling to see such blatant discrimination in our property's history.

Mill Valley years, 1972-1976, were good ones. Sarah quickly became a leader in the San Francisco Junior League, where she made many wonderful friendships that sustain us to this day. We especially enjoyed rekindling her friendship with former Mount Vernon classmate Pam Sporl Elliott (no relation) and her husband and Wells Fargo colleague of mine, Terry. Muffie Graham was another close friend who we are delighted to see has recently announced her engagement to Sarah's cousin, Sam. Sarah became chair of a number of Junior League committees and was elected to the Board of Directors.

Among Sarah's ventures was the Chinatown After-School Program. The success that many Asian families have had in adapting to their new homeland in the U.S. obscures some difficult problems. Often both parents have consuming jobs, leaving latchkey children to fend for themselves. Delayed assimilation and gang activity were often the result. Sarah decided to draw upon her related experience with Latin immigrant children, and together with another Junior League leader, devised an enrichment program for after-school hours. The children were taken to museums, markets, readings, sports activities – all designed to help them improve their English, learn American culture, and cultivate friendships.

So successful was this endeavor that the San Francisco School District sought to incorporate it as a regular part of their program. We will never forget the scene at the school board meeting when Sarah's program was presented for adoption. The meeting was held in a large room filled with strident advocates of special interests.

Among them was a band of neo-Nazis in uniforms with swastika arm bands. Just before Sarah's presentation, the board chair called an unscheduled recess. When we inquired what was happening, the board chair replied that we were taking a "chaos break." Somehow, Sarah was able to maintain her composure throughout and make a successful presentation.

Our home in Mill Valley was at 79 Bolsa Avenue. It was on a steep hillside lot, several blocks above town in a quiet, woodsy setting of oaks and bay laurel trees. Neighbors included the *San Francisco Chronicle* dog writer and their bird writer, Mrs. Terwilliger, who took us on a fascinating tour of the marshes. Above us was a concert pianist whose beautiful music floated down the draw to envelop and transfix us. Just below us were the Denickes and their young child and our favorite neighbors, Walt and Lisa Guthrie and their baby, Annie.

Walt Guthrie was a landscape architect for the Thomas Church firm, the ones who did the landscaping at my parents' home. Lisa was also a landscape architect, but her renderings of plants were so well done that clients began framing them as works of art. Thus encouraged, Lisa began a career as a landscape artist. We attended her first gallery showing in Larkspur and were especially attracted to an impressionistic watercolor of Sausalito. At first, Lisa stoutly resisted our buying it out of concern that we were just being neighborly. Finally convinced that we were genuine in our desire, we held an elaborate "red dot ceremony" wherein the marker was affixed to indicate her very first sale. Subsequently, we have bought four more of her paintings as her artistic career has flourished in Marin County and in Italy where she teaches every summer.

Lisa Guthrie also has a great comic touch. Her kitchen hung out over the road I walked on my way home. Whenever she saw me, she would heckle me with clever insults, usually about my starchy banker's suit or my briefcase. The most memorable shot was when she yelled out, "Hey banker, when you were little, did you wear pinstriped diapers?"

A tragic recent chapter in their life occurred in 2006 when a record rainstorm triggered a mud and rock slide that engulfed their home and claimed Walter's life.

Mill Valley was perfect for running with beautiful byways and views at every turn. Just a few blocks up the hill began a firebreak into the wilderness that led all the way to the top of Mt. Tamalpais. Another favorite activity there was occasionally having the time to commute by ferry from the docks at Tiburon. A pageant of Bay scenes unfolded during the trip. If I found myself troubled over something, I liked to go to the stern of the boat and mentally cast away my concerns into the churning wake.

I remember another ferry boat ride at about that time. One of my responsibilities at the bank was managing a sales force selling a service for merchants. We often held sales contests with various appealing prizes as incentives. This time, the prize was a ferry boat ride from San Francisco to Sausalito for a dockside dinner. It was won by a sales rep from Orange County, a beautiful, tall strawberry blonde. Of course, I certainly didn't mind being in the company of such a head-turner. It was fortunate, though, that the envious males on the boat could not hear her conversation. Entranced by the lovely scene, she kept gushing, "This is just like Disneyland!" – perhaps her only memorable point of reference.

In 1972, I joined the Bohemian Club. Before my first visit to the Bohemian Grove, Sarah told me to be sure to look up "Bob" who was also a brand new member and who was the husband of one of her Junior League chums. I promised to look up Bob when I got to the Grove. When I got there, my roommate turned out to be none other than Bob. I saw his bedroll and such, but didn't see him. After a night of partying on the River Road, I returned back to my cabin shortly after midnight. Still no Bob. The next morning I saw a large lump in the sleeping bag across the room, evidently a sleeping Bob. I got dressed and went about my day. The next evening and the next morning were a repeat of the previous day. In time I left for home. Sarah was delighted that I had roomed with Bob but incredulous that somehow we had never met. A year or so later, I finally did meet the elusive Bob, a very genial fellow, and commented on our earlier non-meeting. He then beamed and said, "Oh yeah, I remember hearing something early in the morning, cracked open an eye, and was revolted to see some a------ doing push-ups."

In the fall of 1974 it became apparent that Sarah was pregnant with the little bundle that would become Elliott Brown. We did not know the gender beforehand, so we adopted the working name of "Herkimer." In fact, we became so captivated by Herkimer's squirming in the womb, it seemed a bit disloyal to abandon that name later. The pregnancy went routinely, and Sarah loved the experience. We enrolled in a La Maze program where I learned how to be her coach. Finally, the big day arrived. Sarah reported feeling contractions. No sooner did I start to time them than she reported having another. Panicked, I asked how long she had been feeling them. "Oh, a couple of hours, I guess," responded my stoic wife.

We rushed across the Golden Gate Bridge to Children's Hospital in San Francisco, stopping only long enough for her to pack a bag. When she saw me packing a bag, too, she was puzzled. I said it was a surprise. That surprise became apparent after Sarah had been installed in one of the birthing rooms. I bounded down the hall and into the room outfitted in coach's regalia – hat, whistle, and a tee shirt that read "Coach, La Maze U." One of us was amused.

On June 20, 1975, the baby arrived, a pink and healthy boy weighing 6 ½ pounds. We decided to name him "Elliott" to honor Sarah's father's family and to accord him the middle name of "Minge" to perpetuate my father's family name. We couldn't wait to tell Brick Elliott of his young namesake, but as was our custom we had to bait him first. I told this paragon of conservatism that we had named the baby "Roosevelt Brown." Brick thought it was a terrible name. Finally, we relented and said that, "The baby was named after another prominent American, Brick Elliott."

The only real complication to Elliott's birth was a scheduling conflict of mine. That very day, I had a long-scheduled press conference announcing the launch of WellService, Wells Fargo's pioneering electronic banking service. As the developer and manager of the program, I had to be there. I barely arrived in time, stopping just long enough to pick up a couple of boxes of cigars and candy to share with the assembled press corp. Elliott's arrival added a very human touch to the event.

Elliott was a delight and was very active physically from the beginning. In fact, he was such an agile little monkey that he literally drove us out of our house. One night when Elliott was only nine months old, we put him down for the night in his crib. Moments after we left the room, we heard a loud thump and then some crying. We rushed back into his room and were shocked to find him on the floor. We figured that by some fluke he had tumbled over the high railing. When Elliott tumbled out again before we had even left the room, it was clear that this was no fluke. Although there was a four foot high railing on our deck, we felt it was just a matter of time before Elliott would scramble over to test the laws of gravity on a 30 foot drop.

Marin County, for all its beauty and spirit of independence, was becoming increasingly inconvenient. We were constantly driving to the San Francisco Peninsula to the airport or to see my parents or to pick up Becky and Kenny or to attend Stanford events. The long drive to Woodside where Becky and Kenny then lived was eased greatly by our oral reading of the Tolkien books. Sarah is an excellent oral reader, and much of the passage to Woodside was evocative of the dark, menacing Mirkwood Forest.

About that time, our church, St. Stephen's in Tiburon, was having a series of lessons on Tolkien, C. S. Lewis, and the other English authors from the 1930's who wrote compelling allegorical myths. One of the other parishioners was Bill Sterling, who I had known from Stanford days. Bill and his wife hosted a hobbit party at their Mill Valley home, perched high above a canyon with a lively creek. We hobbits in our slippers and other hobbit habits were led on an adventure down a trail into the canyon. We then were blindfolded before proceeding up a path along the stream. As we approached a small cascade in the stream, the babble of the water took on a melodic quality. We lifted our blindfolds to see that the music of the stream had been supplemented by a lithe young man in elfin costume playing a stringed lyre. The party wound up on the Sterlings' deck with warm buns and mead. Mead is fermented honey and sounds much better than it tastes. In all, a uniquely Marin experience.

Brick and Ruth Elliott with Sarah

Bride and bridesmaids:
Penny Gill, Liz Morphy, Alison Kuehn,
Lucy Ross, Kathy Rose, and Caroline Darsie

Corporate Development

I returned to San Francisco in early 1972 as a corporate development officer of Wells Fargo's newly formed holding company. A recent Federal Reserve regulation had allowed commercial banks to form holding companies to engage in a limited roster of commercial activities that were deemed to be closely related to banking. Together with colleagues Paul Erickson and Bob Joss, we started up business finance, mortgage banking, insurance agency and other companies within the regulatory purview.

Ernie Arbuckle established the practice of "overstocking the pond" with executive talent, bringing in stars such as Bob Joss who would eventually become Stanford's Business School Dean himself. In fact, while serving on the Stanford Board, I had the satisfaction of advancing Bob's name to John Lillie, chair of the search committee. The secret of Ernie's strategy is that top talent keeps enlarging the pond.

Some of Ernie's "top talent" brought a new element to the bank. Jack Kopec was a brilliant fellow who I first met at a corporate retreat while he was zipping through the *New York Times* Sunday crossword puzzle – in ink. His wife, equally bright and wonderfully iconoclastic, was on the faculty at the University of California, Berkeley. When a female employee in Jack's department approached Mrs. Kopec at a social gathering to say how impressed she was with Jack, Mrs. K. responded "Obviously, you haven't seen him naked!"

The Corporate Development effort was directed by Bob Kemper who reported to Carl Reichardt, who was destined to become Dick Cooley's successor as Wells Fargo's CEO. Carl was brilliant, relentless, and earthy. He was a very tight controller of expenses, and he also understood the power of symbolic communication. When a bank officer would come to him for a spending request,

Carl would be very cordial and invite the officer to join him in the comfortable furniture in his office. Carl would station himself in a big overstuffed easy chair that was falling apart – literally. As the officer presented his or her request, Carl would absently start picking out little tufts of the stuffing in his chair. Usually it wouldn't be long before the requesting officer slinked away and abandoned the attempt.

Another time, Carl was trying to impress the management team with the need to boost our profit margins. At the annual managers meeting, he rolled out a poster of a gigantic bloated goose. Leading into the goose's beak was a conveyor belt stuffing the goose with all manner of resources. Below the goose was shown a golden egg, a miniscule golden egg. Under Carl's leadership as CEO, the bank in fact became much more profitable, in time becoming a favored investment of Warren Buffett.

Carl generally had limited appetite for broad scale consumer banking. When I later became Marketing Director, IRA accounts had just been authorized, and I was pushing for an aggressive campaign. Carl felt that those accounts were too small to be worth pursuing. Reluctantly, he let me continue our efforts, as I was convinced that the deposit totals would rise sharply as account maximums were raised and with rollovers from pension accounts. IRA's are now one of the principal ways Americans save, and Wells Fargo became the nation's leader in that field.

Carl was also thorough. We took a trip to Houston together to check out a mortgage company for potential acquisition. I had a package for Carl that was complete, or so I thought. Over dinner at the hotel, he grilled me on the usual financial aspects and then turned to me to ask how confident was I that the target company's CEO would stay and run it for us. He wasn't in a mood for best guesses and probed further with questions such as, "What kind of house does he live in?" After dinner I sneaked off to rent a car, and thanks to the target company CEO's having a distinctive name and being listed in the phone book, I was able to drive to survey his home in The Woodlands development north of town. It was a nice suburban house but not palatial. Significantly, there was a tricycle in the driveway, suggesting there were probably young children in the house. At breakfast the next morning, Carl seemed pleased with the report of my midnight meandering.

Carl could be harsh, but the results were usually beneficial. When Wells bought Crocker, he assembled the Crocker officers and told them bluntly, "This is not a merger. It is an acquisition, and we are the acquirers." He went on to emphasize that most of the value of this deal was in eliminating duplicated resources, especially manpower. Instead of the usual CEO palaver about being one big team, he told everyone that they should get their resumes ready. This candor helped spur Crocker executives not to cling to false hope and to get moving on their job searches.

For all Carl's gruff manner, he made the most humanitarian corporate decision I've ever seen. I happened to play a catalytic role in the whole affair. When Wells asked me to take over as president of an unconsolidated subsidiary, a consequence of leaving the main bank was that I would have to take a massive cut in my retirement benefit. Our plan was a "defined benefit" plan with deep discounts for early departure. I was then age 45, and with normal salary increases, my pension at the early retirement age of 55 projected out to $81,000 per year. Leaving now after 23 years at the bank would cut that figure to only $18,000. The bank recognized this sacrifice was unacceptable and asked me to propose a scheme to compensate for this loss. With the help of a creative insurance executive and with a big assist from the sky high interest rates of the early 1980's, they were able to buy me a lifetime annuity yielding 12.6%. For a lump sum annuity premium payment of only $236,000, the entire retirement pay differential was overcome.

I then wondered whether this scheme could have much wider application for the bank. I approached our Human Resources chiefs, Steve Enna and John Hancock, to suggest they look at converting the entire bank's pension obligation to one similar to my deal. Our actuarial earnings assumption for the pension plan at that time was that it would remain fully funded if we could earn 6.75% on the invested funds. By locking up an investment at almost twice that rate, the plan would be massively over-funded. The bank did indeed pursue this course, terminating the "defined benefit" plan in favor of a "defined contribution" plan for the future that offered employees portability of their retirement funds. The big surprise is what Carl decided to do with the surplus. Instead of returning it to the company, he decided the old pension plan had been too stingy and poured the money into doubling the employee retirement benefits. He did so even for past retirees, some of whom had retired years ago with meager income streams that had been ravaged by the inflation of the late 70's and early 80's.

Carl Reichardt's drive for efficiency turned retail banking from a relationship business into a transaction-oriented one. The local branch manager became a referral source to specialty departments in remote locations. All major banks have followed this trend. Given the increasing complexity and regulation of banking transactions, this strategy is inevitable to some extent. I just don't like it. Many customers don't either, leading to a steady migration of customers to local independent banks and credit unions which often have more staff stability and trade more on relationships. These units then grow and often get acquired by larger banks, whereupon they adopt the transactional pattern, and the cycle begins anew.

Working to expand the Wells holding company was my first experience with a heavy travel schedule. For the next 30 years, most of my jobs required plane flights every few weeks. Just a few years into this period, I came to realize I had visited all 50 states. One never gets fully used to it, but there is no substitute for hitting the road and seeing the troops or customers or prospects in person. I came to appreciate Joe Brown's comment when struggling to close a suitcase, "I think suitcases are designed for people with three hands."

A memorable trip was in 1996 when Sarah and I were returning from a conference back East. Our Delta flight connecting from Dallas seemed routine until we were on final approach to Albuquerque. Only then did we learn that one of the landing gears had not deployed, and we were told to brace ourselves. The pilot did a good job maintaining control, but the plane spun into the infield with the wing crumpled. We were told to stay in our seats until told to exit and to leave all carry-ons aboard. As we sat there, we got a whiff of jet fuel. Heightening our concerns were repeated shrieks of "We'll all be killed" coming from the rear of the plane. All of us shared the feeling of one neighbor who said, "Why doesn't the parent shut that kid up!" Next, we saw the flight crew up front summarily exit – with their carry-ons, of course. Left to our own with no additional instructions, we decided to make our own way up the tilted plane to the rear exit where slides had been unfurled. The source of the shrieking then became apparent – it was one of the flight attendants! After sliding down the chute, we could see why there were no instructions heard. The batteries in the pilot's bullhorn were dead. As the plane was being foamed to retard fire and explosion potential, some of the passengers started walking across the tarmac, oblivious of it being an active runway frequented not only by airliners but by high-speed touch-and-go Air Force sorties. Finally, a bus came for us. Once in the terminal, Delta tried to keep us sequestered in an abandoned U. S. Customs office. I suspected that it was to keep us from the press and from Delta passengers in the terminal. Sarah and I simply left, disregarding the protests of Delta officials. We stopped by the ticket counter on the way out to see what they were telling passengers who were scheduled to board our plane for the next leg to El Paso. They were being told that there would be a slight delay because of a mechanical problem. All this I captured in a letter to the Delta CEO to advise him on some needed changes. No reply. Finally, months later I did receive a perfunctory apology and $200 voucher, but only after I had escalated the matter to the FAA via Senator Jeff Bingaman.

Sarah in BoraBora – 1974

Launching the "SayRah" – 1994

WellService

After the corporate development job, I was asked to implement a project that had been conceived by colleagues Frank Newman and Dick Rosenberg. They noted that each credit card company had its own primitive electronic authorization system. This situation was untenable for retailers. Space at checkout counters is at a premium and is best used for point-of-sale materials. The last thing retailers need is separate clunky machines for each credit card. The concept for what became known as WellService was for one compact terminal that would connect to the databases of all the major card issuers. After a year of lining up hardware suppliers (TRW and Texas Instruments), programming, and negotiating with the card companies, we hired a sales force and started calling on merchants. Until credit cards were provided magnetic stripes, card numbers had to be input on a keypad. In 1975, calculators were still new and cost over $100. To deter thieves who began stealing our terminals, believing them to be calculators, we had to affix stickers reading "This is NOT a calculator."

The negotiation for access to American Express was a challenge. Negotiations with the two bank-sponsored cards, VISA and Master Card, were easy, as they were fellow bankers. Amex, plus their portal to Carte Blanche and Diners, was another story. We had no leverage, and the unit was headed by a seasoned executive, Maurice Segal. I wrangled an appointment to see him in New York. Dick Rosenberg instructed me to agree to pay Amex no more than 2 cents per transaction. At the airport, waiting to board my flight, I picked up a book by Karrass on negotiation. By the time I landed I had resolved on a different strategy. Projecting myself into Segal's shoes, I realized we were providing them a valuable service. I opened by requesting that we charge them 2 cents per transaction. After much bellowing and posturing, we agreed to provide Amex our service for free. Thank you, Mr. Karrass!

Speaking of negotiation, I soon had another opportunity to practice. Wells had recently bought a local bank in Fresno and found that their leased space was bigger and better located than our nearby office. Our branch people then arranged to sell our old office and began moving into theirs. "Not so fast," said the landlord. There turned out to be an alienation clause in the lease that allowed the landlord to boost the rent upon an adverse change of tenancy. This fellow argued that despite Wells Fargo's size, its equity ratios were not as strong as the former independent bank, and therefore, he was proposing to double the rent. I heard about this dilemma at a Wells Executive Committee meeting and then perked up when I heard the name of the landlord. He was someone I knew, and in fact was a member of my fundraising team for Stanford. He was a tough cookie, but with my solid connection, he agreed to see me at his office. As is typical of many negotiators, he sought to intimidate me by having me cool my heels in his waiting room. Costly mistake. With nothing to do for about 45 minutes, I picked up from the coffee table a report he had made recently to his syndicate of investors. Right there on page seven was a discussion of the Fresno bank property. He speculated to his investors that he thought he would be able to negotiate a 10% rental increase from Wells. When finally ushered into his office, I fairly quickly got to the point where I maintained that Wells' management had authorized me to pay him 10% more. Final offer, or we'll settle it in court. After some ceremonial moaning, he agreed. This news stunned my Wells Fargo superiors, although I did come clean to Dick Rosenberg about the circumstances, lest I be assigned to negotiate with nasty people for the balance of my career.

WellService also taught me the value of Public Relations. PR is both cheaper and more believable than advertising, as someone else is touting the virtues of your product instead of you. It can also be a great enhancement to the impact of advertising. At WellService we had no advertising budget, so PR was our only recourse. We wanted to make a big splash in the press conference announcing our launch, but business news seldom gets much of a play. Enter Alan Doran. Alan was the classic old style salesman – always with a rose for the receptionist to help him get through. We had only six pilot locations as possible sites to host our demonstration and were thinking of holding the conference at a slightly shoddy restaurant that was one of the six. Instead, Alan sold us on doing it at the British Motor Car dealership and announcing it as the "Rolls Royce" of electronic banking. The invitation to the press conference was a life-sized poster of a Rolls Royce grill with the invitation printed in the corner. Most corporate product announcements attract just a few members of the press. This one brought 40, including representatives of all three network TV stations. In addition to a huge publicity splash that led to lots of inquiries, there was what I call an "echo effect." For a year afterwards, our announcement popped up in all kinds of periodicals that were not present at our launch. Many were sister publications, always desperate to fill their perishable space; hence our eventual inclusion in such magazines as *Field and Stream* and *Women's Wear Daily*.

WellService was my first direct experience in a sales management role, and it provided a true learning laboratory for me. Three invaluable rules of selling emerged, ones that are widely neglected. Always get the customer to talk about his or her needs before pitching your product. This practice yields valuable clues as to points of appeal as well as guidance as to the best way to present them. Secondly, always stress the benefits to the customer, not the features of the product. As Dick Rosenberg liked to say, "The customer doesn't really want a 3/8 inch drill bit; the customer wants 3/8 inch holes!" Finally, know when to stop selling. Successful salespeople know that after making the closing sales pitch, "silence is golden." (My idea of the dream salesperson would be that pillow salesperson who convinced home decorators everywhere that beds need an avalanche of pillows).

Always, prospects are buying you as much as they are buying your product or service. Creating good rapport is essential to establishing the trust necessary for a successful sale. Today's Internet access provides a great advantage in learning about a prospect company and will pay dividends in suggesting productive topics of conversation. It also yields valuable clues as to a company's values, style, and practices. I have found it remarkable how top management's habits will permeate entire organizations, affecting the type of language used and corporate dress all down the line. Little things count, too. If a client orders dessert, forget your diet and order one, too (and he or she probably won't notice if you barely touch yours).

If you are entering the sales arena, prepare to be surprised. One of the surprises in selling WellService was its acceptance by car dealerships. These prospects were well down our list of targeted retailers, as their only credit card transactions were a trickle of parts and service purchases. But the dealers loved WellService. The reason turned out to be mainly that these guys loved gadgets. Dealers who spend all day up-selling customers on moon roofs and all manner of automatic accessories are often gadget junkies. At the other end of the spectrum, a WellService sales rep was doomed if led down the hall to talk to the security chief. These folks were invariably beefy ex-cops who could care less about transactional efficiency. They just wanted to catch crooks. One even suggested he might buy our product if we could rig a device that would clamp down on the wrist of the presenter of a bad credit card, immobilizing the suspect until the cops arrived. I could just imagine faulty card data trapping the editor of the local paper or the mayor.

A unique sales technique was practiced by Jim Magid, a former Army buddy. Jim was a skilled investment manager who employed an ingenious little demonstration of the value of his trade. He would pull out his HP12C and ask if one recalled when the Dutch acquired Manhattan (1626) and for how much (supposedly, $24 in beads). He then asked if we knew how much Manhattan was worth today. Predictably, Jim had an answer – about $22 trillion according to the Manhattan assessor's office. He then entered these factors along with today's date into his calculator and solved for the annual compound interest rate required for the funds to grow from $24 to $22 trillion over all those years. Surprisingly, the answer was a modest 7 1/2%. Jim then concluded, "You see, it wasn't that the Algonquins were gypped – they just didn't have good investment counsel."

Competitive juices can get extra stimulation from having a "booby prize" awarded to the worst-performing sales rep, in addition to prizes for top achievers. Such a practice has a touch of cruelty to it, but it does serve to keep the laggards in the game until the end, and it can add an element of fun. One variation of this format is to have a winning team be served a steak dinner by the losing team, which has to dine on beans. My favorite such contest was one where the winner got a $500 gift certificate to spend at the tony clothing store, Wilkes Bashford. The lowest producer "won" a $5 gift certificate from Wilkes Bashford – the gag being that $5 wouldn't even pay the sales tax on any item from that pricey establishment.

Within a couple of years we had several thousand customers and growing acclaim. In the days before interstate banking, banks commonly shared business practices with banks in other parts of the country. I made six presentations at national banking conferences. In fact, inquiries from other banks became so frequent that we decided to hold a seminar in Chicago where we gave guidance to 90 other banks for a sizable fee. Wells Fargo later decided to sell its rights to this service to Control Data Corp. for a significant payday.

I had one major frustration while running WellService. I knew the CEO of NCR socially and visited him in Dayton to offer an idea. At that time NCR dominated the cash register business. When the register rang up a transaction, it captured the description of the merchandise being purchased along with the amount of purchase. All NCR would need to process credit card transactions straight from the cash register would be to install a device that could capture credit card data and perform authorizations. In other words, integrate WellService into their machines. I was taken down the hall to meet somebody who introduced me to someone else, etc. After 18 months of beating on their door, I got nowhere. In the meantime, several Japanese companies developed just such devices and made major inroads into NCR's market dominance.

The bank then asked me to take on several other business services in addition to WellService. Later, Dave Weymouth would succeed me in that job, one of the three times he would do so.

Staff Services

After only a year as head of Business Services, I was asked to take over the Staff Services Division, a clutch of seven departments supporting the branch banking system. Now privy to the bank's salary roster, I learned that I was the lowest paid of the nearly 300 vice presidents of the bank – by a factor of 30%. When I pointed out that fact to my boss, it resulted in an immediate 33% boost, a boost which enabled us to buy the house in Hillsborough.

That staff was so talented, and all would go on to senior positions at Wells and elsewhere. Their very names evoke pleasant memories: Earl Aurelius, Mary Barnacle, Bob De Mattei, Tom Petersen, Roger Smith, and Dave Weymouth. Several years later, when they threw a farewell party for me at Monroe's on Lombard, our laughing (usually stimulated by Roger) grew so loud that we drove table after table of other patrons to far corners of the room. In addition to having fun, we accomplished a great deal, including the creation of a large network of Personal Bankers, who would serve us well in later marketing campaigns.

Quiet, unassuming Earl had quite an experience during this time. He was so well regarded for his expertise in Human Resources matters that he would occasionally be asked to consult with other banks. Wells Fargo at that time had a significant position in a Costa Rican bank, and Earl journeyed to help them. One evening, his hosts escorted him to dinner at a hacienda at the edge of town. It was a "gentlemen's club," and one by one his hosts disappeared in the company of female companions. When faithful Earl refused the offering of a brunette and then a blonde, the proprietor seemed puzzled, but then flashed a look of enlightenment. Shortly thereafter, up sashayed a male escort. Earl said he fled to the car in dread of next being offered members of the animal kingdom.

Tom Peterson's adventures were not as colorful, but they represented an important development for Wells Fargo, its first installation of ATM's. We decided on a pilot project in 13 Contra Costa County branches. The big decision was which vendor to choose. IBM, NCR, Mosler, and Diebold were the major suppliers at that time, and Tom and I visited their plants to assess their merits. We were in the process of formulating our recommendations to senior management when the head of Wells' computer operation said there wasn't any choice. He said that only a little-known company named Incoterm had the right network architecture and that their approach would soon become the industry standard. We hastily arranged for a visit to Incoterm's small factory on the outskirts of Waltham, Massachusetts. Although dubious, we proceeded with a recommendation of Incoterm to the Executive Committee. It was an ominous portent when Dick Cooley asked, "Who? Isotherm?" We did install the Incoterm ATM's, and then uninstalled them in favor of Diebold about six months later due to horrendous reliability and service problems. One of the hallmarks of a company successful in innovations is that it will tolerate occasional well-intentioned failures. Tom went on to a highly successful career, eventually becoming a Vice Chairman at B of A. And Bill Zeundt, the champion of the nefarious Incoterm, eventually became President of Wells Fargo Bank.

Picking up from Carl Reichardt's effective use of dramatic symbolism, I relished the opportunity to protest a computer services invoice that I thought was several times too high. I called a luncheon meeting with the head of the project to discuss the bill. I reserved a large conference room and had 16 lunches placed around the table. When only 2 computer people came, they seemed puzzled by the array of lunches. I remarked that knowing their hourly rate and the amount of our bill, I figured there must have been at least 14 of them working on our project. Our office staff consumed the unclaimed lunches, and our bill got cut in half.

My bosses were Dick Jackson and his deputy Dick Rosenberg. Dick Jackson was a very capable, mellow, sensitive man. When other officers in the executive suite were saying that it would be a great convenience to install a buzzer system to summon one's assistant, Dick quashed the plan with one comment. "The convenience factor depends on which end of the buzzer you're on." Dick Jackson was always very attentive to his staff and was kind to drop by a gathering of my staff at our home in Mill Valley. After a pleasant visit, he and his wife Pat headed for the door. As he mistakenly reached for the door of the coat closet next to the front door, a devilish impulse overtook me. I just watched to see this bit of vaudeville unfold. Darned if he didn't usher Pat in and then follow all the way in to the darkened nest of coats and such. Belatedly, Sarah and I sprung to the rescue. To this day I don't know if Dick was unaware of my connivance or simply forgiving.

I have felt such a strong admiration and affection for Dick Rosenberg ever since we met. There were not many bankers who truly "got" marketing. Dick literally invented bank marketing. Before Dick, Wells Fargo's stagecoach was a forgotten relic tucked away in a dusty storage room upstairs in a San Francisco building. Thanks to its resuscitation by Dick, that iconic logo has become one of America's best recognized symbols. Through use of pictured checks (a first), signs, merchandise, and all manner of advertising, the stagecoach became Wells Fargo. Dick was very disciplined in his depiction and use of the coach – always in low light and in natural settings. The coach and rugged drivers were a metaphor for reliability; they were never used as pitchmen for products. A theatrical agent once offered John Wayne as a spokesman, but Dick rightly declined for reasons of authenticity. Dick was the developer of the first packaged approach to deposit products and was the driving force behind Master Card, the first shared bank credit card. Later as the CEO of B of A, Dick introduced VISA to China. The list of his initiatives and achievements goes on and on.

We shared an intensely personal experience with the Rosenbergs early in our friendship. We went to see a reading of Mark Twain's works by Hal Holbrook. Earlier that day, Barbara and Dick's younger son, nine year-old Peter, had left with a group of Marin County kids on a ski trip to Bear Valley. Ever prudent, Dick and Barb alerted the theater management as to their identity and seat location in case any emergency arose.

Midway through the performance, an usher summoned the Rosenbergs with distressing news. Upon taking roll on the bus at the end of the day's skiing, Peter and another boy were missing. A thorough search of the lodge and surroundings revealed no trace of them. A check of other transport vehicles was also fruitless. For an hour or so, the ski patrol combed the slopes, but winter darkness soon halted the search. Sarah stayed with Barbara at their home in Lucas Valley while I ran back to our house to get parkas and such for Dick. A friend then drove him to the mountains.

Spirits sank further when the night turned cold and snowy. At first light of dawn, the search began anew, aided greatly by a host of skiers there for a celebrity ski race. Fanning out to adjacent valleys, one of the searchers was startled to hear a young voice ask, "Sir, could you please tell me the way to Bear Valley?" When the searcher asked if he was Peter Rosenberg, Peter seemed surprised – evidently unaware that a considerable portion of the Western World was looking for him.

Peter and friend had become disoriented during conditions of poor visibility. Once they realized they were lost, they had the presence to craft a crude lean-to and huddle together until the morning light. Neither boy had any scout training or survival experience, just common sense and uncommon intelligence. We have greatly enjoyed attending Peter's and Michael's bar mitzvahs and weddings and the Rosenbergs' glorious 50th wedding anniversary, but our thoughts often drift back to that blessed occasion for this blessed family.

Hillsborough

Our free-spirited Marin days were replaced by the comfort and stability of Hillsborough. Hillsborough is a place of lovely weather, lovely gardens, and lovely people. The majestic trees are a legacy from grand estates whose owners engaged in a competition for specimen and exotic species. There are no commercial establishments in the town, not even a church. The only non-residential structures are a few schools, police and fire stations, the Racquet Club and the Burlingame Country Club. The Burlingame Country Club is housed in a beautiful former Crocker mansion set among verdant gardens and a tight little golf course. "The Club" is the social core of the town. Without family ties or impeccable preppy credentials, it is impossible to join. Despite misgivings about its exclusivity, our family has enjoyed use of The Club and our many friends there. Recently, we decided to discontinue our membership only when it became apparent we would not be returning to live in Hillsborough.

Our Hillsborough house was our first "real house," as Sarah put it. It was in final stages of completion in a woodsy setting at 1140 Barroilhet Ave. It backed onto Ralston where we cut a gate for easy access to the adjacent grade school and soccer fields. The house was on a nicely landscaped half-acre and contained four bedrooms in its 4,200 square feet. Builder Bob Corrucini was very conscientious, and when some settlement problems occurred, he immediately arranged for floating jacks under the foundation – entirely at his expense. One feature that I especially enjoyed was the built-in vacuum system. The house was piped with tubes leading to a canister in the garage. While it was a useful convenience for housecleaning, my favorite usage was sucking up errant flies and mosquitoes if they dared to invade my domain. There was nothing quite like the satisfying "thoop" of a fly destined for interment in the garage canister.

Buying this home was a stretch for us in 1976. We had managed to sell our Mill Valley house for $114,000 and had hoped to limit our purchase to $200,000, but it was another hot real estate market, and our bid on a San Mateo Park house had been trumped by bids well over the asking price. I had just received a big raise which helped, and we drained our investment holdings to provide the down payment on a $275,000 purchase. The mortgage rate was 7 1/2% vs. the 6% we had in Mill Valley and 5% on my Fremont and Pasadena homes. We had a "now-or-never" feeling about being able to afford a Hillsborough house. Those feelings were borne out when we sold the house for more than triple the purchase price eight years later.

Hillsborough has undergone quite a transformation during my life. When I was young, the town had a few large homes, but was generally solidly middle income. Home prices there were little different from those in the surrounding communities. The Peninsula communities had not yet fused into a seamless megapolis, as I remember fields and crops between each town. Over the years, Hillsborough, Woodside, and Atherton separated from the others to become pricey enclaves. I believe that this phenomenon was driven by the presence of good schools and the absence of any negative factors. There also seems to be a tipping point wherein small differences magnify over time.

Dad and Mom built their Hillsborough home at 943 Hayne Road in 1939 for about $30,000 from money inherited from my mother's family. For several years they had assembled scrapbooks of house features they liked. They drew heavily from design features from the Gillingham family home in Berkeley. These features were transformed into a stately Georgian home with a beautiful curving staircase by noted architect, William Wurster. Just a few years ago, Wurster was honored with a retrospective display at the San Francisco Museum of Modern Art. The garden was designed by Tommy Church who also had a national reputation. We always told visitors seeking directions, "We're the last house on Hayne Road." There was a secluded cul-de-sac below our house that turned out to be a favorite parking spot for amorous couples.

Growing up, our favorite feature of the home was its location at the edge of a wilderness. From our back door to Skyline Blvd stretched two miles of meadows, cypress groves, and eucalyptus forests. It was a personal playground for my brother and me. It's sad to see the area covered with mini-mansions today and to see sleepy Hayne Road become a thoroughfare connecting to the 280 freeway. I was pleased, though, to see that the current owners of 943 Hayne, Bob and Veronica Faussner, have been so conscientious in incorporating Wurster design features into their beautiful remodel.

Except for the episodic earthquakes, the Bay Area is seldom subject to violent storms, floods, or other natural disasters. One winter morning it was a blustery day when my parents dropped by for a visit. Suddenly, there was a dramatic change. Rain came pounding straight at the windows with such force, we thought they might break. Then we heard the ominous thumps of large trees toppling. This frenzy lasted only a few minutes, followed by a dry, eerie calm. Our property was OK, and we quickly left to check on my parents' place. Our trip involved threading our way around dozens of fallen trees. When we got to 943 Hayne, there was another one, strewn across the back yard, but having bounced off the roof. Superficial roof damage was extensive, but there appeared to be no significant structural damage. Then Mom shrieked from downstairs, "Look at this!" There was a track of gouges the length of the dining room table. That table top was a favorite roost for Rusty, the cat. When the tree fell on the house, poor Rusty must have felt he was inside a giant drum, and his reaction was evident on the table.

The highlight of our Hillsborough years was the arrival of Joseph Gillingham Brown. He was born March 10, 1980, also at Children's Hospital in San Francisco. Joseph's conception was a bit of a surprise to us. We traced his happening to a vacation trip to Cabo San Lucas some nine months earlier. We thought that if the child turned out to be a girl, we should name her "Margarita," in honor of the circumstances.

While Sarah's pregnancy was relatively uneventful, her delivery was anything but. Her obstetrician, who had sent her to the hospital for the delivery, unexplainably never showed up himself.

Fortunately, Dr. Green, a most competent OB/GYN was able to fill in, and she did a superb job. By that time the hospital allowed the father to spend the night in the room with mother and the newborn.

It was a special delight to have Elliott come to the hospital by taxi and to witness his joy at welcoming his younger brother. We had previously engaged in the classic parental briefing of the older sibling about the imminent arrival of a younger one. This conversation led to Elliott's probing questions about the process. Sarah and I believe that if a child is old enough to ask a question, generally the child is old enough to get the answer. We engaged in a rather clinical discussion of conception and the role of the egg and the sperm. Five year-old Elliott then riveted me with a stern look and demanded to know, "When were you and Mommy sperming?"

Perhaps our favorite photos of the boys were taken when they were about six and one. The photographer was a genial middle-aged woman, Margaret Peterson, from Menlo Park. Some twenty years later, several of these color photos had begun to fade significantly. Sarah wondered whether we might be able to locate Margaret to see if she still had the negatives. Upon learning that there was no longer a listing for her in the Menlo Park area, I turned to the Internet and logged on to one of the people-searching services. From my entry of her name, approximate current age of 75, and last known location, four suspects were offered. My attention was drawn to one in Sebastopol in Sonoma County, a likely retirement destination. When I called the number provided, Margaret confirmed that indeed she was the long-lost photographer. She remembered our boys and indicated that she did indeed keep the negatives and would be pleased to send them to us. She then expressed astonishment at how I had been able to locate her. When I revealed my Internet source, she exclaimed in a most naive and charming manner, "My goodness, you mean I'm on the Internet!"

During the boys' early childhood years, we had a series of "*au pairs*" living with us. They were teenage girls from abroad who had six month visas to come to America to live in and help with childcare. They were wonderful young girls who added a great deal to our lives.

An especially memorable one was Ulrica from Sweden. I had fantasized over the arrival of a leggy Swedish goddess. What we got was a short punk-rocker, all in black leather with spiky black hair and sullen looks. It soon became clear that this formidable exterior masked a heart of gold. Our bonding occurred when, unaccustomed to the size of our station wagon, she ran it into the garage wall. Expecting to be sent home on the next plane, Ulrica was elated to find us to be understanding and forgiving. By the time she departed for home, she was a vision in pink, restored to her natural blond hair, and wreathed in smiles.

We have special fondness for a Tongan girl, Keasi Utumoengalu, who had immigrated to the U. S. with her family. She just loved our boys and endlessly played on the floor with them. In turn, during our year together we helped her with her English, enrolled her in the local junior college and bought an old car for her. Her confidence grew to the point she qualified for a clerical job with the county. We then didn't see Keasi for several years. One day our doorbell rang, and we were so pleased to see Keasi again. Our delight turned to concern when we saw that Keasi was six months pregnant. The father had taken off, and Keasi's family was unsupportive. We invited her to move back in with us. When little Tevita "David" was born, we raised him together with our Joseph for the next three years. After we moved south to San Marino in 1984, Keasi and David lived with us briefly, but there was no Tongan church or other support system there, so she moved back to Northern California. We have been pleased to be able to stay in touch and to see Keasi craft a successful career in government service, buy a home, and raise David to be a fine young man.

Our lot in Hillsborough had a spacious backyard, and Sarah acceded to Elliott's desire to take in a couple of baby chicks from school. I built a chicken coop that was probably the most over-engineered structure on the planet. The hens proved to be delightful company and were very productive. Their calls in the morning gave our days a perky start. Then one day, a policeman appeared to inform us that it was not legal to raise poultry on a lot our size. Our property backed onto an empty schoolyard, and all of our immediate neighbors had told us they loved the country sounds. Apparently, some distant curmudgeon had cranked up a complaint, which led to a traumatic separation. Fortunately, Pozo had a small flock of chickens and was able to accommodate our brood.

For all of Elliott's accelerated childhood development, in one area he was significantly retarded – potty training. We went through the usual drills without much success. Then one day when we were using our best persuasion, Elliott countered, "But I find diapers to be rather convenient." Simultaneously, Sarah and I echoed a chorus of "Convenient for you, maybe!" and resolved to accelerate his conversion to civilized behavior.

Three year-old Elliott was beyond cranky one morning. His final outburst led to his being packed off to his room for an extended "time out." On these occasions the crying and caterwauling would persist for a short while. Then the mood would mellow, and he would emerge in better humor. Not this time. From downstairs in the kitchen Sarah could hear the wailing continuing and continuing. Rather than subsiding, it was actually getting louder. After maybe twenty minutes of this, she decided to check it out for fear that Elliott was harming himself. Sarah opened his bedroom door to be greeted by a grinning Elliott. Secure on his lap was a tape recorder on which he had recorded one of his outbursts, which he then proceeded to replay, ever louder! Clearly, we were overmatched.

Actually, young Elliott was seldom cranky, but was always full of energy. On a visit to grandparents in Austin, we had definitely pushed his limits. It was probably nine p.m. before we got back to the Driscoll Hotel for dinner, and his fidgeting was escalating. We were enjoying their house specialty, a towering tureen of Bananas Foster, when pacification was clearly in order. We hope the Statute of Limitations has run on this parental transgression. We decided to calm Elliott by spooning him some of the delicious rum-laden syrup. He loved it and wanted more. After a couple of spoonsful, we thought we had reached maximum dosage. Then the games began. Whatever calming effect the alcohol may have had was trumped by a soaring sugar high. For hours afterwards, we felt we were scraping him off the ceiling. Divine retribution, no doubt.

About the same era, Elliott was upstairs taking one of his long baths while we were in the kitchen preparing for a dinner party. Then I thought I heard the sound of water dripping nearby. Turning the corner to the front hallway, I was alarmed to see a stream of water pouring off the light fixture. I raced upstairs, bent on homicide, and found a joyous Elliott making giant bathtub waves that cascaded over the edge of the tub. There was over an inch of standing water on the bathroom floor when I shrieked, "What are you doing"?! He calmly replied, "I'm playing 'abandon ship'." Touched by the hilarity of the situation, I said, "Well, knock it off or we'll all be playing 'abandon house'."

Five year-old Elliott loved his GI Joe's and his battle gear. One day he traipsed into the kitchen in his camouflaged outfit and toy gun. He announced to Sarah that he was going to defend us against "the Bolivians." He proceeded to station himself in the bushes right outside the front door. A few minutes later he popped back inside to ask Sarah, "Mom, what do Bolivians look like?" Sarah responded that they were generally short of stature, stocky, with brown complexions. Elliott then returned a few minutes later to offer that there were lots of nationalities who might fit that description, so he asked, "What do they talk like?" Sarah with her excellent Spanish offered a few likely phrases. Elliott seemed satisfied and resumed his vigil for several more hours. When I came home that evening, Sarah and I shared our puzzlement as to how Elliott could have thought that the gentle, peace-loving Bolivians presented a threat to our security. The puzzle was solved later that evening when we learned that the Libyans had staged a menacing fly-by of a U.S. military installation, news that Elliott must have picked up in an earlier broadcast.

From his earliest days, Elliott has been quite a sports fan. While playing in the outfield during a Little League game, his coach noticed that Elliott's attention had drifted over to an adjacent game. The coach yelled, "Hey, Elliott, what game are you watching?" Not appreciating the rhetorical nature of the question, Elliott responded with a virtual play-by-play description. "Well, coach, it's the bottom of the fifth inning and the Sharks have runners on first and third, and --." The coach cut it short, saying, "Elliott, you're supposed to be watching this game."

Raising children brings poignant moments. One of those came when Elliott was seven. He approached Sarah and me with the question, "Do I really have to die someday?" Although couching our reply in terms of his long life ahead and the prospect of an afterlife, we were honest in our answer. Just writing about it still brings tears to my eyes, though.

Hillsborough Friends

Our move to Hillsborough brought a set of new friends. Sarah's "baby group" were a wonderful group of young mothers. Peggy Kappler she had known while acting as her "big sister" at Mount Vernon College. Candy Blanchard, Tori Hazelrig, Virginia Roberts, Jane Scribner, and Linda Woo were the others.

As usual, Sarah provided my entrée to a great group of new buddies. "Doc" Blanchard, Frank Kappler, Paul Hazelrig, Ross Roberts, Bob Scribner, and Max Woo were all ardent tennis players. Seldom did a weekend pass without some rousing matches, usually punctuated by good-natured needling ("You would have gotten to that ball last year!")

On a visit to Pozo with the Kappler family, we adults were enjoying a pleasant time in the kitchen preparing dinner. Suddenly, we came to one of those moments of parental awareness that our toddlers were being just too quiet. We peeked around the corner to spy three year-old Elliott and Kate Kappler on the floor having a tea party with little tins of food. Closer inspection revealed that they were tins of warfarin, a deadly rat poison. We rushed them to the San Luis Obispo hospital for a quick stomach pump, the first of a number of parental trips to the ER. Somehow all the kids have survived into adulthood, including my lovely goddaughter, Kate. I was so flattered to be asked to serve as an usher at her wedding to a delightful dynamo, Travis Parsons.

Another memorable social occasion was Dave Jackson's 40th birthday. Dave is a warm and happy fellow, but is somewhat reserved. His darling live-wire wife, Jane, wanted to throw a nice party for Dave. He was adamant in his refusal and asked Jane to swear there would be no party. Grudgingly, she agreed. The afternoon of his big day, Dave was out working in his front garden. Slowly, he became aware of an approaching clamor and band music. Around the corner came an entourage of 80 of his friends, all in costume, plus assorted vehicles, a fire engine, and the Burlingame High School marching band. When Dave fixed his gaze on Jane saying, "I thought you agreed there would be no party!", Jane smiled sweetly in response, "Honey, you didn't say anything about not having a parade." As you may suspect, Dave ended up having the best time of anyone there.

We regret that our relocations have put distance between us and our Hillsborough friends, but we have enjoyed the Albuquerque visits of the "baby group," plus the Berwicks, Cooksons, Fosters, Parsons, and Currys. It was also fun to share visits from Peggy Jones, Betty Horn, a contingent from the Hillsborough Garden Club, and our favorite housekeeper and expert won ton chef, Ying Chu.

A relocation to Chicago by neighbors Ann and Rob Krebs (who eventually became CEO of Burlington Northern Santa Fe) prompted a block party where we wished them a fond farewell. As we were lamenting their departure and predicting that we would never leave Hillsborough, little did Sarah and I realize that just three months later, there would be a farewell party for us.

Several of my parents' friends became our friends as well, a transition that is especially gratifying. Bill Barkan was a Navy colleague of Dad's who I later came to know as a mentor at Wells Fargo, and Joan Barkan was my mother's best friend before she became friends with Sarah through the Hillsborough Garden Club. Bill Barkan was the kind of grown-up who endeared himself to children of friends because he made a special effort to get their identities and interests straight. Ernie Arbuckle was another special older generation friend. He had been an usher in Dad's wedding and had a distinguished corporate career. I first got to know him personally when he was serving as Dean of Stanford's Business School when I enrolled. He was a very effective leader and fund-raiser, a record that was extended by his successor, Arjay Miller. The two of them lifted Stanford from the second tier of MBA programs to the top of the heap. I like to remind alums on fundraising calls that their commitment to the school's continued improvement is a reinvestment in their own credentials. At the end of his ten-year deanship, Ernie famously declared that he was ready for "re-potting" and signed on as Chairman at Wells Fargo.

Sarah, Joseph, and Elliott – 1981

Elliott and Joe in Alaska – 1989

San Francisco Main

One day in 1978, I got a call from Dick Cooley to ask if I was free to meet him for lunch. I quickly became free. Dick suggested it was time I got back to traditional banking and asked me to take over management of the San Francisco Main Office. This branch alone held over $1 billion in assets and was the bank's flagship. It was a great re-immersion into mainline banking. It was also a welcome change for Sarah, as she said "For the first time in six years, I think I understand what it is that you do."

Becoming manager at San Francisco Main was a dream job, literally. When I first joined the bank, I came to admire Harry East Miller, the debonair manager of that office. He was the bank's ambassador to the downtown San Francisco business establishment. He was a senior vice president! I thought that job would be an ambitious ultimate career goal. But wait a minute, not halfway into my career, I already had that job. What now? Since then, I've abandoned career goal-setting and have just gone after opportunities that intrigue me.

San Francisco Main had 80 employees, about one-third of whom were gay. This staff composition generally didn't have any effect on work performance except for one gay supervisor who tended to discriminate against straights, an ironic twist that we soon addressed. Halloween at San Francisco Main was especially memorable - like Mardi Gras on steroids.

This job was my first experience with several layers of management reporting to me. I felt a need to connect with the first line employees without subverting the authority of intervening managers. My tactic was to institute periodic "brown bag lunches" for groups of five or six tellers or clerks. The message from their level was generally more candid and unfiltered than messages from direct reports, who were more inclined to tell me what they thought I wanted to hear. I have continued the brown bag lunch program throughout my corporate career.

A major challenge erupted just one week into the new job. A Japanese importer of electronic components had been a customer in good standing for almost a decade. Apparently, he encountered financial problems with stale inventory and began a "check kiting" scheme. That's the term for the practice of depositing a check with insufficient funds behind it, but covering that deficiency with a deposit of another bad check, and so on. Some kites involve dozens of banks. The kite will stay in the air until some bank in the chain decides to hold their deposit until the funds are confirmed to be good. Then the kite comes crashing down upon the last bank in the series. We were that last bank – with an overdraft of $270,000. I immediately reported the problem to Auditing, but it was apparent that their collection efforts would take weeks to get underway. Knowing that pace would be much too slow to catch our thief, and darned if I would take a loss like that, I decided on direct action. As many Asian families love real estate, I called a buddy at a title company to check, and sure enough, this guy owned a number of properties out in the Sunset District. My friend agreed to "put a cloud" on the titles to prevent transfer of these properties. Within a day, our elusive thief was thwarted in trying to transfer the properties to relatives of his. What I had done was dubious legally, but I figured the courts would not smile on him or his motives. We eventually collected our loss in full.

Buddies are essential to cope with the bureaucratic processes of large enterprises. Often a needed resource person is swamped with a backlog of work, and a good relationship can do wonders to move one's request up in priority or to find a creative solution to a problem. As an example, the carpet in our downstairs safe deposit area was badly worn. My request for replacement was summarily declined due to a prevailing budget freeze. I called Henry Polanshek, the bank's chief purchasing officer, to see if there could be an exception. Henry and I had played tennis periodically and were on good terms. He said that the only exception would be if the carpet were torn and represented a safety hazard. I replied that it was threadbare but not torn. He then pressed the issue by saying, "Are you sure it's not torn?" Finally picking up on the hint, I reported that a tear was just now appearing. Within weeks we had a nice new carpet.

On another occasion in another office, we had just gotten a nice plush new carpet throughout the office. The first customer in the door noticed it immediately, gave an appreciative little bounce and then said, "How much is my loan rate going to go up?" Customers appreciate nice surroundings, but opulence can backfire. One of Dick Rosenberg's maxims is "Occasionally, you may have to spend more to make something look cheap."

One of the minor advantages of a job that involves being the bank's principal face on the street is visibility. Visibility can have its dark side, too. Our office was at a prominent downtown location, adjacent to the main offices of four other banks. First one and then another of the other bank managers' wives were briefly kidnapped. For about a year, we took various extra precautions for the safety of our family.

In twenty-eight years of banking, I was never personally involved in a bank robbery, but a number of offices under my supervision were. The problem was especially acute in Los Angeles where easy freeway access expedited getaways. Robberies are very traumatic for the staff and no laughing matter. But one incident early in my career did seem amusing. A robber held up our New Montgomery Office. It was strict bank policy to be sure to pull the alarm, to get a good look at the robber, to delay a little if possible, but by all means to comply and not to engage in any heroics. A new young teller had a different idea. He leaped over the barrier and chased the robber down the street. The two were wrestling on the sidewalk when the police came to take control of the situation. Shortly thereafter, the head of the San Francisco Region called the young man to his office to reprimand him for being so foolhardy and endangering himself and others around him. The young man apologized, but expressed confusion. The executive thundered whatever could be confusing about his message? The young man then said, "Well, sir, just before you called, Chairman Hellman called me to his office and gave me this." At that, he displayed a gold watch given to him by the octogenarian chairman to reward his heroism. The exasperated executive then threw up his hands, another victim of the old school/ new school divide.

If you are in a service business, your company's reputation is on the line every day and is in the hands of employees whose commitment to service is not always there. As Arjay Miller noted when he was President of over 100,000 employees at Ford, it was discomforting to know that on a daily basis someone somewhere in your company was probably doing something absolutely appalling. In Wells Fargo's case, Hal Hankinson related that when he was a neurosurgery resident at UCSF, he dropped by a Wells Fargo branch to apply for a credit card. In vain, he tried to explain to the clerk that he was not in medical practice yet, but was soon to complete his prestigious residency and was serving as chief of the residents. The clerk finally replied, "Why don't you come back when you're a real doctor?" While Hal is the last person ever to be vindictive, the fact he is telling this story 30 years later shows the powerful effect of a negative service encounter.

I found dealing with customers to be one of the fascinations of the job. One of our borrowers was a leading Bay Area street sweeping contractor. For years he had won the bid to sweep the roads in several East Bay counties. One day he came to see me, the picture of gloom. A new market entrant had come from nowhere and had substantially underbid him and his traditional competitors. My customer was facing difficult expense cuts. Next week, he reappeared beaming. It seems that the novice competitor had neglected to figure that there were two sides to the streets and hastily withdrew from the field.

Another customer was Bob, a lively young bachelor who was just getting going as a commercial real estate dealer. Somehow he got an option to purchase an older office building on the corner of Mission and New Montgomery for $4 million. He then went next door to the phone company headquarters and got them to agree to buy it for $9 million. He closed the deal in escrow without ever putting up a dollar of his own and walked off with $5 million. Actually, he drove off – in his new red Aston Martin. He drove straight to the airport, resolved to take whichever international flight left next. He returned from Rio two weeks later, having established a new standard of how to deal with a windfall.

Three customers of mine had what I regarded as dream business models. Mike and Dave were paving contractors whose father's business had expanded out of control and lost everything. The two sons settled on a different business plan. They had only two customers, the phone company and the power company, for whom they patched up street work. They could schedule well in advance, always got paid, and took all of August off to spend at their duplex at Tahoe. The wives handled bookkeeping and logistics out of the house and the two families coined money! The second ideal business model was Jim's, a former Shell Oil chemist who figured a way to extract one more round of fuel value out of refinery residuals. As the opportunity wasn't big enough to interest Shell, they gave him a release to pursue it personally. Jim contracted for a processing plant in the South Pacific near the Australian fuel oil markets. From his perch high on a Belvedere hill, he could watch his leased tankers float by three times per year, each trip netting him about $500,000. The third dream job was a wholesale antique dealer in Pasadena. Virgil would make three trips a year abroad. He would spend a month shopping for items that were ordinary to the locals but exotic to American buyers. He would then spend the next two months arranging for shipping and getting ready for his warehouse sale to retail antique dealers from all over the West. After selling out, he would take the fourth month off. The mark-ups were astonishing. A load of school clocks from Singapore cost him $2 each. He then wholesaled them to retailers at $50 each who in turn sold them for about $200 retail. Virgil made a fortune and enjoyed every day doing it.

Losing some big customers turned into the biggest career opportunity of my life. During the Carter administration, the Treasury Secretary was Bert Lance. Lance had been a Georgia banker who engaged in some practices that we regard today as highly unethical. He and his board buddies gave themselves loans with little credit scrutiny and at extremely preferential rates. In response to a rash of defaults on these loans, Congress passed the Financial Institutions

Reform Act. As is typical of government regulation, the pendulum swung far to the other side, to the point that bank directors risked going to jail for any deviation from proper procedures at their home banks. In response, three of my biggest accounts, ones controlled by directors of Wells Fargo, set sail for safer harbors. I was lamenting this loss when the light bulb went on that would illuminate the rest of my career. I figured that directors of other banks were in the same pickle. I then deputized one of my vice presidents as a bank director loan specialist, had him come up to speed on all aspects of the regulation, and then sent out over 400 letters to directors of other California banks, alerting them to their peril and offering to help. To replace my three lost accounts, I got twenty-six new ones. Just as this surge of business was winding down, a distinguished looking gentleman appeared in my office, flopped my letter onto my desk, and asked if I was "Brown." "Yes," I responded, and glancing at the top of the letter, I asked if he was Walter Haas, Jr., the CEO of Levi Strauss Company. Indeed he was. He then confirmed the current rumor that he and his family were seeking to buy the Oakland A's from Charley Finley and asked if Wells would like to bid for the acquisition loan along with two other banks. Naturally, I agreed to bid.

In assembling Wells Fargo's bid, I started by thinking through why the Haas family wanted to buy the A's. The celebrity that comes from owning a major league sports franchise may have been a factor, but why Oakland? Given the stellar philanthropic record of the Haas family, I figured that a major part of their motivation was to do something to help boost downtrodden Oakland, recently abandoned by the Oakland Raiders' moving to Los Angeles. We packaged our loan proposal with supplemental sections discussing ticket distribution through our branches, help with relocation of players and their families, advertising commitments, coordination with local Boys and Girls Clubs, and access to career counseling and off-season vocational opportunities for the players. All this was bound in a handsome leather portfolio with a window for a photo of an arrangement of an A's hat, a scuffed baseball, and a miniature stagecoach.

Once again, a few weeks later, I was paid a visit by Mr. Haas. He tossed my proposal onto my desk and then said, "You have the crappiest rate and the crappiest terms, but you're going to get our business because you're the only ones who understand us." We later heard that the other two banks had submitted only loan proposals, sheaves of paper with staples in the corner.

Our relationship with the Haas family blossomed and included watching the opening night game with them in the Owner's box. Thanks to wonderful nurturing by account officer Don Rego, the entire Levi Strauss corporate relationship soon followed. It was the largest new account ever won by Wells Fargo at that time, and Don and I had a full page picture in the Wells annual report that year, flanking team executives Wally Haas III and his brother-in-law, Roy Eisenhart.

Marketing

In 1981, I agreed to become Marketing Director for the bank, answering to the dean of bank marketing, Dick Rosenberg. It was an exciting time for bank marketing, as the Federal Reserve was beginning to peel back the regulations that prevented rate competition on deposit accounts and began authorizing a whole new family of deposit products such as IRA's. It struck me as similar to the Sooner land rush in Oklahoma, a mad dash to gain favored position in a brand new marketplace. We were well positioned for this competition with a crack Marketing Dept. led by Nancy Thelen, Pat Pope and Lynnette King, an excellent advertising agency in McCann Erickson, and an ideal delivery system of hundreds of well-trained "Personal Banking Officers" in the branch offices.

After years in the field as a user of Marketing's efforts, I was determined to improve a practice which had developed during the reign of Dick Rosenberg's successors. Expensive campaigns would be rolled out, only to discover there were minor flaws in the program or materials. The flaws ranged from the brochures not fitting in the racks to copy that was slightly off target. Why didn't they simply check in with the users in the field before proceeding to production? Upon assuming my new post, I discovered why. Marketing officers didn't like to expose their work until it was ready to show in full color, final form. I told them they were like chefs who relish emerging from the kitchen with spectacular flaming desserts, only to learn that the diners are diabetic. I counseled that while a new practice of working closely with the field would deny them the thrill of surprise, the reward of greater acceptance by the delivery system would more than compensate. And indeed it did.

Another discovery on this job was that the copy presented to me for final approval would frequently contain typographical errors.

If I didn't catch them, millions of copies of the pieces might be printed with an error. Once, I dialed the toll-free phone number on a brochure and found it to be wrong. My exhortations were of no avail, and the typos kept coming. Suddenly, a new approach occurred to me. My assistant, Sharon, and I went shopping in some local junk stores for the biggest, ugliest trophy we could find. I then presented it to my staff as the "Tpyo" trophy (a typo of "typo") and announced that henceforth, anyone who presented me with final work that contained a typo would have to display this trophy on their desk for a week as a mark of shame. Glumly, the staff left the meeting. But for six months the typos stopped. Then one day, there was another typo. I paraded up and down the department, brandishing the dreaded trophy while the Marketing staff recoiled from me. Finally, I stopped at Rich Martino's office and placed it on his desk. For the next week there it remained, only under a black shroud that Rich brought to the office to hide his humiliation. Over a year passed before the next typo appeared.

Six successive marketing campaigns were a success beyond our highest expectations. We exceeded our normal market share in all six campaigns and beat B of A in actual totals in three of them, quite a feat in light of their being over twice as large as Wells at the time.

Our biggest success was a revival of the Gold Account deposit package pioneered several years earlier by Dick Rosenberg. With some trepidation we launched a revised version with interest on checking included. The concern was that we might cannibalize the existing Gold Account base of some 90,000 non-interest bearing accounts with few new accounts to show for it. We mobilized our stalwart branch network and let it fly. I was on a speaking assignment in Ecuador on the actual date of the launch. I will always treasure the telegram I received there from Bob McGlinchey, announcing skyrocketing success and signed "Roberto del Oro." The campaign finally topped out at 220,000 accounts.

A large contributor to our success was lively competition among the branch offices for generation of accounts. Most banks employ these sorts of contests. We went one step further by pairing up similar branches in different regions and encouraging personal side bets among competing managers. The effect was electric. One branch officer repainted his car gold to help in soliciting accounts. A Bay Area manager and colleague drove all the way to Whittier in Southern California to toss the effigy of a cat into the lobby of their rival, as the Mafioso symbol of contempt. Later, at Crocker Bank we employed similar competitions with equally good results.

Once again, I had a gem of an assistant, Sharon Anderson, a lovely Filipina American woman. She was very competent, highly engaged with our mission, and of endless good cheer. It has been a joy to get to know her parents and later her husband and to see their young family flourish.

We especially remember the occasion of Sharon's 21st birthday. That event is a celebrated milestone in Philippine culture, as we were to witness in a most dramatic fashion. All of the guests, perhaps thirty couples, were instructed to wear white, head to toe. Shortly after the party assembled at the family home, we learned the reason for our costumes of white. Down the spiral stairs came Sharon in a spectacular bright red dress. Throughout the evening, one could catch glimpses of Sharon, like a cardinal in a snowfield. It was a beautifully choreographed tribute.

An ad campaign doesn't need to be slick to be successful. My favorite example was when the town of Burlingame was voting on a rent control measure. Building owners had cause for concern as about 60% of voters lived in rental housing. Jane Fonda and her then-husband, Tom Hayden, came to lobby for its passage. The counter-campaign was brilliant. Posters depicted a frumpy Burlingame housewife who was well-regarded locally. Her message was, "If Jane is for it, I'm against it." The measure was soundly defeated.

Another unorthodox political advertising ploy was deviously effective. Just as I was about to toss a Republican Party mail solicitation, I noticed this message sniped across the envelope, "Ted Kennedy wants you to throw this away!"

The power of Wells Fargo's corporate symbol gave the bank a major advertising advantage. The presence of the stagecoach in an ad gave an indelible impression of the bank's identity. Advertising research has shown that shortly after viewing a bank

TV advertisement, 30 to 40% of viewers will have mistaken the identity of the bank. But when our ad depicted the stagecoach, the mis-identification shrank to about 5%. I was curious, though, as to whether that strong identification might cause us to import fewer mis-identifications from our competitors' ads. Our ad agency executive, Priscilla List, did some quick research and found that we did receive a normal share of spillage from other banks' ads. It was a one-way street headed in our direction when the stagecoach was on it.

Mandated government notices have become the wallpaper of marketing. Required disclosures, full of legal jargon, have zero communications benefit. To prove the point, Paul Eisen, then Marketing Director for Norwest Bank, decided to have some fun with a legal notice he was required to send to their credit card holders. It was several pages of dense legalistic prose. Paul inserted a phrase, completely out of context, lost in the middle of the notice, saying that he would send $25 to anyone who called. Some six hundred thousand notices were mailed. No one called. Only after Paul publicized this folly did a few people try to claim a reward, unsuccessfully.

Working with Dick Rosenberg presented one peculiar challenge. He would often ask me if I had read some item, perhaps about deploying ATM machines. Gee, no, I hadn't. "Well, it was in *North Carolina Banker*, a very good publication" Dick would say. Immediately upon returning to the office, I would fire off a subscription request. Next week, he might ask whether I had seen an item regarding point-of-sale displays. As usual, I hadn't. He said, "Well, it was in *Hardware News*." By the time I had reached 35 subscriptions, I limped into his office one day to say that I couldn't keep up with the reading burden. To which he said, "Oh, you don't need to read all that stuff." He then related that because of a massive print advertising campaign he had launched some years before, he was on the mailing list for scores of publications. Most of them he tossed unread, but during occasional bouts of insomnia, he would grab a few of them to scan. We agreed that he would be my clipping service rather than the reverse.

Shortly before leaving Marketing, I was in a meeting when a new secretary interrupted saying, "There's this gruff man who keeps calling for you even after I tell him you're busy. His name is Mr. Richard, or something like that." Oh, blazes, I thought, I'll bet it was CEO Reichardt. Sure enough, it was Carl, who was seldom patient to begin with. He wanted to know why we were still printing wallet-sized calendars in a time of expense stringency. I had no idea which of our folks might be responsible, but I committed to finding out. It turned out to be a real challenge. No one in Marketing or Purchasing claimed any knowledge. Finally, we tracked down an obscure clerk who had taken it upon himself to reorder them year after year. Sometimes in large organizations, programs can take on lives of their own. A clever scam periodically surfaced to take advantage of this phenomenon. Bank branches would get $20 invoices to renew their subscriptions to "the business directory." For $20, few bothered to check whether they were receiving this imaginary publication. I admired a ploy of Dick Rosenberg's wherein he would periodically cancel almost all subscriptions throughout his units and then quickly restore them as complaints were registered. Usually, there was a substantial savings from cancellations that were unnoticed.

That same secretary who didn't recognize "Mr. Richard" made another memorable contribution to my aging process. I had sent a letter to Goodyear proposing a program for their retail outlets. It resulted in a nice bit of business. I then took the Goodyear letter and marked it up with appropriate modifications to send to Firestone. A week later I got a call from the contact at Firestone expressing confusion about a letter he had received from me that was to Goodyear, but all marked up in pen to direct it to him. Fortunately, he had a good sense of humor when I explained what must have happened. As to the secretary, she was clearly unsuited to the job, but I took pains to find her another spot that would be less demanding. So, where did she end up about a year later? – as none other than the CEO's appointment secretary. It was yet another example of the value of never burning one's bridges.

A fascinating interlude was a three-week consulting assignment in Germany. Wells had a big investment in a floundering regional bank there and dispatched Bill Ford, Perry Wilder, and me to recommend fixes. It quickly became apparent that the German bankers were in total denial of their problems. Perhaps the most disturbing manifestation was their having no reserves for loan losses. I'm not sure whether they took any of our recommendations, and the bank was absorbed by a competitor several years later.

In the meantime, the hospitality was excellent, perhaps overly so on our last morning. As round after round of toasts proceeded, I became concerned about the time. We were in Bremen, 200 miles north of Frankfurt where my noon flight was to depart. As ten a.m. approached, I became more insistent, to which my hosts kept responding, "Don't worry, Hans will get you there." With less than two hours to go, I finally extracted myself and climbed into Hans' Mercedes 600 limo. I watched with alarm as the speedometer climbed to a steady 245 kph (152 mph) on the Autobahn. The scenery was a blur. It started to rain with flurries of sleet. When I tried to tell Hans that I could take tomorrow's flight, he turned around to assure me we would make it – traversing about a half-mile in the process. As we wound into the airport, barely on time, I asked Hans what happened when accidents occur at those speeds. At first, he gave the usual denials that they ever had accidents, but then he grinned and said, "The people, they end up in the trees!"

Quito or Bust[*]

My trip to Quito, Ecuador in June, 1981 to give a presentation was a big deal for me. It was a gathering of 300 top banking officials at an international conference. It was also Sarah's and my first visit together to South America, and we worked in a little sight-seeing before the conference. After a few days in Bogotá and a side trip to the Peruvian Andes, we had scheduled a leisurely day of travel to proceed from Cuzco to Quito via Lima. In fact, we were at the Cuzco airport when the trouble began. Were there omens for the practiced eye to detect? Was there portent in the neglect of our tour guides to meet us in either Bogotá or Cuzco? Should we have taken special note when our train to Machu Picchu was delayed half an hour due to a stray pig that refused to leave the tracks? No, we had been prepared to accept such minor matters as part of our adventure. The prospects for our trip to Lima and on to Quito seemed as bright as the crisp Sunday morning that greeted us at the Cuzco airport.

As we stood by the gate, boarding passes in hand, the only blot on the horizon was a small plane set at an odd angle at the end of the runway. A military pilot had just made a hard landing, and the plane was temporarily disabled. He was unhurt, and in fact, could be seen across the way in the coffee shop munching on a sandwich. A grand congress of officials had gathered by the plane to decide what to do. "There will be a short delay in your flight," came the announcement. Minutes passed. Then more minutes stretched into hours. Finally, after the delay had extended to three hours, we were informed that the disabled plane could not be moved and that Cuzco airport was closed for the day. But, we were assured, there was "no problem, travelers, we can get you out on the first plane tomorrow."

A review of transportation alternatives revealed an absence

---

[*]   This chapter was published in *Stanford Busines*, March, 1995

of realistic options. The trip from Cuzco to Quito would be two to three days by car or rail. Suddenly, a hideous specter began to crowd other thoughts from my mind. It was the chilling possibility that I might - just might - *miss my appointment*. For months I had been scheduled to be at the conference. Speech preparation, Spanish lessons, and 8,000 miles of travel had gone into this. To miss this appointment because of a sight-seeing tour would be unthinkable.

Definitely, it was time to call upon my loyal friend: my positive, problem-solving attitude. After all, my speech wasn't scheduled until Tuesday morning, two days hence. An interesting challenge, this. Thus fortified, I was unfazed upon learning that all Peruvian airline offices were closed due to it being Sunday and that there was no way that day to reschedule my connections to Quito. We would just have to get to the airport early enough on Monday to get aboard the plane. And perhaps, during our flight to Lima tomorrow, the flight crew could radio ahead to reestablish connections for that day. I made a phone call to our office in Lima to ask them to duplicate the effort and then sent a telex to Quito to tell conference officials that I would arrive Monday instead of Sunday. The pieces were falling back into place.

We turned our attention to making the most of our unscheduled Sunday in Cuzco. A marvelous day unfolded. Our visit to the markets of Pisac and the ruins nearby was one of the highlights of our trip. That evening we reveled in a mood of serendipity. As we lingered over pisco sours in the hotel courtyard, we shared our impressions of the rich textures of the marketplace and of the soaring Incan terraces. A basketful of weavings and other artifacts of the Altiplano joined our mound of baggage. We had cashed in one of life's little dividends.

Our buoyancy was not to endure. A guide enlightened us with the inside story of our canceled flight. Moments after we had all left the airport that morning, the "disabled" plane had been moved aside with dispatch. It had simply been a matter of the airport officials deciding from the outset that it was not in our best interest to fly out that day. Why ever? Well, it was Sunday the seventh. The quaint American superstition about Friday the thirteenth pales alongside the dark forebodings that attend Cuzceños on Sunday the seventh.

Clearly, my can-do attitude was to be in for a stern test.

Monday began with a rush to the airport at 5 a.m. to get ahead of the expected mob of anxious travelers. And a mob it was, pushing forward in a desperate quest for service and information. A couple of clerks with rubber stamps in hand and heads bowed met the group with bureaucratic aplomb. Eight or ten of their less stalwart colleagues could be glimpsed through a doorway, hiding from the pressures of the travelers' demands. At last, the situation was sorted out, and our plane lifted off the runway at 7 a.m. Passengers aboard responded with applause, and a young woman waved a yellow ribbon to symbolize our liberation.

Although the flight crew was unsuccessful at arranging our connections to Quito, we arrived in Lima with renewed confidence. It was only 8:30 a.m., and we had all day to find a way between the two neighboring capital cities. We had heard there were three airlines that made daily flights to Quito.

One by one, the array of options vanished like shimmering mirages. Varig's flight was indeed every day - except Monday. All Ecuatoriana flights from Lima to Quito had been canceled due to recent border hostilities. Aeroperu? Pilots out on strike. How about connections to Quito via other points – Bogotá, Santiago, Panama? No luck. Auto travel was risky and probably too slow. It was as if Monday had been torn from the calendar.

We were now left with trying to find a way to get to Quito on time Tuesday, the very day of my speech. *Gracias a Dios* for Varig. They had a 6 a.m. flight via Guayaquil, Ecuador and on to Quito, arrival time: 9:30. My talk was scheduled for 11:30. Conference officials in Quito agreed by phone that the timing was close, but workable. They could not reschedule me to Wednesday due to the limited availability of interpreters, but they could delay my speech until noon through minor reshuffling, if necessary. They would arrange for a guide to hustle me through immigration and to the conference site. As a fall-back position, if I did not arrive by noon, they had a copy of my speech, which someone else could read to the group - a distressing prospect for me, but at least we had the bases covered.

Tuesday morning, we arose at 3:30 a.m., our fifth straight day of predawn awakening. We approached our day with calm resolve. We were going to make it. We checked in at the Lima airport at 5 a.m., got some Ecuadorian sucres, paid the airport tax, and then waited for the immigration official to arrive. And waited. And waited. As the airport staff conducted a languid search for the missing official, the scheduled 6 a.m. departure time slid by. With nothing to do but wait with mounting anxiety, we became more aware of our surroundings. The immigration area was cluttered with boxes, and in the corner was a pile of blankets. Suddenly the pile of blankets began to stir. Then it rose up. Blankets fell away to reveal a rumpled immigration official.

When we arrived in Guayaquil only 30 minutes late, I felt the odds had definitely shifted in our favor. We should be in Quito by 10 a.m. Allowing half an hour for immigration, taxi, etc., I would have about an hour and a half left to meet the noon deadline.

Our spirits took another dive when we heard the next announcement. An unseasonal fog in Quito would delay our takeoff for 45 minutes. I had less than an hour of margin now, plus an added dose of uncertainty. As usual, there were no progress reports or assurances as the 45 minutes ticked slowly by.

Then, good news. Quito airport had reopened. There were five Quito-bound planes on the tarmac at Guayaquil, and of course we were the fifth in line to take off. No, I could not hop aboard one of the other planes because their terminal facilities were not staffed with the omnipotent immigration officials. At 10:15 we took off. I projected landing at 11:00 – leaving about thirty minutes of margin. That margin slipped away as we circled Quito awaiting our turn to land. My numbing anxiety was joined by a dash of apprehension as we surveyed the snow-capped peaks poking up through the cloud cover. My thoughts drifted to that story of the gripping ordeal of the soccer players downed in the Andes. Then - at last - clearance. Our descent began, and our wheels rumbled into place, locked for landing. On our final approach, we could see houses through the patchy fog, just a few hundred feet below.

Then I froze. I felt the sudden thrust of the engines and the pitch of our plane on a climb. The airport was closed again. News that the other four planes from Guayaquil had been able to land came across the loudspeaker like a gleeful cackle from the devil himself. As we climbed to circle some more, my time margin vanished. I was now late. Two days of margin had disappeared utterly. The pilot announced that we could circle for about 30 minutes. If no weather break occurred by then, we would proceed to our alternate landing site – Bogotá, Columbia.

My unrelenting anxiety was swept away by a wave of relief. Better to go to Bogotá. And then home. My speech was just not meant to be. How much easier to explain an aborted flight than a late one. We would have an extra day or two - maybe we could spend it in some sunny place to lick our wounds and recover. Explanations and apologies would be due, and I would have to reimburse my hosts for the several thousand dollars in expenses they had paid for me. At least my odyssey would be over.

Again, the devil appeared and cackled over the loudspeaker. We were cleared for landing, denying my escape to Bogotá. It was already noon. Only two slim possibilities remained to save me from the nightmare of having to mill around the conference for the next two days, endlessly repeating excuses as to why I had not gotten there in time to give my speech. The possibility remained that they were monitoring my progress closely and making appropriate adjustments. Or maybe the conference schedule had slipped enough for me to make it in time.

I busied myself with last-minute mobilization. My dear Sarah agreed to take care of the bags and catch up with me later. I was told that exiting from the rear of the plane was faster, so I stationed myself by that door. The plane pulled up to the gate at 12: 15. Adrenaline pumping, I poised for a burst out the door and across the runway. The door swung open - to a yawning hole. The pavement was 20 feet below. The ground crew had not gotten around to placing the stairway ramp. "Ladies and gentlemen, we will exit through the front door only."

Last off the plane, I dashed to the terminal to meet my waiting guide. No waiting guide. That meant no close monitoring of my progress and scant prospect of the program schedule having been adjusted for me. As my cab hurtled toward the conference, one hope remained: the faint, flickering possibility that the conference schedule was running sufficiently late. Text of speech in hand, I plunged into the conference room at 12:45.

Miracle of miracles. The previous speaker was just winding up. They had delayed a bit for me, and my stand-in was ready. But I had made it. I was on.

As I mounted the platform to deliver my remarks, I could not help thinking how mundane my topic was compared with the high adventure of getting there.

WESTNET

My next port-of-call was to head up WESTNET. During the early 1980's, there were the first cracks in the dike of interstate banking. Large regional banks felt especially vulnerable to the threat of banks such as Citi and Chase that they knew someday would be national competitors. Guided by McKinsey & Company Consultants, five western banks formed a consortium to develop ways to gain the power of their collective strength without sacrificing their sovereignty as individual banks. Two representatives from each of the participants comprised the Board of Directors, the banks being Bank of Hawaii, Seafirst, United Banks of Colorado, Valley of Arizona, and Wells Fargo. Berne Hart of United was elected Board Chair of the company, and I agreed to take on the job of President and CEO.

The company took the form of a "banker's bank" we named WESTNET Bank. We got off to a promising start, forming a nifty discount stock brokerage, a budding insurance agency, a loan syndication effort, a joint purchasing program, and a lively discussion forum for sharing operating ideas. It was enlightening to see one bank moving towards centralizing a function while another was de-centralizing, each unaware of some of the disadvantages of the new model they were adopting. I appreciated the comment of one colleague regarding re-organizations, "Different tree, same old monkeys."

Scholars occasionally speak of a "horseshoe nail" theory of history, referring to the story (likely apocryphal) that a faulty horseshoe nail hobbled Napoleon's horse, fatefully delaying his arrival at Waterloo. WESTNET's version of this phenomenon occurred at a board meeting in Honolulu. Our consortium's viability was critically dependent upon enlarging the network of participating banks to a national scope. First Bank System of Minneapolis with its market dominance in nine Midwestern states had agreed to join, but on the condition that Texas Commerce Bank would do so simultaneously. TCB had indicated they would, and we arranged for a conference call from their board to ours and to Minneapolis to share the news and to welcome them and First Bank to WESTNET. Upon hooking up the call, we learned that the Chairman of TCB, the champion of our cause there, had fallen in his garden over the weekend and had injured his knee. We postponed our call for a week. During that week, an infection to the injured knee developed, which soon progressed to a life-threatening condition and a month-long hospitalization. By the time the Chairman was back on the job, the moment had clearly passed. Our alliance began to fray as member banks started to go in separate directions in launching some new initiatives. WESTNET was probably not slated for long-term survival anyway, but its demise was surely hastened by this "horseshoe nail".

Crocker

The timing of WESTNET'S collapse was fortuitous. In early 1984, Midland Bank of England decided to bring in a new management team to shore up their sagging investment in Crocker Bank. They brought in brilliant, relentless Frank Cahouet from Security Pacific to be their new CEO and Dick Rosenberg to be President and COO. When Dick called me to take over as Executive Vice President of Crocker's branch operation in Los Angeles, I jumped at the chance, not only to reunite with him, but to take on a line management responsibility much larger than I'd experienced previously, 120 branch offices and over 2,500 employees.

One of the factors that had weakened Crocker Bank was a large burden of corporate "Goodwill" whose write-off created a significant drag on their earnings. While engaged in the holding company corporate development job at Wells Fargo several years earlier, I had been part of the team that assembled Wells Fargo's bid to buy an independent bank with a strong regional presence in San Diego. This bank had failed due to poor (and corrupt) management, but had a strong network of branch offices in a marketplace we were keenly interested in entering. After crunching the projected numbers and relating them to a targeted rate of return on investment, we concluded that we could justify a purchase price in the low $40 million range. Adding some value for the desirability of the market led to a recommended bid to CEO Dick Cooley of $49 million. He pondered a bit and then said that he really wanted that franchise and that Crocker would probably be submitting an aggressive bid of maybe $50 million. With some misgivings from staff, we boosted our bid to $51 million.

When the bids were opened, Crocker had indeed bid aggressively and "won" the prize at the staggering price of $92 million! As accounting rules require writing down any premium paid over tangible value, Crocker assumed a multi-million dollar annual after-tax expense burden. This circumstance seemed to us to add an element of justification to our team's takeover of Crocker management.

Relocation to Los Angeles required a yearlong separation from the family for most of the week, as Elliott was just finishing primary school. It was a trial, but the job was a wonderful challenge. We quickly ramped up business production and chopped hunks of expenses. Some of the expense cuts were not difficult. As a prime example, when I arrived at the office, I was surprised to see five black limos at the curb. I asked my staff whether some head of state was visiting. I was told, "No, sir, they're yours." By that, he meant one was for my personal use, another for directors if they appeared, another for visiting San Francisco dignitaries, etc. Quickly we pared the fleet down to one we used for courier service and for occasional trips by me or members of my staff.

Frank Cahouet was a very bright and effective but demanding boss. He expected his key execs to be at their desks before 7 a.m. In fact, he advised us always to wear black socks. That way, when we awoke and got dressed in the dark so as not to awaken our spouses, we could dig into the sock drawer and be assured of always finding a matching pair. He even berated Dick Rosenberg upon learning of Dick's intention to take a two-week vacation with "We don't allow sabbaticals around here." So, it was no surprise when at an Executive Committee meeting of the top 20 officers, Frank announced that he was scheduling a special weekend meeting in two weeks to deal with some crisis or other. Attendance was mandatory – no excuses allowed! John Jenkins, my counterpart who ran Northern California, then raised his hand and suggested to Frank that he might have to miss the meeting due to his 26th wedding anniversary. "Your 26th?" questioned Frank. Yes, John said, "If I renege on our 25th wedding anniversary in two weeks, there won't be a 26th." He got a pass.

Despite being an amalgam of bankers from several different organizations, the team worked well together and helped each other succeed. Unity among this disparate group was helped by frequent dinner meetings and such tactics as insisting that we wear our Crocker lapel pins on our suits. The only acceptable excuse for failing to do so was "I left it on my pajamas."

A great moment was provided by Vice Chair David Brooks. David is barely five feet tall, and his darling wife Carole is shorter still. For Halloween, the two of them dressed up in full costume with masks, looking for all the world like pre-teens in pirate gear and such. They then called on some of David's subordinates. Mark Brandin related that this cute little pair showed up and chirped, "Trick or treat!" When Mark reached for the Milk Duds, a baritone voice boomed out, "Hey, what about a scotch!"

At Crocker, I enjoyed one of my most successful and satisfying business development programs. Accountants and lawyers are often well-positioned to refer clients to their bankers. I especially liked to cultivate lawyers because they were generally more inclined to make referrals. However, I reasoned that they would be much more likely to make referrals if they were themselves satisfied customers. The mission then became how to attract the accounts of lawyers. Rather than just assuming that lawyers would be attracted by a standard approach, I decided to host three after-hours focus groups of lawyers to probe what might especially appeal to them. The answer surprised me. There turned out to be three distinct cohorts of lawyers, each with different needs. The new young lawyer, often from out of town, needed access – to a credit card and to a deposit account where it wouldn't require weeks for checks to clear. The second group were the journeymen, often with young families, who were acquiring things and were attracted by good rates on home and car loans. The third group were the partners and senior associates, a harried bunch who mainly wanted convenience and service. For example, upon the sudden realization that taxes were due today, they wanted to get instant credit, often not that mindful of the rate. A key player with the starter lawyers was "Millie," my name for the battle-hardened office manager who helped the new lawyers sign up for benefits and who was pivotal in directing them to a bank. The "Millies" got lots of attention from us. The results were astounding. At our downtown office alone, we began averaging 60 new lawyer accounts per month. An especially satisfying haul came from a firm which was the principal counsel for a rival bank.

We decided to settle in San Marino at 800 Canterbury. As with "Chaucer" and other nearby streets, the name reflected the book collections acquired by the adjacent Huntington Library with the proceeds of the sale of those lots. It was a handsome low-slung adobe home in a lovely garden. We later remarked on the irony of moving from a genuine adobe in San Marino to a fake one in New Mexico, the land of adobe. That adobe exterior was a new material for me. As I was hosing off the front porch one day, I noticed how dusty the walls were. Training the hose on the walls produced a flow of silty water. As I continued to spray, the stream of water never got any cleaner. Finally, it dawned on me. That wall was nothing but dirt, and I was busy washing my house away!

A troubling aspect about San Marino, though, was a growing resentment on the part of many long-time residents about a recent influx of Asian families. To us, these quiet, industrious neighbors couldn't be more welcome. The source of the animus was mainly that Asian students began monopolizing the high school honor rolls, perhaps dimming the prospects for Anglo kids to gain admission to top colleges. Our feeling was that our kids had better start learning to compete now because surely they will need to later in this global economy. A source of concern about the Asian parents was their lack of participation in PTA and other school events. Sarah concluded that it was really a cultural problem and that the Asians were reluctant to volunteer unless specifically invited. When she undertook to escort some of our new Asian friends to school parent gatherings, they readily accepted.

My moment of the golden repartee came shortly after we moved into our San Marino home. I was out working in the front yard when a fellow walked by and asked if I was the new owner. When I answered in the affirmative, he said, "Well, I'm sure glad you're not Chinese." To which I replied, "No, but would you like to meet my wife, May Lin?" He scurried off, hopefully with a dent in his shell of bigotry.

After two years, Crocker was in the midst of an impressive turnaround. All the numbers were moving in the right direction. A retreat of the Executive Committee at Silverado in February, 1986 was a celebration as well as a time to plan next steps.

Just two nights later, I got a call that woke me from sleep. The call was from a Wells Fargo executive, who I was in the midst of recruiting to my team at Crocker. In a panic, he implored me to disavow our plans, as he had just learned that Wells was acquiring Crocker.

Not even our CEO knew that Midland was selling their Crocker franchise to Wells Fargo. As a crowning blow, Midland practically gave it away, at a price of just book value, obliterating the value of our stock options. The stock market quickly recognized Wells Fargo's coup with a doubling of its share price over the next month. What possessed Midland to abandon Crocker just when all signs were pointing up? After laboring ten years with a lagging turnaround effort, they jumped at the chance to exit. But why not engage in a bidding process? I'll never know. I had developed some disdain for Midland management over the two years. We would get periodic visits from Midland senior management, "the Sirs" my staff liked to call them. At first I would arrange tours to showcase various aspects of our operation. It quickly became apparent they had no interest in such matters and often departed with spouses for shopping tours on Rodeo Drive. At the dinner table they showed no interest in personal or corporate accomplishments but perked up upon hearing that my mother's cousin was chaplain to the royal family.

While I was at Wells Fargo, colleague Alan Holroyde was assigned to take over our London office. He reported that he expected to find a lazier work ethic among the British employees and resolved to tolerate this situation as a cultural difference. But his fuse was lit when July 4th came. The American workers, realizing that British banking didn't pause for this holiday, all came to work, whereas their British colleagues stayed home due to it being a "Yank holiday."

As the merger with Wells Fargo was an in-market merger, it was clear there would be major management attrition. To help my direct reports get on with their corporate lives, I asked to see their resumes on my desk within a week. All but one of the eight did so, and those seven all found good jobs before consummation of the merger four months later. The one hold-out, "grasshopper" we called him, was sure that his skills would be appreciated and that he would be retained by Wells. He wasn't and finally ended up in a modest level job at FDIC, the federal banking regulator.

I was approached by Wells management and asked if I had an interest in staying on. The job would actually be an expansion of my responsibilities – from 120 offices to 160. However, my title would be downgraded from Executive VP to Senior VP, and I would be expected to take a salary cut of some 20%. I also felt that I would probably suffer adverse discrimination, both as a former defector from Wells and as a handy scapegoat for the inevitable problems that crop up in the aftermath of a merger. As if I needed additional incentive to decline Wells' approach, I would have had to forego a very generous severance payment that an incensed Frank Cahouet had negotiated for his team.

When Crocker Bank wound up in June, 1986, we wanted to mark the occasion of the end of a proud 125-year corporate history. In Northern California, they decided to have a fancy dinner at a downtown San Francisco hotel. It attracted several hundred employees and was an elegant event. I decided to go a different route, as I was concerned that lower paid employees couldn't afford the dress, the parking, etc. that such an event would entail. Instead, we decided our party would be to attend a Dodgers game with hot dogs and kegs in the parking lot beforehand. It was so popular that the 5,000 tickets we sold represented the Dodgers' biggest corporate night in years. One of the perks for bringing so many fans to the stadium was to throw in the ceremonial first pitch – on the mound in front of 55,000 fans. At the last minute I turned to Art Martinez, Manager of our South Gate office and coach of our league champion softball team, and asked if he would like to be pitcher. As Elliott and his buddy Sumner Miller got to be ball boys for the game, I thought I already had enough glory. I assumed the position of umpire behind catcher Bob Altobello, a regional manager. When Art let fly, he was petrified of the prospect of the ball falling short, so he threw it almost over Bob's head – to which I called, "stee-rike!"

As a sequel to the takeover of Crocker, part of our severance payment was withheld because of uncertainty over the amount of allowable severance compensation. Treasury Rule 280G had been tentatively interpreted by the Feds in a manner that would favor full payment, but Treasury never got around to issuing a final ruling. For Wells Fargo, the potential penalties were significant. It was a classic government "gotcha." There were heavy penalties for violating a rule they hadn't gotten around to defining! I took on the cause of the 14 senior ex-Crocker officials affected. After 13 years, with a boost from Keith Smith and Frank Cahouet, we finally got a reasonable settlement out of Wells Fargo. In aggregate, the amount was about $10 million. In the years since the demise of Crocker, we had lost track of one of our cohort. Through the Internet, I was finally able to track him down – at a consumer finance company in Massachusetts. I will never forget that phone call. When I reported that he would be receiving some $900,000, he was silent. He then said, "You have saved my life – my wife has left, my jobs haven't worked out, and I'm in debt. You have saved my life." All those years of working the case were amply rewarded by that one call.

With the banking and thrift crisis of the mid-1980's, there was a brisk demand for executives with demonstrated experience in successful turnarounds, just not in Los Angeles. It was very disappointing, as we loved our home in San Marino and our friends there. I resolved to cast a wide net and contacted by letter and follow-up phone calls over 100 persons I felt might be able to help me find a spot. The results were surprising. Several persons I felt close to and who had great networks in the corporate world did nothing, whereas several more remote acquaintances went way out of their way to be helpful. Fred Stern, a Stanford fundraising teammate and Beverly Hills stockbroker wrote a bunch of letters on my behalf. So did Bob Swanson, the CEO of Genentech, who just a few years later succumbed tragically to brain cancer.

My acquaintance with Bob Swanson began in a rather dramatic fashion. He was an eager young venture capitalist who was backed in part by Wells Fargo's venture capital group. Bob had taken office space down the hall from my office at Wells Fargo, and we had passing conversations. One evening I was just leaving the office shortly after six when I witnessed quite a fuss in the office lobby. Bob was trying to gain after-hours admission to his office to pick up some presentation materials for a key meeting in New York the next morning. He was scheduled to take the "red eye" flight in just a few hours. The burly security guard was adamant in his refusal and said that only a senior bank official could authorize Bob's re-entry. The guard acquiesced when I offered my credentials and vouched for him, and the day was saved. Once again, "What goes around, comes around."

My job search was narrowing down to two choices, both in the Bay Area. One was for president and chief operating officer of a small venture capital firm, and the other was a similar position at Citibank in California. While both jobs were decent and in desirable locations, I did not like either prospective boss. Both were abrasive and somewhat quirky. Then I got a call from Russell Reynolds executive search firm about taking over a troubled financial firm in Albuquerque. They had initially approached a Crocker colleague, Don Vodra, on the theory that a real estate specialist was needed, but Don told them that they should consider a retail banker and referred the lead to me.

I was at the kitchen table in the process of weighing the pros and cons of these three alternatives when an incident occurred that struck me as an omen. Elliott entered the kitchen looking uncharacteristically morose. He lamented that his bike had just been stolen. He and his buddy, Tommy, had biked to a nearby grocery store to play video games. When they emerged, the bikes were gone. He admitted that they had forgotten to lock them securely as he always did at school.

We then sat down and worked out a deal. Elliott needed a bike for school, but clearly bore fault for its disappearance. Our deal went as follows. He needed about $75 to buy a basic coaster bike. He had $23 in his bank account. By stepping up chores, car washes, etc., and by my matching his contribution, he could accumulate the necessary funds in about three weeks. We shook hands on the deal. Just then, we heard a call for Elliott from outside the kitchen. It was Tommy. He had ridden up on his brand new bike, even better than the old one, paid for entirely by his indulgent dad. Elliott then looked "daggers" at me. I turned to Sarah and asked whether that would have happened in New Mexico. We agreed that it was unlikely and that maybe New Mexico was a better place to raise our kids.

Albuquerque

I flew to Dallas where most of the Board members lived. They were a group of wealthy investors drawn to the turnaround potential of AmeriWest Financial. While the company's loan troubles were daunting, it was also a leading landowner in both Albuquerque and Las Cruces, two strong growth markets. The company's 18,000 acres at the fringes of these cities included parcels with cost bases as low as $100 per acre.

The potential upside was terrific, and the directors were great. Randy Talbot, only in his mid-30's, had taken the helm on an interim basis after the Board had removed the former CEO. Randy was such a dynamic, focused, and decent fellow who has become a pleasure to know over the years. The Texans were a very capable, impressive young group. I came to love their hilarious expressions. After one rather dubious proposal at a Board meeting, Jim Sowell expressed skepticism by saying, "I may have been born at night, but it wasn't last night." Another was, "The meek may inherit the earth – but not the mineral rights." Jim Bosler reacted to a loan proposal on a horse farm by saying, "Never lend on something with a tongue attached – horses, trailers, or preachers!" One expression that took on more meaning as the company's condition deteriorated was, "Once the mouse is in the trap, it tends to forget about the cheese."

Even during the interview process, there was good natured banter. At the hotel before my final interview dinner in Albuquerque, I couldn't decide whether to wear the usual necktie or a Southwestern bolo tie I had brought along, just in case. Sarah had noticed that all the men at the airport were wearing normal ties. Sure enough, so were the six directors who took us to dinner. At dinner I asked whether they ever wore bolos. The response was, "No, that's generally for yahoos from Arizona." I then brought out the bolo from my pocket and said, "This is how close I came to being a yahoo from Arizona." Then, to enjoy a chuckle at their expense, I fished out Randy Talbot's calling card from my pocket and said, "You guys should put the Area Code on your calling cards – it makes it <u>look</u> like you know someone from out of state." (Only recently has New Mexico added a second area code. In Los Angeles, my eight direct reports hailed from six different area codes.)

The next day, while the directors were meeting with me, several wives took Sarah on a tour of one of the nicer neighborhoods, the area known as Sandia Heights. We have come to appreciate that area's dramatic beauty as the years have gone by, but at lunch when we reunited, Sarah looked stricken and said, "They took me to an area that looked like the backside of the moon." Quickly, I asked our hosts whether there was any part of town that might be similar to lush, floral San Marino. Fortunately, the North Valley was just such a place and now has been our home for over 20 years.

My new office had a sweeping view of the mountains to the north and east and the barren mesa on the west. When I commented to a colleague how brown it looked, he told me that after a while it would begin to look greener. He said it was like adjusting to night blindness.

Compared to the high-voltage intensity of California, the measured pace and easy access of New Mexico was quite an adjustment for us. In July, 1986, I moved to Albuquerque ahead of my family to get started on my new job. On my very first day on the job, a friendly fellow on the elevator turned to me and asked whether I was "Brown – the guy who is coming to take over AmeriWest." Startled, I responded in the affirmative. There had been a fair amount of publicity preceding my arrival, as the company was one of the state's largest. The elevator passenger introduced himself as John Porter, a fellow Stanford alum. When he learned that I was without family for a little while, he asked whether I might like to join him and his wife for dinner that evening. Contemplating the alternative of hotel food, and taken by the sincerity of his offer, I agreed.

When I arrived at John's handsome adobe home in the North Valley, I was greeted by his charming wife Roseann and introduced to their other guests, Elaine and Toney. Elaine was a high-powered realtor who was full of lively conversation. Finally, I turned to Toney who was a pleasant but quiet sort. When I asked what line of work he pursued, he said that he worked for the state government. When I then asked about what area, he calmly responded that he was the governor. The Governor of the State of New Mexico! In 48 years in California, I had hardly met a mayor, much less a sitting governor. Here in New Mexico, on my first full day, I was having dinner with one.

Sarah and the boys soon joined me, and we stayed for several months in a small, two bedroom apartment in the heights. It was perhaps one-third the size of both the home we had moved from and the one we would later move to, but we found it warm and intimate. That is, until one Saturday morning in October when Sarah and I had slept in. We were unaware of an unusual early snow that had fallen that night. This climatic event abruptly became a traumatic event when our two boys bounded eagerly into our bedroom, bombarding us with snowballs.

One of my first tasks upon taking on the job was to host a press conference. The conference went well until a most unexpected question arose, "Do you pray in public?" To be overly dismissive of this question was to risk offending persons of faith, so I answered simply, "No, I pray in private." The reporter then asked whether I believed in the prophets. At this point I felt I could take the liberty of saying, "I believe in both kinds." Later, I asked my staff whatever had prompted that line of inquiry. It was then I learned that my predecessor did conduct public prayer services, and in fact went so far as to convene meetings in his office where he would encourage his staff to proceed to a trance-like state and "speak in tongues." Among the sources of bad loans were applicants with shaky credit credentials presenting themselves as fellow religious zealots and getting unquestioned credit. I remember reading somewhere that Utah has the nation's highest incidence of consumer fraud as unscrupulous types prey on the faith connection to devout Mormons.

The secular version of this phenomenon was the shaky borrower who would lure the former CEO into making a bad loan by purchasing a few shares of stock and posing as a "fellow owner." This status led to a bypassing of credit checks, appraisals and other prudent procedures.

I must confess to an instance where I took benign advantage of my predecessor's strong religious inclinations. Although he had been gone for six months before I arrived, it was up to me to settle his severance arrangements. He had written himself a four-year salary continuance shortly before his departure, signing it both as grantor/CEO and as employee/CEO. I told him that the Feds would agree to no more than two years and could act to block the whole deal if he insisted on more. I suggested that he should pray on it for guidance. A few days later, he reappeared having had "a vision" that two years would be appropriate.

Thus began a three-year ride to the heights of promise, followed by a plunge to the depths of despair. Job one became continuing the clean-out of unproductive employees begun by interim CEO Talbot. Some targets were easy, such as the Chief Financial Officer who suggested that I probably wanted to get rid of him. When I responded that he had just taken a big step in that direction, he then said he was planning to move East and asked whether I would like to buy his house for my residence. I quickly declined this rather bizarre offer, as even if I found it to be our dream house, I would always be susceptible to the claim that I had let him go to get his house. A second easy mark was our Las Cruces manager. This market was booming, but our operation there wasn't. The reason quickly became apparent on my first visit to the office. For some unexplained reason, he wasn't there to greet me. When ushered into his office to wait, I noticed that there was only one item on his desk, a partially completed crossword puzzle. For the first time ever, I performed a Trump-style firing on the spot.

The payoff was in securing highly qualified replacements. Once again, Dave Weymouth rode to the rescue when he agreed to become our Chief Financial Officer and later President. Dave had a most unusual background for a financial executive. He and his wife Susan were both from Covelo, California, which is a tiny logging town in the Trinity Alps area. Despite very modest family finances, stretched further by multiple parental divorces (for one of his serial stepmothers, it was her 13th marriage), Dave managed to get himself through college. Actually, it was six different colleges as he patched together his undergraduate program while in the Army. He was an accounting specialist, but when I came to observe the breadth of his talents, I encouraged him to take on several general management responsibilities. After I left Wells for Crocker, Dave was promoted to Senior Vice President in charge of Wells Fargo's $100 billion Trust Department. I was delighted to have the opportunity to work together again. When other former Wells colleagues, Ralph Peters and Tim Shahen, agreed to join us, they blended with our inherited talent to form a fine team.

Dave's calm profile belied a venturesome spirit. For several years he took time off to serve as a banker on cruise ships sailing all over the Pacific. He described the passenger manifest as "elderly people – and their parents." Dave was also a motorcycle enthusiast. One venture he decided not to take was while attending a financial meeting at the La Costa Resort. La Costa is also a frequent meeting place for union groups and reputed mobsters. As Dave was checking in, a gorgeous young woman approached and asked, "Are you Mr. Costello?" For just a moment Dave pondered the benefit of being Mr. Costello for the next little while. But his unfailing moral compass asserted itself, along with the realization that the real Mr. C. probably had a menacing bulge under his breast pocket.

When I arrived in Albuquerque, once again I was shown to a palatial office. Two personal secretaries awaited. I quickly moved down the hall to a modest office where I shared one secretary with a colleague. My old office suite was sublet to the Sutin law firm, who converted it to offices for six lawyers. Trappings of opulence are one of the hallmarks of businesses that careen out of control.

We also made a number of vendor changes, including our law firm. I was unimpressed by our laconic counsel, and a change was hastened by an unbelievable incident. The bank had a pending lawsuit against another party, and the matter was proceeding through the discovery process. In response to a request from opposing counsel, our law firm asked a clerk in our note department to send them certain documents from the file. The clerk wasn't sure which documents to send, so she sent the whole file – to our law firm. An employee of that firm then made the grave mistake of sending not only the requested documents, but the entire file to the opposing lawyer. This file included a memo from our lawyer that outlined our lawyer's opinion of the strengths and weaknesses of the case! The other lawyer gleefully returned the file several days later, their copy machine doubtless having run overtime. As if the matter weren't already bad enough, our lawyer then drew up a letter absolving himself and his firm of all responsibility for the mistake and presented it to our frightened clerk to sign. When she came upstairs to ask what she should do was when the matter first came to our attention. We summarily sacked the firm and held a competition for new legal representation. The Sutin Thayer firm under the leadership of Steve Moise won hands down, and the subsequent representation by Steve and his colleagues, Robbie Heyman and Jonathan Sutin, could not have been better.

All the financial metrics began turning in the right direction with income up and expenses down. In particular, Chuck Haegelin and his land development group produced a steady flow of profitable deals. The loan recovery program was very productive, and we even had time to devote to social concerns, such as a highly successful smoking cessation program. Female managers made great progress as did minorities. Our company was awarded the "Vision Award" by the New Mexico Commission on the Status of Women, as the best company in the state in that regard. A very successful new account promotion featured little stuffed dolls of "Louie the Lobo," the iconic mascot of UNM. Bad loans kept bubbling up from the past, but we felt we had the resources to continue overall progress.

With the upswing seemingly assured, we decided on a name change. The holding company and main subsidiaries had long, awkward and different names. Picking up on our city's short crisp airport designation, I decided on the name "ABQ" – ABQ Corp, ABQ Bank, etc. in turquoise, a perfect southwest color, but one not used by any competitors in our marketplace. Being short, ABQ Bank could appear big and be easily legible on signs. Also, at that time ABQ was used by only one forlorn little radio station, KABQ. As an unexpected outcome, ABQ has subsequently become the principal abbreviation for the city with scores of companies now using ABQ as a prefix.

Slowly, the wheels began coming off ABQ Bank. One cause was that we underestimated the extent of loss due to faulty documentation. Many of our liens were not recorded properly or were otherwise invalid, denying us access to collateral. The main cause, though, was continuing deterioration of the real estate market in the oil patch. What a contrast – our New Mexico domiciled loans had a delinquency of 3% whereas the large out-of-state portfolio was 50% delinquent. The collapse of the Houston market was unbelievable. In California, the worst one might see in a down market would be a decline of 10% to 20% in residential real estate value. Parts of Houston dropped by over 90%. Some brand new $50,000 homes were going to the auction block for under $4,000 each. There were entire city blocks where every home on both sides was in foreclosure. Brand new homes were being bulldozed, as the improvements added no value and created maintenance expenses. One of our commercial real estate loans was on a new office building on Houston's inner ring, near the Astrodome. It was built for $20 million, and our loan was for $16 million. By the time I came aboard, the loan had been written down to $12 million. Some two years later we were finally able to sell the property for $2.1 million. That price came to $9 per square foot for brand new office space. In normal markets, that rate would be a bargain rental rate, not a purchase price!

We knew from the outset that the bank was vulnerable to failure, but we had comfort in knowing that there was substantial value in the holding company's three independent subsidiaries. The land development, mortgage banking, and insurance operations were all profitable and were the state's largest in their fields. The Feds then rolled a grenade into our boardroom. Unbeknownst to current Board and management, the company's previous management had signed a "Net Worth Maintenance Agreement", giving the bank regulators unfettered access to the assets of the other holding company subsidiaries in the event of bank weakness. This agreement had not been revealed in any of the corporation's public filings. Apparently, the company's previous lawyers did not regard as significant the existence of a corporate death sentence.

Witch Hunt

The most pernicious cause of our failure was Federal policy. Lost in all the Fed's recriminations against the management of savings and loans (also known as "thrifts") was that the Feds demanded in the early 1980's that thrifts diversify into commercial real estate. Then just a few years later, Congress passed the Tax Reform Act of 1986, stretching out depreciation schedules, which significantly devalued commercial real estate. To complete the trifecta, just as thrifts were trying to unload their foreclosed commercial properties, in 1989 the Feds ruled that troubled thrifts couldn't make any new commercial real estate loans. That prohibition extended to selling foreclosed real estate by offering "carry-back" loan financing, which is the only practical way to do it. We had to back away from a deal, negotiated but not closed, that would have off-loaded $26 million in remote motel properties to a highly creditworthy buyer for $9 million down and a carry-back mortgage of $17 million at 9% interest. On an appeal to the regulators in Dallas I was told that it made great sense to do it, but they couldn't stand behind us. Business losses are one thing, but criminal violations are quite another – I wanted to keep the pinstripes going in the right direction! Next, I called FDIC chief Bill Seidman. He commiserated, saying, "Sometimes I think our job amounts to going into the battlefield after the battle is over and shooting all the wounded." He said it was Congress's law and that only they could make a change. Next I went to see Pete Domenici, our senior U. S. Senator. We were on friendly terms, and he clearly understood the injustice, but he then held up a copy of that week's *Time Magazine* that featured the "Keating Five," the five U. S. Senators implicated in doing favors for indicted thrift CEO Charles Keating. He said that under the current circumstances, there was no way Congress could pass any legislation that might be deemed to be cutting some slack for thrift organizations.

This folly was followed shortly by a new rule restricting thrifts from holding high yield debt instruments. Our sizable portfolio was highly profitable, and we had been well advised by Morgan Stanley (a regulator later commented, "I've never heard of either Morgan or Stanley"). With this dictum, the market was suddenly flooded with debt being disgorged by thrifts, leading to these positions being liquidated at big discounts.

Then the blame game began in earnest. Of the 43 thrifts with a billion dollars or more in assets serving the public in the Sunbelt area, all 43 failed. One might suspect that there was a systemic problem. The Feds concluded that there was systemic negligence, and the managements and boards of all 43 faced negligence lawsuits from the Feds. The case against us was predicated on 17 documents that the Feds claimed were missing – appraisals, financial statements and such. With the help of an investigator I hired to search the files, we located 15 of the 17 documents and found strong evidence of the existence of the other two. The response from the Fed's lawyers was that we might win in court, but they could string it out with endless discovery, appeals, etc. The Feds disallowed all corporate indemnity agreements and director and officer insurance coverage, so our defense costs became a burdensome personal expense. As was the case with many of the Fed's suits, they did not pursue the former management who were the principal cause of the failure. They went after the firemen, not the arsonists. Statutes of Limitation played a role, but mostly it was a pursuit of deeper pockets. Pure extortion.

Perhaps the darkest part of this chapter was a series of troubling incidents that suggested strongly that the Feds were engaged in all manner of illegal searches of my property. Our home telephone calls were interrupted by unusual static, and neighbors reported men in suits trespassing on our property taking pictures. The manager of the storage facility we used called to say that our unit, and only our unit, had been broken into. We had secured it with a circular "Kryptonite" lock that defies usual thieves. Inside, nothing appeared to have been taken, but from the papers tossed, someone had searched vigorously for documents or property.

Then Mary Sandoval made a visit to my office. She was one of the regulatory investigators and had previously examined ABQ as a regulatory auditor. Rather reluctantly, she asked me about the source of funds for a recent significant donation I had made to the University of New Mexico. I was stunned. That gift had been made with no publicity and with a check from my account at another bank. It was a memorial to my mother who had died just a few months before. Ms. Sandoval said she did not know how her supervisors had obtained the information.

Ms. Sandoval then confided that, "They're after me, too." She said that investigators had put her under suspicion after she related to them that her previous audits of ABQ had found management to be competent and honorable. Shortly thereafter, the investigators gleefully confronted Ms. Sandoval with a "smoking gun" – evidence that she had violated Federal rules by applying for a job at ABQ while conducting her audits. This "evidence" turned out to be her one-paragraph resume they found in my files. The ready explanation was that I always asked for such resumes from visiting auditors to distribute to my management team by way of introduction and to encourage my team's cooperation with the auditors. There were about 30 such brief resumes in the file. The investigators rejected Ms. Sandoval's explanation and threatened her with criminal prosecution. Shortly after our conversation, Ms. Sandoval resigned her position and moved out of the area.

Another less-than-stellar governmental performance was turned in by Congressman Steve Schiff. I had supported Steve from when he first announced his candidacy for the Republican primary in 1988. He was in a free-for-all with ten other candidates competing for a vacated seat. Steve had been an aggressive District Attorney and was given good marks by his former colleagues at the Sutin firm. I am generally leery of politicians who climb the prosecutorial ladder to higher office (Nixon, Giuliani, Spitzer, etc.), as I feel their zeal for high profile victories can compromise their objectivity, but Steve seemed to be the best of the field. He went on to victory and subsequent re-election. Then I got a call from Steve saying that he would have to return my campaign contribution because I was under investigation by the Feds. No assurances about my lack of culpability served to allay his concern. The returned check was for $300. I wrote back indicating that I would not cash his check in hopes that someday I might once again be deemed worthy of his association. I also pointed out that as long as he felt disposed to return my contributions, that over the years I had contributed about $2,000 to his various campaigns. No reply.

Then, about nine months later, I got another call from Steve Schiff. A thorough journalistic investigation by the *Albuquerque Tribune* painted a very favorable picture of our valiant effort to rescue ABQ. Schiff called to congratulate me on my "favorable publicity." I responded that our deeds were indeed favorable and inquired whether he now might be confident in my returning his check. He mumbled something non-committal and again congratulated me on "my publicity." I should add that neither Senator Bingaman nor Senator Domenici felt compelled to return my contributions.

Simultaneously, I was sued for $150 million by the FDIC in connection with my service as a director of Century Bank in Phoenix. ABQ Bank was a major shareholder of Century as a result of converting collateral on yet another bad loan. I had two other ABQ executives join me on the Board of this troubled bank. It, too, was loaded with bad loans, but the long-term prospects of the Phoenix market were excellent as was the prospect of enhancing ABQ's value through a possible merger, thereby establishing a presence across the Southwest. Century finally succumbed to insolvency and the FDIC took over. We ABQ directors had arrived late in the game and had not participated in making any of Century's bad loans. The FDIC wouldn't back off from their negligence claim against us even after we showed them an unsolicited letter of commendation from Arizona Banking Commissioner Mary Short, praising our service and expressing the view that we might have saved Century if only we had arrived sooner. As I couldn't afford to fight legal battles on two fronts, I reluctantly agreed to settle the ABQ suit, but took the Century suit to court. Thanks in part to excellent representation by Bob Harrell of the Fulbright and Jaworski firm in Houston (a referral by Steve Moise), the suit against us was dismissed in a summary judgment. I note with regret that my father did not live to witness my exoneration.

When organizations' fortunes fade, the employees involved often engage in various forms of gallows humor. At Crocker, the multi-pointed logo, which was generally known as the "pinwheel," was renamed the "buzz saw." At a savings and loan conference, a group of us were discussing our "MTF" ratios – which stood for "Months 'Til Failure." The sports world is replete with such expressions for losing teams. One of my favorites was when the New Orleans Saints were mired in the bottom of the NFL standings, their fans began referring to them as the "Aints," and while in the stands, took to wearing bags over their heads with holes cut out so they wouldn't be recognized. Humor can be an indispensable companion when dealing with adversity.

More Albuquerque

Albuquerque is such an open, friendly place. In fact, a visitor one time described its residents as being "relentlessly friendly." Strangers greet you and people talk on elevators. Parking is often free, and traffic generally moves well even during rush hour. Neighbors will pick up newspapers for you when you're away.

Concern for others extends beyond the neighborhood. During my first week here, I had to slam on my brakes to avoid colliding with a convoy of traffic that had slowed to a crawl. A funeral procession? No, a school zone. Here drivers really do observe the 15 mph speed limit. Californians generally slow a little, glance around for kiddos, and then shoot on through.

When we say we live in Albuquerque, we should do so with an asterisk. We actually live in an adjoining little town called the Village of Los Ranchos de Albuquerque. Mayor Larry Abraham is always getting after us to make this distinction, and using this designation helps Village revenues from cell phone providers, but it looks cumbersome on a letterhead and doesn't fit when filling out forms. Larry's leadership resulted in our finally getting a cell tower to cure our deficient cell phone coverage. While there was strong popular support for the tower, there was understandable resistance from the immediate neighbors who remained unconvinced that masking the tower as a giant pine tree would obscure its monstrosity. While I disagreed with their position, I had to admire their term of derision for the tower, the "Frankenpine."

Albuquerque is accessible. While destinations here are often scattered about in this rather disorganized city, nothing is very far away. Our neighbor, Robert Anderson, spent several days a week commuting to an office in Beverly Hills. I commiserated, saying,

"Well, at least you're not too far from LAX." He replied, "That's what everyone in L.A. tells me. Only it often takes me up to an hour to get from my office in Beverly Hills to LAX. In Albuquerque I don't live especially close to the airport, but I can be there in 20 minutes."

The most powerful initial impression of Albuquerque comes from its hypnotic vistas. Because our predecessors had broad horizons, ours will forever be preserved. Ordinances prevent building above the foothills of the magnificent Sandia range ("Sandia" is Spanish for watermelon, the color the mountains become at sunset). Where else would guys call other guys to say, "Hey, buddy, check out the sunset!" Nowhere else would a business meeting be distracted by the visage of Goofy floating by on a hot air balloon.

Life here is quiet. Days pass without hearing a car honk. Like its adobe architecture, New Mexico life has rounded corners. One recent newcomer to the state described her adobe home as being "the same color as the earth – it looks like it grew there."

The city's amenities, restaurants, and cultural attractions are spotty, but good music and theatre and sports can be found. When we arrived here, a quaint custom at the old minor league ballpark was when one of our players hit a home run, he would run a victory lap by the stands to collect dollar bills thrust through the fence. The University of New Mexico's "Pit" is an historic basketball arena where many an epic battle has been waged, including Jimmy Valvano's upset victory in the 1983 NCAA championship game. The world-class attractions of Santa Fe are only an hour away, and outdoor recreation abounds.

Albuquerque's medical care is first-rate. Neurosurgeon Hal Hankinson, cardiologist Paul Cochran, gastroenterologist Ed Pierce, ophthalmologist Bob Reidy, and allergist Steve Tolber are all at the top of their profession. And my current primary care physician, Dr. Richard Todd, is the best I've experienced. The same can be said for dentists Jim Fanning, David Hillson, Jack Kennedy, and Mark Yarbrough.

Our culinary introduction to Albuquerque was not auspicious. At one of the leading local restaurants, the server announced the specials, including a salad with house dressing. When we asked what the house dressing was, she said she would have to check. She returned and proudly proclaimed that the house dressing was "maison!" I was reminded of a Herb Caen item in the *San Francisco Chronicle* when he asked a server whether the fish was frozen. The server responded, "Oh no, sir, it's thawed out."

Albuquerque is a delightful compote. Partly desert, partly mountain. Almost big. Its mile-high altitude produces four real seasons, all comfortable, but bring your ChapStick. Its people represent a unique blend of Anglo, Hispanic, and Indian cultures. A factor that helps these groups assimilate better than elsewhere is that Albuquerque has few suburbs to polarize the population. There is a remarkable lack of pretension. Stretch limos generally appear only on prom night. Ever been to a no-host bar at a wedding reception? Neither had we.

Albuquerque is affordable. Median house prices hover around the national average. It may be the country's cheapest among the really terrific places to live. When I went to Motor Vehicles to re-register my car, the clerk apologized that their fee schedule had risen sharply from the year before, from $9 to $11. Absorbing this blow was eased by my noting that the previous year in California I had paid $236. New Mexico's property taxes are the second lowest in the nation. We paid more tax on our little 1,000 square foot Laguna Beach condo than on our 5,500 square foot Albuquerque home on four acres. Albuquerque landscaping is variously described, but my favorite is, "bare dirt yard, surrounded by chain link fence and guarded by a large dog named Lobo, who doubles as a doorbell."

Even our crime and scandals have a downscale cast to them. Recently, a Santa Fe judge was arrested – for extortion? for bribery? No – for stealing tires from a tire store. Years ago, one of our Lt. Governors was weaving his way up a Santa Fe street one night when he lost control of his car and plunged through a fence into the kitchen of a house. When the police arrived, he greeted them with a glass of milk in hand – obviously, his beverage of choice.

Like other states, New Mexico has a State Bird, a State Tree, etc., but no other state has a State Question. It is "Red or Green?", which refers to our State Addiction to chile peppers. Here, you'll find it in burgers, pizza, omelets, even candy.

New Mexicans can be prickly about being lumped together with their cactus-ridden neighbors in Arizona. Few Californians realize that Phoenix is actually closer to Los Angeles than to Albuquerque. Ads or graphics depicting Arizona's *saguaro* cactus in New Mexico are certain to raise local dander. The ire of New Mexico sports fans is aroused from the NFL's insistence on piping Arizona Cardinals games to us instead of local favorites, the Dallas Cowboys and Denver Broncos.

The ultimate insult to New Mexicans is to be excluded from the United States entirely. I read recently that some 30% of U.S. high school grads cannot find France on an unlabeled map of Europe. This cohort is probably the source of questions such as, "Is the dollar accepted in New Mexico?", "Do I need a passport?", "How about shots?" A delightful little book, "*One of our Fifty is Missing*" chronicles some of these follies. Even fewer Americans realize that New Mexico was settled by Europeans well before Jamestown. In fact, there was already a published history of colonial New Mexico in 1605, two years before Jamestown was founded.

New Mexico does have its challenges. The state is relatively poor in financial resources and is low in all the social metrics. A majority of New Mexican babies are born to single mothers. In California one scrolls down a list of states from the top to see where the state stands; here one starts at the bottom. A local wag suggested that our state motto should be "Thank God for Mississippi." Visit the gas pump and note that often the previous purchase was only a couple of dollars. Many New Mexicans lurch from station to station because their cash is so limited. As Rick Johnson puts it, "All you need to know about Albuquerque is that the car dealers are the richest guys in town."

Another problem is our spirit. We carry self-deprecation to an extreme. When Albuquerque held a contest for a city motto, one of the entries was "Next 19 Exits." While New Mexico's tolerance of others is one of its most endearing attributes, it can lead to undue toleration of mediocrity. I cringe when I hear, "Well, what can you expect, it's only New Mexico." This attitude can be a debilitating, self-fulfilling prophecy.

As the Albuquerque metro area approaches a million in population, various elements of sophistication are being added. There is now direct air service to most major U. S. cities. But we will probably remain somewhat provincial as one of the most isolated urban centers in the country. I received a potent reminder of this isolation when in the early 1990's, I was asked by our neighborhood group to see if I could persuade a particular Albuquerque City Councilman to oppose a proposed river bridge. He was impervious to the economic arguments, so I played my trump card. I pointed out the potential disruption of the rural nature of our North Valley neighborhood. I related how all great cities have distinctive neighborhoods, cities such as Boston, New York, and San Francisco. If we weren't attentive to our unique neighborhoods and proceeded to grid the city with boulevards every half mile or so, we might become "another San Jose." His response? "I don't know. I've never been to any of those places." Maybe by now he has.

When we arrived in Albuquerque, the airport was in the late stages of a major renovation that had lasted for years. Locally, it became known as "Beirut International" for its torn-apart state. Curious about the eventual outcome, I visited the airport office to view the model of the completed project. I was very favorably impressed. It was to be modern and spacious, yet very Southwestern in its motif. When I next saw the mayor, I asked what kind of a grand re-opening was being planned. There were no plans, and he asked if I might head up the effort. The mayor's wife and I then gathered a widely diverse committee and began planning a series of events, climaxing in an elegant dinner. Our secret weapon was the Albuquerque Junior League. Breda Bova and her chums contributed generously of their time and boundless competence. Slowly, the event took shape under the theme "New Mexico is Taking Off."

The dinner for 700 occupied the newly-built Concourse B. The mayor, both U.S. Senators and the Governor were there to deliver remarks. We were fortunate to have this political firepower on hand to deal with an impasse that developed at the airport security checkpoint where the Kirtland Air Force Base color guard, equipped with rifles and gleaming bayonets, was being detained.

I was the emcee for the event which led to a curious incident. As I returned to the head table after giving some brief introductory remarks, I found my seat occupied by a large woman who wanted to visit with my dinner partner, Senator Pete Domenici. I stood by patiently until their conversation wound down a bit, then gently excused myself and asked to reclaim my seat. Ignoring my half-eaten salad, she maintained her ground, insisting this was her seat – "I'm a big supporter of Pete's." Not wanting to tarnish the evening with an unseemly confrontation, I found an empty chair several tables away. When Pete finally caught the drift of what was going on, he managed to get another place added to our table – fortunately, away from the intruder. I gather that dealing with such folks is one of the occupational hazards of holding higher office.

To celebrate our move to New Mexico, Ruth Elliott, Sarah's grandmother in Austin, kindly sent us a prized New Mexico artifact. It was a handsome black pot that she said had been crafted by "Maria." "Maria" refers to Maria Martinez from the Pueblo of San Ildefonso, the pre-eminent New Mexico potter. I thought it would be prudent to have it appraised for insurance purposes and sought out a well-regarded pottery expert. He was a fussy little guy who lived in a modest home with every room lined with pots on shelves from floor to ceiling. He took our pot, and cradling it lovingly, said, "Yes, yes." I asked whether it was in fact a Maria. He said with a wry look, "Well, it might be a Mary, but it is not a Maria." He then asked where Sarah's grandparents had acquired it. I said I thought it was at some roadside stand. Again, "Yes, yes." Finally, he said that it was a 1940's era "popcorn pot." When they sold a bottle of Coca Cola, they often threw in a cheap pot of popcorn. That was what we had. I asked what it might be worth. He said it looked like it was probably waterproof, in which case it was worth maybe $15. We decided not to apprise grandmother of the true nature of her "Maria" pot.

Albuquerque has delightful oddities.   Perhaps it started with a misspelling of the city's name. The founder, the Duke of Alburquerque, had his first "r" surgically removed by some early postal clerk. Local signs are often curious. One nearby us indicates the directions to the zoo and the country club. However, the words are run together to read, "Zoo Country Club," creating the specter of giraffes hitting out of sand traps. Then there's the highway sign just outside town with the rather existential message, "Gusty Winds May Exist." Or they may not. Perhaps the odd aspect of our hometown was best portrayed in a *New Yorker* cartoon that featured a large chess piece standing in a barren desert scene. The caption read, "Obscure chess move – queen's pawn to Albuquerque."

Talbot

Talbot Insurance Agency was one of the subsidiaries of ABQ Corp. It had been founded and built by Lyle Talbot and then his son Randy into the state's largest agency. One of their successful programs was the distribution of fixed annuities through the ABQ Bank branches. The commissions were good; the SAFECO products they sold were sound and of good value; and they offered improved yields for customers who were living off the income from bank certificates of deposit.

Despite the disappointment over the failure of ABQ Bank and several attractive offers to return to California, we wanted to remain in Albuquerque. We loved the place; our boys were thriving; and I wanted to stay to lead in the resolution of our legal wrangles. Randy Talbot and I agreed that I would head up a new activity called Talbot Financial Services to distribute annuities through bankers around the country. Banks were just getting into this activity, making it a wide open field. Randy knew annuities, and I knew banks. My network of senior bankers got a major boost from Wells Fargo's pension termination whereby many of their senior officers became free agents and left for promotion elsewhere. Then my Crocker colleagues went far afield to add to my network of ex-WESTNET colleagues.

In July, 1990, I hunkered into a 75 square foot windowless former closet at the modest Talbot offices south of the freeway and began dialing for dollars. Our first nibble came from B of A's Seafirst subsidiary where Dick Rosenberg had become President. At the final presentation, Dick Fulp, our champion there, gave us the needle by asking, "I hope you don't mind if we say you're from Dallas." Upon winning the account, we hired and trained a sales force and began selling. Within a year this program had become three times as productive as B of A's California program with another vendor.

Several years later we were finally able to crack B of A's California market. An impediment was that their current vendor, GNA, had a year left on their five-year exclusive contract. Given our productivity in Washington State, B of A persuaded GNA to let us in. A condition of the deal, though, was that we had to allow GNA into our Seafirst program. GNA was highly suspicious that we would make only token sales efforts of their products and insisted on strong contractual terms to enforce compliance. In fact, our sales reps found that GNA products were useful in filling some niches in our product line. What ensued gave us a great deal of satisfaction. Each year, GNA posted their top ten sales reps nationally from among their several dozen bank programs. By the second year, our Talbot reps were holding down numbers one, three, and seven nationally. Embarrassed, GNA stopped publishing that list. Ironically, our forced involvement with GNA produced another benefit. In the competition for Wachovia, which we subsequently won, one of their criteria was demonstrated ability to sell GNA products. Victories also came at Bank of Hawaii, Mellon, Nations, and Washington Mutual. The portfolio expanded to variable annuities and to mutual funds, and the vendors broadened to include American General, Transamerica, and Physicians Mutual, each with particular features to fill out our product line.

The keys to success in selling through banks are good products, constant communication, attentive service, and keeping the sales message simple. I was especially grateful for the superb sales management contribution by Norm Howard. In running an outfit that grew to hundreds of employees in twenty states, I tried to keep on top of what was going on in the field, but there were occasional surprises. One of our reps in rural Pennsylvania was quite successful, but we heard reports that she used intimidating sales tactics. Then came the horrifying specifics. One of her closing lines was, "Buy this annuity or God will punish you!" We parted company shortly thereafter.

The insurance business likes to reward high producers with trips, which gave us glorious opportunities to visit Australia, New

Zealand, France, and Hawaii, as well as great stateside events, such as the U.S. Tennis Open. Nothing will quite match the sumptuous banquet in the Hall of Battles at Versailles, followed by spectacular fireworks over the reflecting pools. Within Talbot we had frequent sales contests and incentives. If one has never spent time selling, one may not realize that sales reps face rejection most of the time. Constant encouragement and incentives are needed to keep spirits up.

One year I decided to reward our top five sales reps with a long weekend in Yosemite. Most of the winners were from the East, and none had been to the Park before. Hiking, horseback riding, and just reveling in the majesty of the canyon made it our best sales trip ever. Sarah couldn't join me on that occasion, so I decided to take my son, Kenny. Our big outing was a hike from the valley floor to Glacier Point 4,000 feet above. Typically, Kenny was mute all during the weekend, but on the return trip, as we neared the group home where he lived, Kenny became increasingly agitated. In fact, I had to restrain him to keep him in the car until we were parked. When we stopped, he burst out the door and into the home, shouting to all, "I climbed Glacier! I climbed Glacier!" It's all in there; it just has a hard time coming out.

Several strategic decisions added greatly to our success. One was that we concentrated on selling only to large banks, which led to continual expansion of our territory as those banks acquired others. Another was Randy Talbot's pricing formula. Our participating banks realized a trailing commission of ¼ of 1% per year which they would forfeit if they were to end their contract with us. We never lost a bank.

Randy was also a genius at managing our corporate fortunes. As an exit from ABQ Corp, he arranged for Talbot to become allied with the ABI network run by Barney Mizel and later owned by Carl Lindner's Cincinnati conglomerate. Randy eventually arranged for Talbot to get bought out from Lindner and into more stable hands at SAFECO Corp. SAFECO was motivated in part for defensive reasons, as over a five-year period we went from accounting for 10% of their annuity sales to over 50%.

As a postscript, SAFECO realized what a gem they acquired in Randy Talbot and quickly "drafted him to the Bigs" by making him President of SAFECO Life. When SAFECO later decided to exit the life insurance business, Randy led a successful buyout financed by private equity sources. The resultant company, renamed Symetra Financial, has continued to make excellent progress. Dave Weymouth returned to Albuquerque to take the reins of Talbot from Randy.

A parallel development occurred within the old line property and casualty arm of Talbot. At first there was some natural skepticism about our Talbot Financial venture and perhaps a little resentment over their profit sharing being shrunk by my travel and other start-up expenses. By the second year, though, my unit was making a solid profit contribution. At the annual dinner, Rob Machacek, who headed the commercial side, presented me with a "hockey stick" award, symbolizing the profit recovery I had been promising and had finally delivered. In part spurred by the growth of our unit, they showed equal growth through both acquisitions and internally generated business. A contributing factor was Randy's canny strategy of keeping commercial insurance margins up by avoiding major urban markets. Another was the strength of internal competition from other high-performing units. Dan Scott's life insurance unit also rose up on the tide of rising expectations. Overall, Talbot grew to over $2 billion in annual sales, and the combined firm became one of the top agencies nationally. Subsequently, Talbot has been acquired by Hub International.

There were some notable characters at Talbot. One was Phil Kneib, a very shrewd analyst and perhaps the thriftiest person I've ever known. Phil would mark his calendar for when you might let him come to pick fruit off your tree. I had to chuckle at Phil's Valentine's Day ploy. He and his wife Martha would visit the greeting card kiosk at the drug store. Each would pick a card, and then exchange them for mutual enjoyment, followed by a return to the rack unpurchased.

We often relied on Shari Lucero for her leadership at the Talbot office. One day I came to her for help with a problem that needed a deft touch. Five women in our office had delivered babies over a short span. One by one, they would visit the office with their little bundles of joy. All work would cease for about an hour while the women in the office would swarm around the baby. We were on a tight deadline when the fifth such interruption occurred. I thought that a message to cut the visit short would be better received if it came from Shari. She was indeed sympathetic to my concern, but then I mentioned that Yolanda's baby was currently stopping all forward progress. Like a shot, Shari bolted from the office to join the adoring throng. Maternal instincts rule!

Speaking of matters maternal, one day an unexpected present arrived at the office for Randy. It was an Indian "storyteller" doll, one of those little pottery statuettes of a mother seated on the ground with children crawling over her. Randy noticed that the doll depicted three such children, whereas they had only their two boys, Nathan and Casey. It finally dawned on him that this was Margaret's precious way of telling him the story that Baby Allison was on the way.

The Boys

As all parents know, the arrival of a second child adds a third dimension. There are the two kids, and then there is the relationship between the two of them. A treasured moment when we were in Hillsborough was when four year-old Joseph was questioning Elliott whether Santa really existed. His final probing question was "Well, why does Santa come down the chimney instead of just coming in the front door?" Elliott's response was quick-witted as well as quintessentially suburban. "Santa uses the chimney so he won't set off the alarm."

A second child also teaches parents how different two offspring can be and serves to humble one as to how much difference parenting really makes. This lesson came home to us during visits to dine at Burlingame's North China Inn. Elliott was about four and kept insisting that he try some of the fiery Szechuan dishes that Sarah and I enjoy. Finally, we decided there was nothing quite like an object lesson. We fed him just a little bit of a capsaicin-laden portion. Predictably, his eyes widened, and he clamored for water, again and again, complaining, "It's coming back!" Fast forward five years to same restaurant, same scene. When four year-old Joseph lobbied for some of our meal, we again discouraged the prospect. This time Elliott weighed in, too, "Joe, you really don't want that!" Once again, it was time for the object lesson. But this time all we got was a smile and a request for more. We gave him more, making sure we loaded on more of the fiery little dark red pieces. He loved it.

Our two boys have generally gotten along well together, as the five-year age difference placed them a mini-generation apart. We did hit a rough patch, though, when the boys were about 7 and 12. Teasing, poking, and bickering became the norm. We found ourselves separating them in the car and restaurants. Slowly the relationship improved until one Sunday morning, there appeared to be a dramatic breakthrough. I went to peek in on sleeping Joseph, only to find his bed empty. Upon checking his older brother's room, I was delighted to find Joseph sound asleep in a blanket on the floor next to Elliott who was asleep in his bed. A little while later, when the boys came into the kitchen, we made sure to reinforce this newfound indication of brotherhood. Sarah said to Joseph, "It is good to see that you are becoming better friends with Elliott." Joe acknowledged, and then added cheerfully, "and it only cost me two dollars!"

Joseph liked to trade with his older brother, a practice we tried to forbid as we were concerned about his being at a disadvantage. We relented, though, when it became apparent that Joe could hold his own. In fact, when Joe was nine we began to receive mail for him from all over the country, as many as 8 or 9 envelopes per day. It turned out that the envelopes all contained checks, as Joe had developed a brisk and profitable business in trading collector cards over the Internet.

Young Joe had nomadic sleeping habits. In the morning we never knew where to find him. One favored spot was under the dining room table. So we wouldn't inadvertently wake him when we entered the main part of the house, we asked him please to try staying in his own bed. He said that his problem was that he found his room boring. When we asked how we might enliven it, Joe had a ready suggestion. He proposed a *trompe l'oile* wall mural, one depicting a dark, menacing "Mugger's Alley," as he called it. We thought his plan might provoke nightmares and that it wouldn't do much for eventual home resale value. We finally settled on a universe theme. Helped by some local artists, a dark blue swirl originated out of a wall socket to envelop the room and eventually disappear into a ceiling vent. Within the swath of universe were planets and other celestial objects. Among Joseph's contributions was an orbiting can of Coke.

In Elliott's middle school years, there was a spell of mediocre academic performance. I gave the usual parental lecture about the importance of qualifying for a good college and how that might impact success in life. He responded with the observation, "Dad, you went to Stanford, but don't you work for a grad of Arizona State?" I had to admire his cheeky response. I then reminded him of Ring Lardner's comment that "The race doesn't always go to the swift, but that's the way to bet it."

The artistic, creative side was apparent early in both boys, but Joseph's affinity for things artistic was profound. When Elliott went off with Sarah to one of his regional tennis tournaments, I decided to take seven year-old Joe to Santa Fe, as I thought he might enjoy seeing some art galleries. As we started up Canyon Road, Joe became riveted. He wanted to go into every gallery and into every room of every gallery, all 40 of them. Then he wanted to go back to galleries previously visited to compare one work to another. I think we got more of a workout than the tennis players.

A year later, when we were visiting family in Los Angeles, we arranged to take Joe to the Art Center School of Design in Pasadena, the place where the Mazda Miata was designed. When told of this plan, eight year-old Joseph said, "I've wanted to go there all my life!" We had no idea how he might have come to know about that premier design school.

Elliott's passion was sports. Early on, he became the "go to" guy on his youth soccer teams. He also had good success in baseball. In fact, his baseball got to be a source of distress when we moved to Albuquerque. Elliott had just been selected to play on the San Gabriel Valley all-star Little League team, and our family's move disqualified him from playing. His morose reaction lasted a few weeks until one day he came peeling around the corner with a broad grin, proclaiming that, "New Mexico rocks!" Elliott had just learned that in his new home state, the driving age was only 15. Elliott had this fantasy of celebrating his 15th birthday by roaring out to California to impress his old buddies with his new red sports car. We let him know that a car would come when we felt he earned it, would be a Volvo, and would be older than he was.

Joe has always been prudent, perhaps the most prudent of all of us in the family. One day when he was about nine, he came to me and asked, "Dad, do you know how much college costs?" I told him I had a pretty good idea. Joe then asked if I was saving for his college expenses. When I answered yes, he followed with, "How much are you saving, Dad?" Not wanting to get into family finances, I said he would have to be satisfied with my general assurances. To which Joe then said, "I hope you don't mind if I save, too." I left with the comforting feeling that there was a kid I was never going to have to worry about.

On the boys' first trip to the East, at ages 6 and 11, they were excited about all the new experiences. Often it was the little things such as curbside pretzel vendors or the elaborate New York subway graffiti that impressed them as much as traditional landmarks like the Statue of Liberty. The Metroliner trip from New York to Washington traversed six states, a big deal for boys from the West. There began a rather metaphysical discussion of what constituted actually "being" in a state. The boys concluded that hurtling through on a train wouldn't count. Fortunately, each state crossed included at least a brief stop. Then, at Trenton, NJ, the boys decided that merely touching down at the platform was entirely too token. The solution to establishing at least brief residency was to conduct a commercial transaction. So, at each station the boys bolted for the local newsstand to buy a candy bar, and at each station their anxious parents awaited last second returns of the boys bearing Zagnut bars.

Elliott did lots of skiing in New Mexico where after-school access to the slopes is so easy. One year he was able to work in 50 days of skiing. But his competitive sport was tennis. Elliott and I had played together for years, and he was able to make the Academy varsity team as a freshman. I remember the warm June day when he got his letter jacket. That jacket was not coming off, even as the temperature soared into the 90's. Together with his good buddy and doubles partner, Todd Hankinson, Elliott made All-District, and his team won the state championship repeatedly. But despite his obvious superior skills, he still couldn't beat the old man. Aided greatly by blatant gamesmanship ("You're playing your father, you realize!"), I prevailed until his junior year. Then one day, Elliott mopped me up 6-2, 6-2. I don't know which of us was more proud.

After participating in the usual youth sports programs (soccer, Little League, etc.), Joe signed up for the Academy cross-country program. The coach was wonderfully supportive, and the scoring formula made every participant's placement count in the team results. Even the slowest of competitors was cheered on by earlier-finishing teammates. Joe related that the highlight of his running career came when he and a competing runner were struggling up the final hill, battling to avoid a last place finish. With delight Joe told how his rival faltered and was compelled to detour to "chuck his cookies." Glorious!

Joe's earlier track career had a most unexpected highlight. As an eight year-old, he spent one summer with the Albuquerque Road Runners youth track team. Joe entered several events at the Southwestern Regional meet with disappointing results. Then he entered the shot put. The dozen or so other boys in his age category were about a head taller and 50 pounds bigger. Somehow, our little lefty managed to uncoil a terrific throw and walked off with the bronze medal.

The boys had always gone to public primary school, and we had every intention of continuing this practice with Joe when we moved to Albuquerque. Joe enrolled in first grade at Alvarado School, just a block from our home. A few months later, his teacher quit. Then a few months after that, the school principal left. This turmoil, plus an uninspiring curriculum led us to enroll him in private Manzano Day School from the second through the fifth grades. Under the leadership of Gloria Mallory, this fine institution provided both excellent instruction and a nurturing environment.

Albuquerque Academy has become an important part of our lives. When considering our move to New Mexico, we were discouraged by what we saw and read about Albuquerque Public Schools at the middle school level. Dick Elkins, then a colleague at the company I was joining, suggested I look into Elliott's attending "the Academy." I was introduced to the Headmaster, dynamic Bob Bovinette. He showed us around the beautiful campus and its first rate laboratories, athletic facilities, drama stage, art studios, etc. He talked about their high faculty salaries, the challenging curriculum, the national championship debate team, and their impressive commitment to diversity and financial aid. From my background as a board chair of Crystal Springs Uplands School in Hillsborough, I knew that such resources cost big bucks. Yet the Academy's tuition at that point (1986) was only $4,200 per year. I speculated that they must have a large endowment to make the finances work, an improbable situation in capital-starved Albuquerque. Bob explained they were one of the top endowed day schools in the nation.

The origin of the Academy's largesse is unique. The school began as a boys school in quarters borrowed from St. Michael's and All Angels Church. Like most start-up schools, they were tuition-driven and fought to keep their doors open. Then one day a new student arrived. Young Albert Simms had been a student at Albuquerque High School. The Simms family had great real estate wealth, as well as connections to the McCormick farm equipment family from Chicago. Young Albert had spent the summer in Florence studying art, and he wanted to stay a week after the start of school in New Mexico to see an exhibition coming to the Uffizi Gallery. The Albuquerque High School officials would not agree to this "truancy," even after the family proposed that young Albert could write a report for the benefit of other students. Exasperated, Albert's parents turned to the fledgling Albuquerque Academy which welcomed the boy's extended stay in Florence. Upon their child's graduation, the Simms family approached the school's Headmaster and said that they would be pleased to make a gift to the school. It was a swath of land a mile wide and eight miles long through the heart of Albuquerque. Today, that holding and its subsequent investment growth have resulted in a beautiful 330 acre campus plus an endowment worth over $300 million. These resources, as well as superb leadership by Bob and then by Andy Watson and Dick Elkins, have enabled the school to continue to reach new heights of excellence and to remain need-blind in its admission policies. Over one-third of the student body are students of color. Both of our boys had the opportunity to spend seven years at the Academy, forging lifelong friendships, as well as benefiting from a superb education.

Fortunately, by the time we were raising Joseph, educators had recognized learning disabilities. We knew Joe was very bright because of his insights and his startling observations such as, "Why do they say 'Don't throw litter?' It isn't litter until you throw it." In watching movies, he would know from the first few minutes of the film what was going to the happen to various characters – by the music played or their dress or various cinematic precursors the rest of us missed. You can imagine our consternation to see him at the kitchen table, sweating over the words in a book, concentrating hard, yet lingering on a page for 20 minutes or more. A visit to learning therapist Lorraine Perlmutter revealed that Joe indeed had significant learning disabilities. Through consummate skill, she helped Joe find more effective learning techniques. Within a year, he was given an award for most improved student at Albuquerque Academy. Joe was so surprised to hear his name called for an academic achievement that the Headmaster had to call his name three times before he responded and hustled to the podium for his prize.

After the fifth of his seven years at the Academy, Joseph started lobbying for a change of pace, perhaps via a semester at a boarding school. We thought this objective might best be achieved with an international experience, and Joe subsequently spent a term at the American School in Madrid. While it did provide a wonderful new exposure, and Joe excelled academically, his host family was overly restrictive. They insisted on taking Joe with them to their mountain retreat every weekend, denying him the opportunity to explore Madrid and its environs as much as he would have liked.

When he first got to Spain, though, Joe had a remarkable sojourn. Sixteen year-old Joe decided to go see Paris. We lined up his first night's lodging in Paris, but he did all the rest on his own. When he arose the next morning, Joe called us to check in and to consult on what sights he might see. We had a map of Paris spread out on the kitchen table and spoke of Montmartre, the Louvre, etc. Sarah then said, "Joe, why don't you start at the Eiffel Tower – it's right nearby." Joe, with classic teenage inflection, responded, "Mom, I'm nowhere near the Eiffel Tower!" Rather sure of her ground, Sarah then said, "Joe, look up." Upon doing so, he then said, "Oh – I guess you're right."

Both of our boys loved the Academy drama program, as actors and as set designers. Both of them also served as class representatives to the student government. Joe hounded the art studio, while Elliott was active in journalism and debate. The Academy is so rich in resources.

Joe's experiences at summer camp were treasured. For seven summers he journeyed to beautiful Orcas Island in the San Juans off Seattle to attend the Four Winds Westward Ho Camp. Many kids from the Bay Area and Los Angeles were there, affording Joe an opportunity to keep in touch with California acquaintances. It was also an opportunity to learn boating skills and to experience a very different environment from our desert home. Perhaps most importantly, it provided Joe personal growth. It was a new role when he vaulted into positions of leadership among the campers. In fact, Joe won the coveted Polaris Award as the top camper. Later, he was enlisted by the camp as a junior instructor in the arts and crafts program. Joe himself put it best when he said, "Dad, you wouldn't know me at camp." The thrill of mastering new and unfamiliar challenges is one of life's most exhilarating experiences.

When it came to Joe Brown's dental structure, I'm afraid he dove into the shallow end of the gene pool. I had four teeth that never came in; Joe had seven. In a vain attempt to fill in the gaps, his teeth began migrating every which way. Our California dentist surveyed the wreckage with the enthusiasm of one who had just been given a lifetime annuity. Fortunately, Don Beck was an extremely skilled practitioner, and he crafted a multi-phase program of remediation. When we got to Albuquerque, our new children's dentist took one look at the plan and urged us to keep going back to Beck, as he didn't feel he had the requisite skill. Over the years, we made many dental trips to California. It all cost about the same as a year of college tuition, but there was such a payoff in seeing Joseph's glorious smile emerge. In family photos before, Joe invariably posed with mouth closed; afterwards his smile and his life opened up.

A creative kiddo will produce some amazing moments. When surveying family members as to what might be an appropriate subject for an outdoor sculpture we thought we'd like to acquire, Joe thought it would be great to install an ATM machine in the garden, fully stocked, of course.

Elliott had excellent grades and test scores. When it came time for college applications, Elliott's first choice was Stanford, which is a long shot under the best of circumstances. The clincher for him was a superb writing sample. Elliott wrote of an incident that occurred during his senior year. A tennis teammate asked Elliott for a ride downtown to a doctor's appointment. Elliott knew his teammate was gay, but he was alarmed to see that the "doctor's appointment" was in fact his teammate's going to learn the result of a test for HIV. As Elliott sat in the waiting room, he scanned an ominous set of posted notices for hospice care. Finally, his friend emerged, joyful that his test was negative. Elliott's vivid account related how his teammate had trusted Elliott to share the most significant moment in his life.

Finally, the envelopes started arriving from colleges. One day, the envelope from Stanford arrived. It was stripped of mystery by the word emblazoned in red on the outside of the envelope, "Congratulations!" Of course, we wanted Elliott to open the envelope to be sure. But no, he had to taunt us by lingering over another piece of correspondence, an ad from a record club. Finally, he opened the Stanford envelope to receive his official acceptance. I know Elliott's decision to attend Stanford pleased my father. He sent Elliott a letter that we treasure, along with the honor Dad valued most, Stanford's Gimbel Medal, given to the Stanford athlete who best manifests good sportsmanship.

We should credit our young friend, Pier Kuehn, with "an assist" in Elliott's scoring with Stanford. Elliott was just a high school freshman when Sarah arranged for him to spend a weekend with Pier at Pier's fraternity at Berkeley. Elliott had the time of his life, attending a class, going to a football game, and enjoying the rollicking camaraderie. His big revelation was, "Gee, Mom and Dad, college is really neat!" Suddenly the goal of attending college was no longer just a vague abstraction pushed by parents, but a highly appealing prospect. We encourage other parents to expose their children early to the excitement of college - to add zest to the quest.

Joe's grades were also excellent, and as he got high percentile scores on his SAT's and ACT's, he clearly was a candidate for a top college. Given a little boost from the legacy factor we enjoy at Stanford, I encouraged him to at least look at the school. He grudgingly agreed. The source of his reluctance was that he was not sports-oriented, but more interested in studio art, literature, and philosophy. When I cited that Stanford had a studio arts department, he replied that their materials were unimpressive. Finally, he agreed to visit the Stanford Studio Arts Dept. and meet with faculty before making his final decision. He did so while Sarah and I visited other parts of the campus. Several hours later we reunited, and Joe related his experience. He had met with three professors. The first was elderly and dozed off during the interview. The second droned on about his ideas and work and spurned all of Joe's attempts to show his portfolio. The third professor, Dr. Rivera, was exciting. He related to Joe's work, and the two shared thoughts about composition, coloration, light, etc. When Joe asked him whether he taught any freshman classes, the professor answered, "Yes, but not here. I'm just visiting here from the University of Texas." Joe went to NYU where he thrived. Not only did Joe graduate with an excellent GPA, he won a Presidential Service award for his service to the youth of the community. Stanford would enter his life in a later chapter.

I've long admired the expression, "None of us is as smart as all of us." The truth of that statement was amply demonstrated by an incident in El Paso at the end of a vacation trip to Mexico. We had stored our car in the basement of the Westin Hotel and had just returned across the border from Juarez in a taxi. We transferred all the bags to our car and then bid farewell to the driver. As the taxi rounded the exit ramp, Sarah suddenly exclaimed, "My purse. I left it in the taxi!" The cab was gone, and we appeared to be goners.

We then caucused on a purse recovery program. It was remarkable the different pieces of the puzzle that each of us could recall. Sarah had chatted with the driver in Spanish the whole way and knew all about his family. Joe remembered details of the driver's appearance and the color of the cab. I could recall the exact location where we were picked up and the amount of the fare. Somehow Elliott recalled several of the digits in the cab's serial number.

Our optimism received a jolt, though, upon Sarah's call to an information operator in Juarez. Sarah asked for the names and numbers of the 3 or 4 cab companies there. She was told it was more like 103 or 104 companies, as the great majority of taxis were run by independent operators. Rather than abandoning hope, as I would have, Sarah pressed on with consummate charm and her Spanish facility. Despite all odds, she was in fact able to locate the driver and got him to send back the wallet and cards, licenses, etc., but to keep the cash for his trouble. It was a stellar family moment.

When we moved to New Mexico, Sarah was excited to find the skiing so good and so accessible. She was an excellent skier, having made many visits to the slopes during her youth and was able to teach the boys to ski by skiing backwards in front of them. My skiing had been confined to a few awkward times in grade school. Also, I had never had much experience on bikes or skates or other activities where balance and weight shifting came into play. And I was over 50. Naturally, the boys quickly became proficient and delighted in my ineptitude. Their derision reached new heights one day at the Santa Fe Ski Lodge. During lunch break, Elliott asked me for my map of ski trails. I asked why didn't he just go over to the rack on the wall and get another. "No, Dad, we want yours!" I knew the boys were up to no good when I saw them over in the corner hooting and laughing. Gleefully, they returned my trail map to me. They had renamed all the novice trails that I had been skiing. Instead of names like "Bluebonnet Trail" and "Forest Glen," they had substituted "Wimp's Way," "Marshmallow" and the like!

We always enjoy Becky's visits to Albuquerque. On one occasion, the visit almost got a little livelier than we had in mind. When packing the car to take Becky to the airport for her return trip, Elliott and Joseph, about 12 and 7 at the time, asked if they could please ride in the trunk. I don't normally accede to such foolishness, but we were having fun and it wasn't far to the airport. As we approached the departure curb, we could tell from the muffled murmur from the trunk that the boys were up to something. Sure enough, they began yelling, "We're being kidnapped!" The nearby police officer must have had boys of his own to let this incident pass.

Once in a while, though, we were able to keep up with the boys. While in San Marino, ten year-old Elliott came home one afternoon having adopted a punk rocker look. His hair was moussed into a spiky peak, and he had torn several holes in his tee shirt.

Recognizing that his script doubtless called for us to get apoplectic, we adopted another course. A few hours later when we gathered for dinner, Sarah and I both sported torn tee shirts and spiky moussed hair. We said that we enjoyed his look so much that we decided to adopt it. At that point, all the appeal drained out of his scheme, and we never again saw him in punk rock mode.

Sarah and I admired Barb Rosenberg's canny way of keeping up with her two lively teenage boys. The boys were perplexed as to how mom always knew when girls had been visiting the house in the parents' absence. The telltale sign? – neatly folded towels in the racks.

When a child approaches you with, "Dad, has the Statute of Limitations run on _ _ _ _ _?," you know whatever is coming next will add a few more grey hairs. One such moment came when Elliott related how he, Todd, and David had raced down Tramway on their in-line skates. Tramway from the top to I-25 is a straight shot six miles downhill. He said they got going so fast, they passed a car. Elliott was an excellent skater, often playing skate hockey at UNM, but this caper was truly death-defying.

Road trips can be fun, but the 1,100 mile drive from Albuquerque to San Francisco is a long slog even when taken over two days. Elliott routinely would have breakfast with us at home and then call us shortly after dinner to say that he was already in San Francisco. When we asked how he managed to stay awake and alert, his response was less than reassuring, "I just keep driving until I start seeing snakes."

Long after the kids are supposedly "out of the nest," a parent's concerns will rise and fall with their fortunes. Stu Sherman put it in a rather anguished way when he said, "You're only as happy as your unhappiest child." Fortunately, the opposite is true, as Sarah and I couldn't have been more elated upon getting a phone call from Elliott while at Stanford. He proclaimed that he had just experienced the best day of his life. Elaborating, he reported getting an "A" on his math exam, followed by a reception for the Dalai Lama where the Dalai Lama for some reason stopped to give Elliott a hug. Then later that same day, Elliott and some buddies decided to take in a

San Francisco Giants game. While sitting in the outfield bleachers, Elliott snagged a home run ball. Ferris Buehler lives!

What a difference a generation brought in the nature of summer jobs for teenagers. Mine invariably involved mind-numbing physical labor, such as digging ditches or picking fruit. Our boys' summers included working for securities firms, service as a Senate intern in Washington, and attending Rhode Island School of Design. I still can't believe that during law school Elliott got paid for spending a summer in Bali formulating policies to protect the coral reefs.

Twenty-first birthdays are very special in our New Mexico crowd, and the usual pattern is to celebrate them with a weekend in Las Vegas under adult supervision. Lest one think that the kids were being inculcated in the ways of sin, it is actually a very safe place for this type of celebration. No one drives, and the gaming and shows provide a diversion from the excesses of alcohol. Elliott had a great time there with four of his Stanford buddies.

When it came time for Joe's big day, he declined a Las Vegas party in favor of another idea. He said that as Thanksgiving had always been his favorite time, he would like to celebrate his March birthday with an extra Thanksgiving dinner. Joined by ten of his chums, we reveled in turkey and all the trimmings. For us, the highlight of this delightful occasion, and perhaps one of the highlights of our lives, was when Joe offered the following toast to his parents, "Thank you for a perfect childhood."

Pets

First Elliott and then Joseph had goldfish, all of them named Fred. When we moved to New Mexico, transporting the current vintage of Fred proved to be a challenge. Obviously, he couldn't be packed up, and we felt he could not survive the many hours of the motion of a car on the highway. It became clear that the solution was for me to carry him aboard a flight to Albuquerque in a jar with holes punched in the lid (before the current limits on liquids aboard planes). As I was preparing to leave, I suddenly found myself confronted by six year-old Joseph. In a very manly tone he said, "Dad, I know you may be tempted to flush Fred down the toilet and get a new goldfish in Albuquerque. I just want to know that I have memorized Fred!" Actually, that devious thought had occurred to me, but I had decided to play it straight. Fred did acquire some bruises from the motion of the plane, but survived to be one of our New Mexico companions.

When we got to Albuquerque, Joe briefly had a cat, "Dirk." It seemed to get along well with Elliott's dog and appeared to be on its way to permanent residence. Then, our friend Steve Moise paid a visit, as he often did. No sooner had he stepped into the doorway, when he asked, "Do you have a cat?" The cat was not in the area, but Steve's allergy was so strong that the dander in the air set off a reaction. If we needed any more reason to wind up our relationship with "el gato," it came later that week. Dick and Barb Rosenberg had visited recently and had brought us a lovely housewarming present, a delicate curtain of green and gold glass by the noted Seattle glass artist, Dale Chihuly. It was proudly displayed over the mantle in our living room. I came home to find it ignominiously displayed in pieces on the living room floor. Perhaps anticipating its imminent demise, the cat had taken off and was never seen again.

A cat of a different sort also made a unique contribution to our household. At Joseph's fourth birthday party we wanted to add a thematic element to his cowboy party by having the local children's zoo lend us a pony. On the day of the party we learned that the promised pony was not available. However, they offered a substitute visitor, a baby tiger cub. The cub was adorable, looking for all the world like a striped house cat except for its enormous paws. It was a big hit with kids and adults alike. Then our little friend decided to make a rather anti-social deposit on our rug. None of us had ever encountered such a foul-smelling concoction – it cleared the party out of the house. Our best hazmat efforts were never able to completely eliminate the stain from the rug.

Our doggies were somewhat more conventional pets. When Elliott was eight, Sarah visited the local pound to find a friendly mutt for him for Christmas. She found this cute ball of fluff that Elliott named, "Black Gem." At Black Gem's initial checkup at the vet's, I noticed a little flyer on pet health insurance. It seemed like a foolish purchase, but the brochure was very well done, so I took the bait for $35 for lifetime surgical coverage. A mere two weeks later, our poor little doggie jumped off the kitchen chair and crumpled to the floor. Her broken leg required two pins to set it. A few months later the same leg was re-broken during a front yard football game and reset. Then within the year, a babysitter fell on her and broke the other leg. In all, over $800 in benefits were paid on my $35 policy, one of the best investments I've ever made. However, after the third claim I did have to field a call from an Ace Ventura-like claims adjuster and assure him that we were not a family of sadists.

Despite the early physical trauma, Black Gem was lively, and she ran all over the fields with the boys. She did have a slight limp, which gave rise to an amusing situation. After we moved to San Marino, our yard couldn't contain her, and on cool winter days Black Gem enjoyed absorbing the warmth from manhole covers on the street. She invariably scampered out of the way of passing cars, but when drivers looked back they would see her limping. Several conscientious drivers rang our doorbell out of concern that they had harmed her – one driver even took her to the vet for treatment. We speculated that Black Gem could have been a very useful accomplice in a damage suit scam.

After the misadventure with Dirk the cat, we decided to get a dog for Joseph. A trip to the Albuquerque pound produced Chelsea, who looked like a sawed-off black Labrador. At first she was bullied by Black Gem, but as she grew older and stronger, Chelsea became the dominant dog. In fact, Chelsea became fearless, chasing after all manner of larger dogs and coyotes. Both dogs loved the open space of our home on Los Poblanos and lived lives of 16 and 17 years.

With the kids grown and our busy travel schedule, we have decided to defer further canine acquisitions for the immediate future. Although we hope someday to get another, we want to make sure it is a breed that doesn't disturb the pheasants. We love "George," Wayne and Elaine Chew's stately poodle, but I am still hoping someday to wear down Sarah's resistance to a big, furry Bernese Mountain Sheepdog.

Houses

Our Albuquerque home was ideal for raising the family. Salamanca Circle is a kidney-shaped loop about a mile around with several cul-de-sacs spoking off of it. The singular entrance to the development had a manned gatehouse, and the 20-mph speed limit and numerous speed bumps made for a safe environment for the many young families. A pleasant surprise was to learn that right across the street lived former Stanford schoolmates, Pat and Nanette Hurley. Our home was spacious, was light and airy, and had attractive outdoor spaces and easy access to the park in the center of the tract. The home was not distinguished architecturally, but suited our needs well and was a place of many happy memories.

In April, 1997, after eleven years at 912 Salamanca, we moved about a half-mile away to our current home at 2030 Los Poblanos Place. Just as Joseph was about to depart for college, and a rational decision would have been to consider a smaller house, we bought a bigger one. We had often walked the neighborhood and had admired the handsome adobe (a real one) on a beautiful, wooded four-acre lot. It was built by Bill and Nancy Anixter with the help of noted architect, Nat Kaplan. Nat was actually trained as an artist, and he created wonderful dynamic spaces, always beautifully oriented to the gardens. His architectural features were generally asymmetrical, and his rooms often had diagonal walls that drew the eye outside. It has been a great joy to us and has been a wonderful venue to host many community events. Thanks to the influence of our superb interior decorators, Suzanne Rheinstein and Joe Nye, we were pleased to have the home featured in the December, 2004 issue of *House Beautiful*.

The Anixters were just splendid in selling their home. When we commented about a pot or bench, they invariably said, "Oh, please keep it." They were so generous that we became reluctant to comment lest they add to our treasure trove. We paid a fairly full price, but the home and the neighborhood are so choice that values have risen nicely. Albuquerque residential real estate finally caught the nationwide real estate boom with prices rising strongly since 2000. But for the previous period, prices were stagnant while California real estate was exploding. We barely recovered our cost basis on the Albuquerque home we owned from 1986 to 1997.

Our Los Poblanos home is in a delightful rural setting, where we are treated to frequent visits from pheasants, rabbits and all manner of other wildlife. There is even an occasional coyote. One day, we noticed two coyotes lingering in our back field. We were very concerned that these swift carnivores might make an hors d'oeuvre out of Chelsea, our little pound puppy. That concern was heightened when I made a visit to the spot where they had been seen and found the beginning of a burrow. This couple was evidently taking up residence there. When Sarah quickly ruled out use of a shotgun, I turned to County Animal Services for advice. They prescribed a baited trap, but warned that coyotes usually do not fall for such lures. Indeed our coyotes were wily and blithely ignored this temptation. I then devised my own very personal deterrent. I kicked in the nascent burrow (making sure no cubs were within) and proceeded to "mark" the territory directly around it, thereby announcing there was an "alpha" in the neighborhood and it wasn't them. The coyotes disappeared, not to be seen again.

With the Farm an easy reach when we lived in the Bay Area and with the convenience of Pozo from Los Angeles, we never felt the need for a vacation home. The move to New Mexico, though, made it an all day event to get to Pozo. Sarah has always had a yearning for the beaches of Southern California, and I had enjoyed renting a place in Laguna Beach years before. A visit to the glorious Montage Resort in Laguna in 2003 clinched the deal. I began an Internet search for a condo there. On a subsequent visit we landed a place that seemed just perfect for us. Its crowning feature was a large deck with a whitewater view of the ocean and dramatic views of Aliso Canyon and the picturesque adjoining mountainscape. The location was ideal, only a long block from the Montage and from a shopping center with an Albertson's and a Starbucks. The condo building was undistinguished, but it was gated and had ample covered parking and storage. We kept our BMW Z-4 there for stylish zipping around the Laguna hills.

Our only initial reservation about the condo was the ugly interior condition of the unit. With two bedrooms, two baths, and a fireplace packed into about 1,000 square feet, plus that glorious deck, it had good bones. Everything else about the place looked like "Wyoming Motel." Guided by Joe Nye, the place underwent a transformation. What emerged was a sleek, modern look that is right out of Park Avenue. The principal negative factor turned out to be its loneliness. Only five of the twenty-one units were occupied as primary residences. Also, we have not been able to break away to use it often and to develop local friendships. With our subsequent commitment to Santa Fe, we decided to sell the Laguna condo.

Our interest in Santa Fe was kindled by our enjoyment of a little rental casita at 810 ½ Abeyta, just off Acequia Madre, when I took on the State Treasurer job. We loved the neighborhood and its easy access to the culinary and artistic delights of Canyon Road. One of the desirable criteria when looking for a place in Eastside Santa Fe is that it be "within warm latté walking distance of the Sub." The Sub is Subscription News coffee house. When I order my nonfat, decaf latté, the delightfully irreverent cashier calls out to the barista, "One 'Why Bother'!"

One day we saw a For Sale sign on a charming little adobe at 412 Sosaya Lane. It was right across the street from our friends, Roy and Tana Bidwell, and just a block away from Peg and Dick Cronin and Paul and Lisa Bardacke. It had been marked down twice because of a circumstance that actually played into our hands. It was under lease for another nine months which served to deter most buyers, but it was just what we wanted, as we were soon to depart for our sabbatical in New York. With so many of our good friends either moving to Santa Fe or having second homes there, we see more friends walking the neighborhood there than we do in Albuquerque. It has also provided an opportunity to make some wonderful new friends, especially the group associated with the splendid Santa Fe

Chamber Music Festival. The timing of our New York adventure allowed us a window of time to plan a remodel with Susie Westbrook, to get it approved, and to begin the construction. The construction is still going on in fits and starts, mostly fits. We had been warned that some local contractors have a unique interpretation of ASAP – "After September, April Possibly."

At this point we don't know how long we'll be keeping our home at Los Poblanos. It has been a happy home, great for entertaining, and the kids love it. It is a peaceful place and provides a showcase for our antiques and paintings. Except for a needed remodel of the twenty year-old kitchen, we are done with any major projects. But it is a lot of work and expense to maintain. In a few years, if we find a small place in a secure community, we may move. Sarah and I love to collaborate on fixing up houses.

Health

The physical dimension of life has long been important to me. I was a chubby kid who would routinely make a tour of the kitchen cupboards after school. When I was about ten, my mother bought me a book on calories. What a horror story that was. Everything I liked was in the high calorie column. Even nuts and cheese!

When I got braces in the 7th grade, for two years I could not eat sweets, which had been a staple of my diet. The pounds melted off in time for high school and helped me make several varsity teams. After a fling at freshmen tennis at Stanford, I kept physically active, but not in an organized way. That changed when I went to Army Basic Training after graduation from college. At Fort Ord, a Stanford football player and I tied for top overall physical performance among our company of 200. Then began my yo-yo years. Under the heavy demands of grad school I slid back to an all-time high of just under 200 pounds (up from 170 in the Army). A tennis buddy warned that I was risking being arrested for "carrying concealed sandwiches." That next summer I dropped 30 pounds with heavy aerobics and portion control. Since then I have kept to the 180 to 185 range with a consistent exercise program of an hour or so each morning (leading to a 4:45 a.m. alarm setting during the work week). Vanity and good health are parts of the motivation for this dedication, but I have found the biggest benefit to be that fitness contributes vitally to mental peace.

It was tough to stop smoking, due in part to peer pressure. In the 1960's, most guys in the bank smoked, and they helped frustrate my attempts to stop by goading me to have another. Then I had a job transfer to Wells Fargo's East Palo Alto branch. No one there knew I smoked, so at the first coffee break with others around me lighting up, I surprised myself by spontaneously declaring "No thanks, I don't smoke." Now I had to live up to that statement. That "cold turkey" moment was 45 years ago. At times, though, I still miss it.

My health has been excellent throughout adulthood. Several times I went over five years without missing a day of work. Then, in February, 1999, on the eve of joining Tuition Plan, I had the incident described in the email below:

TO: TUITION PLAN BOARD OF DIRECTORS
FROM: DOUGLAS BROWN, PRESIDENT & CEO – ELECT

I want you to be informed of the events of my week. Once my appointment at Tuition Plan was set, I decided to replace my term insurance coverage from Talbot with a new policy. As I am a bit of a fitness fanatic, I usually gloat about the results of physical exams. This time, though, my EKG showed a small irregularity, despite an Olympian performance on the treadmill (gloat) with no pain or discomfort whatever. To run down the source of the anomaly (or to dismiss it as a "false positive"), I had an echocardiogram on Wednesday. This exam confirmed an irregularity, and an angiogram on Friday pinpointed the source as a small blockage in one of my coronary arteries. Unfortunately, it is lodged at a fork in the arteries which makes routine angioplasty unsuitable.

I could decide to do nothing, as I feel no symptoms at all and have been continuing my workouts unaffected. The doctors tell me, though, that my sense of well-being is due to the collateral arteries having grown so strong that my weakness has been masked. They say I run the risk of the blockage breaking free and doing permanent damage to the heart muscle. A bypass appears to be a very good and permanent solution, so I am going in for the "grand opening" on Tuesday. The docs predict a recovery period of two to four weeks of gradually increasing activity permitted, after which I should be 100%.

I wanted to disclose my situation fully, even though I don't officially come on board until April 1st. I can assure you that I am as surprised as you must be. I certainly understand if some of you may feel that you are getting damaged merchandise, but I am fully committed to doing the job for you at Tuition Plan. I'll come back fit as a fiddle -- I may even look like one.

I did indeed recover quickly from the bypass surgery. Within two months, I was back to my usual levels on the stairmaster, bike, and treadmill. Then came a surprise. We were enjoying a delightful weekend visit with Jane Scribner's family at her parents' ranch. It is located in the San Luis Valley of Colorado at about 8,000 foot altitude, aside a picturesque stream among majestic mountains. On a routine hike up the stream, I found I couldn't catch my breath. The terrain and the pace were easy; others of ordinary fitness who had just come from homes at low altitude were having no trouble; but I, with all my aerobics and living at 5,000 feet, had hit a wall.

Upon return to Albuquerque, I had a pulmonary test which revealed that my overall lung capacity was about 20% below normal, compared to about 25% above on tests previous to the surgery. A neurological exam pinpointed the problem – that my phrenic nerve had apparently been damaged during my operation. This nerve commands the diaphragm muscle on the left side to force the expansion and contraction of the left lung. For the most part, my left lung had stopped functioning, and one cannot regenerate phrenic nerve tissue. From consultation with experts at Johns Hopkins and from my own research, I learned that this problem occurs when coolant applied to the heart muscle to preserve its function during open-heart surgery damages adjacent nerve tissue. About 14% of patients who undergo this surgery emerge with some degree of nerve impairment, but as the average age of such patients is 74, and they aren't usually hiking in the Rockies, it usually goes unnoticed.

I believe my heart surgeon may have noticed it, though, as in a follow-up exam shortly after my operation, he kept asking pointedly, "Are you <u>sure</u> you're feeling OK?" I had not been apprised of the risk of loss of lung function, and some friends thought I should pursue a malpractice claim. However, even if I had been told of the risk, I know I would have gone ahead, and I know the doctors did their best. I remain grateful for all the health that I do enjoy, and I am especially grateful to Northwestern Mutual agent Bill Ebel and to the anonymous clerk in Milwaukee who noticed the anomaly upon reading my EKG.

I also had some mental/emotional setbacks along the way. 1969 was such a devastating year for me: going to my beloved brother's funeral three days after being Best Man at his wedding, enduring a divorce, and dealing with Kenny's autism. At the end of my life, I hope I can still say that 1969 was the worst year of my life, as I never wish to experience its equal. Although I was coping reasonably well superficially, I began to have periodic dizzy spells. One of my customers was a leading psychologist, Dr. Glaser, and his counseling helped greatly to get me through that dark period.

Another rough patch occurred a few years later in 1974. I had every reason to feel at the top of my game with a happy marriage, a pleasant home in Mill Valley, and good career progress. Yet something was clearly wrong, as my dizzy spells had returned. About a year of visits to Dr. Cartwright, a skilled psychiatrist, helped me to discover the apparent source of my distress. I had never been able to feel I had won my father's approval. Every time I approached him about some achievement of mine, he would respond in a way that would seem to me to qualify or belittle the achievement. I am sure that wasn't his intent, but the effect was undeniable. If I was tops in a class, invariably he would say, "How many were in the class?" When I achieved a personal best in the high jump at a high school meet, it was "What's the school record?"

I resolved that I would avoid these letdowns by simply not telling Dad about my achievements. When shortly thereafter I was promoted to Vice President at Wells Fargo, I kept it to myself. A few months later, Dad called with true elation in his voice, "I understand you were promoted to Vice President. That's terrific." Never have I felt such a sea change. Again and again, the same pattern was repeated. In fact, such a balance shift occurred that he started coming to me for approval (which I readily gave).

Progress of a different sort came from two programs sponsored by Wells Fargo. The first was a seminar on listening. As the program emphasized, "Listen to the music as well as the words." I clearly saw where I had followed the common managerial (and parental) practice of responding to the explicit message in a rational manner instead of listening also for the emotions behind the message. When an employee asks angrily, "Why wasn't I included on the memo?," the rational response that you didn't think the employee needed to get a copy is not likely to satisfy. Instead, if one responds "You seem upset, would you like to talk about it?", one is more likely to elicit information such as the employee's being disappointed at not getting a recent promotion.

The other program taught how to achieve goals through vivid fantasies that envision attainment of those goals. Sarah and I attended together. One imagines the bathroom scale coming to the desired weight or the calming influence of a still pond. I have a dozen such affirmations that I perform daily, usually in conjunction with daily prayers. I have never been a routine churchgoer, but I am deeply spiritual.

Achieving career success has always been a high-order goal for me. In fact, I believe the desire to succeed may be the single most important contributor to success. With that orientation, one is ever watchful for what works and what doesn't in others. I have found that having an absence of weaknesses is probably a more important factor in business success than exhibiting towering strengths. If someone is a "B+" in team building, counseling, public speaking, written communications, on-time delivery, analytical skills, good personal appearance, etc, that person will vault ahead of someone who is "A+" in some attribute but failing in others.

An area where I felt I was a "C+" at best was public speaking. To improve in this area, I spent years in practice with Toastmasters. Unlike some others, I was not petrified at the prospect of speaking, I was just too methodical. Toastmasters teaches useful skills, but just as important, they are a wonderfully supportive group. They are dedicated to positive reinforcement, and the improvement they stimulate is remarkable. I did find it amusing, though, when one of our new members rose to give a rambling, halting monologue that was painful to hear. Upon his conclusion, we were to comment on the performance, always leading with the positive. The silence in the room was getting embarrassing until one member commented, "George, your posture was good."

I am reminded of the scene in the Wild West town when a thoroughly disreputable character went to his final rest. A few cowpokes gathered at Boot Hill to pay their last respects. There was some shuffling of feet as they struggled to find something nice to say about this lying, thieving rascal. Finally, one of them stepped forward and said, "Some say his brother was worse!"

Regarding self improvement, perhaps the master of that practice was Benjamin Franklin. In his autobiography, he outlined his elaborate and highly disciplined program. Various desirable behaviors were assigned to each day within overriding themes for the week or month. Today might be thrift day within piety week, and so on. When Franklin related his program to a friend, that friend listened with admiration, but then suggested that Franklin might consider adding another virtue to the list – humility, as "by some you are regarded as a bit proud." The fact that Franklin related the story serves to indicate that the message hit home.

A different perspective was provided by a Spanish friend as he was showing us around Barcelona. Sarah and I refused his offer to join him in smoking cigarettes, and at mealtime we followed our usual practice of moderating our intake of food and beverages. Javier then turned to us and said with a twinkle, "We Spaniards have an expression for people like you – we call it 'Fear of Living'."

A comment about aging. The physical effects are uneven. Back pain took me out of tennis in my early fifties, and ankle pain curbed my jogging by mid-fifties. I will try not to think of Stu Sherman's rueful comment, "I'm beginning to run out of sports to give up." I used to have "good hops" with a vertical jump of about 25 inches. It's about half that amount now – which is probably just as well, as some body part would probably give way if I came down from any higher. I envy mid-60's neighbor Gig Brummell who doesn't seem to have slowed one bit from his days as an Athletic Hall of Famer at UNM. My hearing in the very highest ranges is off a bit, causing difficulty hearing female voices in crowds. It also makes turn signal indicators hard to hear, which is why elderly drivers go around all day with their turn lights blinking. Thanks to lasik in one eye, I can still read unaided with the uncorrected other one. One of the most noticeable effects of age is the slowdown in recovery time from any injury. One area that seems only slightly diminished is strength. I can still lift as much weight and do almost as many push-ups and chin-ups as ever. It is encouraging to note that there have been Olympic champs in the discus in their late 40's. But it takes rigorous maintenance to keep the old machine in tune and to ward off the weight gain that can come from a lower metabolism. I do appreciate the advice given to me by Curt Brewer on the occasion of my 70th birthday, "Remember, today you're not a year older; today you're just a day older."

Morgan Sparks struck me as a role model for gracious, constructive living in one's later years. We recently lost this eminent former head of Sandia Labs at age 91, but even in his late 80's he was as engaged and engaging as ever. A favorite moment for me was when he was serving as Chair of the Albuquerque Academy Board. He was ever attentive to the need for care in spending despite the Academy's ample endowment. He reacted to an expensive landscaping proposal to relocate some large trees with the skeptical comment, "That's what God might have done if He had the money!"

The years bring a definite decline in social stamina. At dinner recently, a pleasant young server asked if we planned to go out that evening. We had to inform her that for us, dinner was going out. However, as Sarah delights in recalling, my social stamina has long been suspect, as even early in our marriage I had a few "chin-down moments" while entertaining guests.

Growing older becomes easier if one can develop a little insouciance. One of our San Marino neighbors asked us to dinner a few weeks after we had moved there. They were an older couple, probably in their late 70's. When the hostess asked the inevitable question, "How is the move going?," we replied that we still had to deal with a mound of boxes in the garage. She then said, "Don't worry, dear, we've lived here 37 years, and we still have three boxes in the attic that we've never unpacked. Someday the children can unpack them."

My favorite story about getting on in years was told at the Grove by Art Linkletter, who is still going strong in his mid 90's. He enjoys doing performances at retirement homes where he is very popular. One day he was walking down the hallway of a nursing home when an elderly woman approached using a walker. Detecting a glimmer of recognition, Art asked, "Young lady, do you know who I am?" "No," said the woman, "but if you go to the front desk, they can tell you."

So far, my mental equipment seems to remain in fairly good working order, although there are occasional bouts of what friend Dick Borda calls "CRS Disease" (euphemistically, Can't Remember Stuff). Even Dad claimed that his mental activity had dulled a bit with age, although I told him that he was like a 300-foot redwood that might have shrunk to 280 – those of us on the ground still couldn't see the top.

Tuition Plan

After almost ten years at Talbot, in 1999 I decided to retire to an office with Steve Moise and to serve on a few boards and such. Within days I got a call from an old friend and former Stanford trustee, Kay Hanson. She asked whether I might be interested in heading up a new non-profit enterprise. A group of Southern private colleges had decided to form a program whereby families could prepay tuition, redeemable at any of the participating colleges. This effort was in part a response to the state-sponsored "529" programs that favored public universities. Obviously, the private college scheme would be successful only if enough colleges joined to provide a wide spectrum of choice. I thought it would be an interesting and worthwhile adventure, so I agreed to meet the Board. It was a good fit, and the next six years were spent building what became known as Tuition Plan Consortium. Best of all, I could do it from Albuquerque, although our location so remote from the majority of private colleges meant lots of travel.

As always, job one was to surround oneself with top talent. I had greatly admired Nancy VanDevender from our service together on the Albuquerque Academy Board. She had a Ph.D, had been a trustee of her university, Vanderbilt, and she and Pace had coped with three private college tuitions for their children – at Duke, MIT, and Northwestern. Nancy also had experience selling educational programs into the collegiate marketplace. The third member of our team was Diane Callahan, our most capable assistant. In addition to all administrative functions, she did the bookkeeping, took corporate minutes, etc, etc. Perhaps best of all, she was always in good humor. For six years, the three of us spent every working day together.

With a big boost from our board members, the list of colleges grew steadily, and as of this writing now numbers 275. Chair Wendy

Libby provided excellent leadership and former Chair Tom Kepple constantly thought of ways to spread the message. It took countless trips, endless hours in booths at educational conferences, and lots of working of leads. Colleges pay a great deal of attention to what their peers do. It was surprising to see how narrowly some schools regarded their peer group. When I approached a Catholic college with the news that Notre Dame had just joined, the arch reply was, "Well, they're not a Jesuit College." – as if Jesuit school parents had unique financial needs.

TIAA-CREF, the teachers' pension people with over $400 billion under management, was our servicer, investment manager, and in effect, our venture capital partner. Finally, we got all our required tax bills passed and cleared away other legal impediments to launch Independent 529 Plan to consumers in September, 2003. We were pleased to see *Business Week* name it as a "Best Product of the Year".

Perhaps the biggest challenge was getting our tax bills through Congress. It took three years of lobbying with more than 20 trips to Washington, D.C. before success was finally achieved. A veteran lobbyist likened getting a bill passed to staying aboard a boat while passing through the rapids. At one point our bill had such widespread support in the Senate that our bi-partisan sponsors decided to place it on a "consent agenda." That is a process whereby a universally popular resolution (Happy Mother's Day!) can bypass committees and proceed to a floor vote if there are no nay votes. Our measure failed, as it attracted one very surprising "nay" - from a Senator who had previously expressed support for it. It turned out that he was upset with one of our bill sponsors for opposition to some law enforcement bill that he had sponsored earlier. It was payback time, and we were the ones who had to pay. Two years later we finally succeeded in gaining passage, thanks to great stewardship by Senator Bingaman's Chief of Staff, Stephen Ward.

A disappointment was the lack of acceptance of Tuition Plan by the Ivy League colleges. Princeton joined, thanks to the influence of our Board member Dick Spies, and we were able to land Chicago, Duke, Johns Hopkins, MIT, Stanford, Vanderbilt, and Washington U, plus most of the fine liberal arts colleges. But the Ivies felt they didn't need us. In time, though, I am confident that their alumni and parent bodies will let them know that they are in need of this tax-free way to prepay private college tuition.

After getting the program well-launched, I gave nine months notice that I wanted to retire. The Board found a most worthy successor in Ms. Nancy Farmer, who subsequently relocated the operation to her hometown of St. Louis. An irony is that Nancy's previous job was that of Missouri State Treasurer. By the time of my retirement party in October, 2005, I had already decided to take on the job of New Mexico State Treasurer. Nancy Farmer added a delightful touch to the evening by giving me a DVD of the movie "Trading Places," which was already a favorite of mine and most appropriate for the occasion. The highlight of the event was when the "Retirement Fairy Godmother" made an appearance. In gauzy gown complete with halo and wand, she swooped in to present me with my "retirement report card," displaying a big "F." No one could have pulled that off better than Nancy VanDevender.

Leaving a job graciously creates an impression that is out of all proportion to whatever may have transpired on the job. A gracious departure amplifies achievements and mitigates shortcomings. I liken it to a plane flight. When a passenger is asked how was the flight, all but the severest bouts of turbulence are overcome by a smooth landing.

Politics

I've never been a highly political person. In fact, I deplore party politics with all its polarizing and demonizing. I was pleased to read recently that George Washington was disappointed to see the nation's body politic divide into political parties. I also resist the notion that the voting public is so stupid or naive as to believe their elected officials need to pose as perfect people and that voters cannot understand the nuances in public issues.

I am a registered Republican with a largely independent voting record. Right wing types call us "RINO's" – Republicans in Name Only. In fact, for over ten years I have headed the Bingaman Circle, the statewide support group for Democrat Senator Jeff Bingaman. Jeff is a graduate of Harvard and Stanford Law, former State Attorney General, and now fifth term Senator. We are indeed fortunate to have such a qualified, hardworking Senator. I have to remind my harder line Republican friends that New Mexico is first in the nation in the ratio of Federal spending received vs. Federal tax dollars collected. We cannot risk upsetting this favorable "balance of payments" by betting on only one side of the political aisle.

Among the college crowd I dealt with at Tuition Plan, though, I had to keep my Republican affiliation under deep cover. There was a near-universal rejection of conservatism and generally of capitalism. In most circles, tales of success in business would bring admiration, or at least benign acceptance. In collegiate circles, success in business is regarded as *prima facie* evidence that you are a cheat and a rogue. These inclinations led to my abandoning an idea that I tried to import from my marketing experience. I proposed giving incentives to members of our consortium who were successful in referring other colleges. The prize was to be a week's vacation at one of several vacation homes that were donated by two Board members and me. This offer was widely viewed as inappropriate in the belief that one shouldn't benefit from doing a good deed. While laudable in some respects, I believe that naiveté about the "real world" can have the perverse effect of making some academics blind to conflicts of interest that most business people would recognize - the student loan scandal being the latest manifestation.

An insight into the parallel universe known as government came a few years later when I joined the boards of New Mexico's public employees and educators pension funds. With over $20 billion invested but billions more in eventual pension obligations, I asked about our strategy for becoming fully funded. A veteran board member pulled me aside to enlighten me that they strive to move in that direction but that it was unwise ever to become fully funded. He said that as government pensions approach full funding, legislators invariably vote in greater benefits, plunging the funds back into deficit.

A variation of this theme of governmental practices came in response to a suggestion I made while on the Cal Water Board to CEO Pete Nelson. Periodically, towns that we serve will consider taking over our franchises and converting them to municipal systems, despite a consistent record of poorer and more expensive service resulting. My thought was that we should add to the argument against public takeover by highlighting the considerable capital needs that will be required for future maintenance and for meeting ever-more-stringent water quality standards. Pete smiled and said that municipalities rarely recognize such costs. They just let things go and then turn to the state government for bail-out when the systems are on the verge of collapse.

Serving on the Salamanca Home Owners Association Board provided government experience of another kind. An HOA is partly a board of owners, partly a social club, and partly a small governmental unit with real enforcement powers. Always a balance is needed between doing maintenance and improvements and keeping expenses down, and between keeping dues low yet minimizing periodic assessments. Beyond the usual concerns of speeding traffic, loud parties, and barking dogs, there was the occasional bizarre element. Of the 87 homes in the association, two or three generated most of the complaints. One of the troublesome types was a psychiatrist who one day went off to a conference in Southern California. Upon his return to his wife and three daughters, he announced that he had met "his soul mate" at the conference and planned to have her move in with the family in a polygamous relationship. The wife booted him out of the house; whereupon our amorous neighbor left for California to move in with said soul mate, only to find that she had already found another soul mate of her own.

The most strident complaint was from a homeowner who insisted that the speed bump outside his home was so high that the impact of cars going over was a seismic event that caused cracks in his home, a structure which was set back about 60 feet from the road. I decided to run a test to measure the relative impact of the speed bumps in our neighborhood. Elliott and Joe agreed to be the judges. They donned blindfolds and rode in the back seat of my car while I set the cruise control at the neighborhood speed limit of 20 mph. Three times we made the circuit of the nine speed bumps while I recorded the subjective impact ratings on a one-to-ten scale as reported by my back seat judges. The speed bump in question registered right in the middle of the pack, which served to settle the issue.

One innovation that I instituted while serving as HOA president worked especially well. Much of the rule violation was caused by teenagers, especially fast driving, loud parties, and occasional graffiti. Who better to help diagnose the causes of the problems and suggest the appropriate remedies but a fellow teenager? Thus began the practice of adding a teenager to our board. This tactic provided us with valuable advice and provided the young board member with valuable experience.

Lobbyists are among the most consistently maligned groups in our society, as all one ever hears about them is that they are overpaid and wheedle influence through financial and other favors. In fact, their name derives from their 19th Century practice of button-holing and plying with drinks members of Congress in the lobby of Washington's Willard Hotel. I have found lobbyists to be an impressive group without whom government could not function. At the New Mexico state level, legislators must cope with up to 2,000 bills presented during a 30 or 60 day legislative session. With only a token staff member or two to help them understand the issues and provisions, lawmakers need lobbyists to apprise them on such matters as the impact of a proposed bill on dairy farmers or chiropractors. As in any field of human endeavor, some practitioners do cross ethical lines, and there can be abuses in lobbyist firms becoming havens for former state officials. However, I prefer someone knowledgeable to someone who is ignorant, and I feel it is up to me to sort out their biases. As a practical matter, New Mexico state government would grind to a halt without the enlightenment provided by the likes of Tom Horan, Dick Minzner, and Richard Romero.

Nancy VanDevender as "Retirement Fairy Godmother" – 2005

*With Haukinsons and Gills at Hal's installation
as neurosurgeons' president – 1990*

SeniorDiscounts.com

Shortly after I turned 60, we were going to the movies with our friends, John and Terri Salazar, when I realized I was now eligible for the theater's "senior discount." Instead of $8.50, I could get in for $4.50! Over the years, I had seen such signs posted at various establishments, and I wondered where I could find a directory for senior discounts. AARP had a collection of discounts they sponsor at some large national chains, but nothing at the local level. Upon finding that there were no private or public sources of reference, I decided to create one. A web-based service was the only practical medium, one that can enable the database to be kept current. Thus was born SeniorDiscounts.com. I became Chairman and Chief Geezer of a company pledged to help seniors "Find the Gold in the Golden Years."

Joining the enterprise as President and CEO was David Smidt, a real go-getter who had been an Academy classmate of Elliott's and who had helped Sarah build her Gold Street Caffé. Dave got the company fully operational in no time. The concept proved to be unique and highly popular with seniors. Even wealthy seniors who may not need to be attentive to bargains greatly appreciate the special attention.

Acquiring data from national firms was easy. The challenge became acquiring data from the millions of local ones. Here, the seniors came to our rescue. Grateful for our making the service available, many seniors volunteered to scout for senior discounts in their areas. One senior made a three-week trip around the mid-Atlantic coastal area and contributed almost 300 new entries for us. We telephone each establishment to verify the accuracy of the data before posting it. Our corps of senior volunteers has also been attentive to correcting and updating our files.

The service asks a user to indicate a city and then to specify the type of business from a list of categories. The results are displayed in alphabetical order and include the specifics of the discount and the firm's location, phone number, and a link to a map to find the location. All this has been for free, but we have begun migrating to a membership model. The industry precedent of free services makes it difficult to create revenue unless one has a commanding presence in the business sector – which we believe we have now acquired. The enterprise should become modestly profitable this year, a feat that only about 1% of Internet companies ever achieve.

In any event, we are proud to have created a service that lists over 150,000 discounts and that attracts over a million unique visitors per year. In 2005, Dave and I were pleased to attend the national conference of the American Society on Aging. In front of 7,000 attendees, SeniorDiscounts.com was judged to be the outstanding small business in America serving the needs of senior citizens.

Volunteering

A great source of satisfaction to me has been service as a volunteer. I had good parental examples, and Hillsborough School encouraged community service, as did the Boy Scouts. Sarah has been an active volunteer at every stage of her life.

Stanford fundraising provided a ladder of leadership experiences for me. Currently, I am serving my ninth national chairmanship for Stanford, including two stints as head of their annual fund. I am proud of 45 years of unbroken service to the school in addition to selection as a member of Stanford's Board of Trustees. A highlight was being awarded the "Gold Spike," the University's highest fundraising honor. However, the peak moment was two years later when I had the honor of presenting to my father his Gold Spike, thereby becoming Stanford's first two-generation honorees.

At about the same time I was appointed to the Stanford Board, Dallas friend Jim Sowell was appointed to the Texas Tech Board of Regents. As the two schools were scheduled to meet in the first round of the upcoming NCAA baseball playoffs, Jim proposed a wager – that the loser would have to wear the winner's sweatshirt to his first board meeting. After agreeing, I belatedly looked up the team records. To my dismay, I saw where Stanford had squeaked into the tournament while Texas Tech was a #2 ranked national powerhouse. Somehow, though, in extra innings, Stanford pulled off an upset. A prized photo shows Jim wearing a Stanford sweatshirt and a sheepish grin, surrounded by the other Tech Regents with their backs turned.

My commitment to higher education extended to our adopted school, the University of New Mexico, where I served as chair of several committees and boards until my selection as a Regent of the University. All the while, Sarah was serving as Trustee of her Mount Vernon College.

On the secondary school level, I was pleased to serve as first a trustee and then Chair of the board at Crystal Springs Uplands School in Hillsborough. My predecessor, Andy Berwick, was such a competent leader, truly a hard act to follow. Upon moving to Albuquerque, I became a trustee at Albuquerque Academy where I served for 15 years including a term as president. Sarah and I were delighted when the school decided to honor our service and philanthropy by naming one of the principal campus buildings, "Brown Hall."

Honoring individuals by naming things after them has a curious history, fraught with unintended consequences. One of history's greatest leaders is now remembered principally in "Caesar" salad, and even that distinction is erroneous, as this salad was actually named after its creator, Mexican chef, Cesar Gardini. At the other end of the scale, an obscure Italian bookkeeper/navigator, Amerigo Vespucci, was honored with the naming of the entire New World. The Earl of Sandwich may have been satisfied with his legacy, but I am less sure whether British inventor, Sir Thomas Crapper was. I remember a radio interview late in his life with celebrated war hero, Admiral Chester Nimitz. He was lamenting the deteriorating condition of the Nimitz Freeway, "All those accidents, all those delays – they should have named it the Tojo Freeway!" Research doctors probably suffer the cruelest blow. For their glorious work, unlocking the secrets of disease for the benefit of all humanity, their usual reward is to have the disease named after them (Alzheimer's, Parkinson's, etc). Counter-balancing such inequities is an occasional incredible windfall. In the early 18th century, The Collegiate School in Connecticut was in dire financial condition. A dubious character, who had made a good deal of money in illegal profiteering while employed at the East India Company, offered to help - with the stipulation that the school would be renamed in his honor. School officials agreed, but then learned that the gift was to be a bequest. Patiently, they waited, and in due time learned that the school was indeed a beneficiary of his estate, to the tune of $5,000 worth of books and other goods. For this modest commitment, their benefactor will forever be honored in Elihu Yale University.

A troubling volunteer moment came while serving at Crystal Springs Uplands School. A fellow trustee's daughter was applying to colleges. The process at that time was for teachers' recommendations to be given to the student in a sealed envelope that the student was not to open but to attach to the application materials for submission to colleges. The father/trustee came storming into a trustees meeting demanding that his daughter's recommendations be redone. The family had ignored the rules, opened the letter, and saw that the student had received mixed reviews in the recommendations. I happened to have first-hand exposure to the daughter's behavior during a recent tennis tournament. I had filled in for her non-playing father, and we had gotten to the finals of the tournament. She was a skilled player, but given to fits of racket-throwing and other manifestations of poor sportsmanship. After one last bout of profanity, I warned her that upon the next outburst we would forfeit the match. When we finally lost the match in a close contest, she was sullen all the way home. From that incident, it was easy to understand how she had earned guarded reviews. And from her parents' failure to observe the rules and their subsequent outrage, it was clear that the apple had not fallen far from the tree. Upon receiving an ultimatum from this trustee to change the record, we accepted his resignation from the Board.

That same Board was the scene of a very revealing exercise. The school had become quite selective and accepted only one of every six applicants. Some of the trustees were questioning why particular applicants were not offered admission. As it was difficult to communicate all the nuances and trade-offs involved in the selection process, I set aside a trustees meeting for a mock admissions committee. Six hypothetical applications were presented, but we could only admit one. There was an Asian boy with high intellectual qualifications but no sports or community involvement; an African American girl with good, but not great all around achievement; a middle-ranking boy who was a top-ranked tennis player; another middling profile who was from a very wealthy local family; and similar profiles from a sibling of a current student and a child of a faculty member. There was a wide variance in the candidates recommended by the participating group which gave way to heated discussion. This immersion in the difficulty of the decisions served to quiet future complaints about declined applicants.

Crystal Springs Uplands School carried a mortgage debt of $400,000. At 9% interest, this obligation was burdensome, especially since non-profits cannot enjoy the offset of tax deductibility. Extinguishing this debt was a desirable goal, but our consultants told us that debt-extinguishment campaigns do poorly. I devised a unique approach. We launched a "Burn the Mortgage" campaign with the kick-off party featuring a melodrama depicting a pig-tailed girl threatened with eviction by a sinister, thin-mustached, cloak-wearing banker. This theme was echoed in a cartoon on campaign stationery. In just nine months the required funds were in hand, whereupon we had a ceremonial burning of the mortgage with the Hillsborough Fire Department in attendance. The villain slinked away, uttering the immortal phrase, "Curses! Foiled Again!" The Council for Advancement and Support of Education (CASE) favored me and the school with an award for the nation's best secondary school campaign of the year. A few years later, CASE gave me their national award to recognize my service to Stanford. I am told that I am the only person to have received their honors at both the secondary school and collegiate levels.

Volunteer activities have provided some worthy challenges. Stanford's Class of 1947 was a tough nut to crack. Many of them were war veterans with families while attending the school and didn't get as caught up in school spirit as their younger cohort. One evening I was working the phones, trying to squeeze some contributions out of a batch of non-givers. One particular guy had excuse after excuse, to which I did my best to give answer after answer. Finally, he said, "You still haven't given me a good reason to donate." I then said, "It's getting late. My coffee's gotten cold. I have this cow bell on my desk to ring whenever we get a donation, and I haven't rung it in almost an hour. Won't you please let me ring my cowbell?" He said, "I don't believe this – how much will it take to let you ring your damn bell?" "$20," I responded. He finally gave in.

Perhaps the best description of fellows like that one was given by Stanford Development head, John Ford, "He had deep pockets, but, unfortunately, he also had short arms."

My most satisfying Stanford fundraising occasion was as co-chair with Barbara Hart of our 45th reunion of the Class of '59. We gathered a superb team, attracted record attendance, and blew the doors off the financial goal. That goal started at $6M, and then moved to $10M (an all-time record for our class). Our class giving total then surged past the all-time 45th reunion mark before roosting at $20.4M, which was 20% more than any Stanford class during any reunion year.

An instructive fundraising incident occurred while I was President of the Board of the Pasadena Mental Health Association. This organization ran a valuable suicide prevention hot line on a budget of only $75,000 per year. Our most significant private benefactor was a woman who gave us $10,000 each year around Christmas. That year, the most welcome check arrived on December 15. Then, a week later, came another $10,000 check from her. Our executive director wanted to deposit it and move on. I was concerned that it might have been an unintended duplicate and that we risked disaffecting our major donor if such was the case. When I called the woman, she indeed did say, "Oh my, did I send two checks?" I offered to return the second check, but she said she so appreciated our honesty that she would let us keep it and hoped to be able to increase her support in the future.

On the social service front, I have served on over 40 different boards, including 20 board presidencies. These experiences have been a source of immense personal satisfaction and have served to broaden my perspective and my circle of acquaintances within the community.

A poignant example of a new perspective came from my service on the Big Brothers Board in San Francisco. We were discussing potential Big Brother candidates. A particular candidate was very forthcoming on his application about his family relationships, admitting that he did not have a good relationship with his mother. At that point an African American board member spoke up and said, "He doesn't like his mama? What kind of a sick guy is that!" This reaction helped me to appreciate the sacred position of mothers in black families where the father has so often abandoned them.

Sarah's and my service to Albuquerque's local food bank yielded another valuable insight. Our boys had always cherished the occasions when winter storms gave rise to "snow days" when school was cancelled. We learned that for families in poverty, these days were dreaded, as school meals were often the only ones their children had.

Another pivotal moment in volunteerism came from my service on the board of the Exploratorium Museum in San Francisco. Dick Cooley had passed the buck to me to volunteer for their board. As usual, I became head of their fundraising. I then recruited a dream team of bright energetic friends to join me, including Mike Painter (noted landscape architect), Jim Robertson (law partner and later judge), and Van Kasper (who started a successful securities firm). Van later served 20 years as Board Chair of the Exploratorium. Together, in two years we ramped up annual fundraising from $200,000 per year to about $700,000. The museum's founder and CEO and stellar human being, Frank Oppenheimer, was delighted. But in the meantime, Frank had escalated spending to absorb every nickel and then some of the new resources. I then called for a dinner meeting with Frank. I told him that I was going to increase my gift from $1,000 to $5,000 that year. Frank was understandably pleased. I then said that there was a condition, though – that it was to be the start of an endowment of permanent funds for the institution. I can still hear Frank's protests, which dissolved into tears before the evening was over. But I stood my ground, as I told him that I could not maintain the enthusiasm of my team if we felt we were just shoveling sand against the tide. Frank finally agreed to my terms, and I am most pleased to see that the seed that I planted has grown to an endowment of $18 million today, thanks to Van's excellent leadership.

It is well that all of us should come to know a bit about Frank Oppenheimer. He had been at Los Alamos with his brother J. Robert, and together they were among the physicists caught in the bombastic web spun by Senator Joseph McCarthy. Stripped of his security clearances and academic privileges, Frank and his family went into self-imposed exile in the desolate altiplano of Colorado where they became sheepherders. When Frank became critical of the primitive level of scientific education at his son's local high school, he began to volunteer his services as a science teacher. Several years later, the secondary school world was astonished to see a national high school science competition won by a heretofore unknown school from Alamosa, Colorado.

Frank then proceeded to relocate to San Francisco to found the Exploratorium, a unique form of science museum. Visitors perform their own science experiments and experience the power and majesty of science first hand. As of this writing, over 100 museums worldwide have been patterned after Frank's model.

There were several other memorable moments at the Exploratorium. One day Frank called me at the office to say, "Come quick – the founder of Polaroid, Edwin Land, is here visiting the museum." Dr. Land was one of America's first billionaires. He was intrigued by Frank's exhibits and offered fascinating commentary on some of the optical effects. He left without further comment or the opportunity for a substantive conversation. Then a few weeks later, unsolicited came a gift from him of $60,000.

The museum was one of the city's tourist attractions and thereby rated an allocation of funds from San Francisco's hotel tax. Frank asked me to join him to make the annual pitch to the Mayor. We were ushered into his enormous office. Behind a large desk flanked by flags was handsome, welcoming Mayor George Moscone. He had just one question for us, "What percentage of your budget is spent on payroll?" For a moment I almost gave in to my corporate habit of minimizing the amount. Then, in mid-thought, I remembered that politicians care more about jobs and voters than efficiency. I was able to assure him that over 70% of our budget went to payroll, a fact that pleased him and helped lead to a renewal of our tax allocation. It was such a tragedy when just a few months later, Mayor Moscone was murdered in that very office by a deranged former City Councilman.

Participation in non-profit leadership provides frequent opportunities for public speaking. Family friend Parmer Fuller, who served as president of a number of Bay Area non-profits, was an excellent speaker whose wicked sense of humor made him a sought-after emcee. A memorable incident came at a large community banquet where he was going through the tedious drill of introducing a number of elected officials, each standing for applause. Finally, Parmer concluded by asking, "Is there anyone else who needs to be recognized to make a living?" Even the politicos seemed to enjoy it.

I was pleased one time to provide Parmer with a merry moment. I called to invite him to lunch to discuss some Exploratorium matter. He responded that he was unavailable on the date offered and then added, "And I've waited all my life to be able to give this excuse – I can't because I'm having my portrait painted" (as outgoing President of the Bohemian Club).

My most challenging speaking engagement arose on January 16, 1991. I was Chair of Albuquerque's United Way campaign and had scheduled that date to celebrate our record-breaking year with over 400 volunteers and agency executives. Then, just a few days before our event, President George H. W. Bush announced that very date and time as the ultimatum for Iraq to withdraw its troops from Kuwait. He scheduled a televised speech to the American people at the time of our long-scheduled event.

We decided to proceed with our gathering and arranged for giant screens for the group to hear the President. After he declared that the Gulf War had begun, I switched off the broadcast and called for a minute of silent prayer. As the group bowed their heads, I signaled for Keith Lancaster's A Cappella singers to mount the stage quietly. The interval of silence was then broken by their stirring rendition of the *Star Spangled Banner*. If there was a dry eye in the house, it certainly was not mine.

Non-profits also present a fertile field for entrepreneurial initiative. Fellow United Way director Ray Ziler and I were appalled to find that in 1996, we were the only two United Way donors in Albuquerque giving at the $10,000 level. With the guidance, commitment, and energy of staffer Christie Bybee, we resolved to create a robust chapter of the de Tocqueville Society, the recognition category for gifts at that level. Thanks to excellent subsequent leadership, Albuquerque has gone from "worst to first" among cities our size with over 400 now giving at the $10,000 level. It was a special moment to be able to share with Ray the United Way's Arthur Spiegel Lifetime Achievement Award.

The Albuquerque Community Foundation has played a vital role in meeting community needs. In a town that has spawned no major corporations, there is a paucity of private capital. (With some anguish, we note that Microsoft was founded here and flourished for seven years before fleeing to Seattle for adequate legal and banking services.) The Community Foundation, under the exceptional Board leadership of Dr. Barry Ramo and now Victor Chavez, helps to fill this void of capital. During my nine years on the Board, the team was able to triple the endowment to almost $60 million. I was honored to serve a term as Board President and to be the 2007 recipient of their Founder's Award to recognize my service to the organization.

At Stanford I had been selected as a trustee of the foundation for the Graduate School of Business. This designation may sound prestigious, but in fact we were stewards of a fund of just over $1 million. It had been founded at the request of a wealthy prospect who had claimed he refused to donate to Stanford out of dissatisfaction with the school's then-lagging investment performance. After much negotiation with the University's Board of Trustees, the Business School was allowed to start its own foundation, advised by a committee of GSB alums who were leaders in the investment community. Then the wealthy donor prospect stiffed us. The orphaned little fund languished while the Board met quarterly to second-guess the investment experts. When I was asked to take over as chair, I agreed to do so on the express condition that we would initiate fundraising. After getting buy-in from the Dean and key Board members, I announced our new direction at the next meeting. Gesturing towards a row of silver loving cups behind me, I acknowledged that for some, "this was not the horse they rode in on" and that they were free to leave with our gratitude if not disposed to give and raise funds. Three board members did resign, paving the way for three energetic replacements, including Chuck Schwab. The other major step was to establish a specific purpose for the distribution of income from the fund. We determined that funding student fellowships would address a compelling need. The response was immediate, and when I turned over the reins two years later, our fund had quadrupled to over four million. Twenty-five years later, that fund has grown to $135 million and provides most of the scholarship needs of the school, as well as being a discretionary fund to address such needs as providing bridge financing until funds are raised to pay for a planned new campus.

Fundraising is also friend-raising. Many of our fondest friendships have come from involvement in supporting worthwhile community endeavors. Diane and Don Chalmers have been behind nearly every good cause in Albuquerque, as have Alice and Trevor Loy and Dick and Eleanor Brenner in Santa Fe. Ken and Cindy Johns have not only been very generous financially, but unflinchingly stepped into the breach for a troubled relative and raised their two daughters as their own. And our friendship with the Hankinsons and Moises has acquired new dimensions through involvement in fundraising. We are also fortunate to have corporate leaders who are willing to give so generously of their time and skill, such as John Ackerman, Jim Hinton, Larry and Dorothy Rainosek, Duffy Swan, and Larry Willard. From my Stanford GSB class, treasured fundraising teammates include Frank Countner, Bob Gee, John Packard, Bill Preston and Fred Rehmus. And all of us are grateful to our globe-trotting classmate who has worked tirelessly to help the school, Edo Vortakien.

Fundraising staffers become valued partners when one is heavily engaged in this endeavor. Laura Bass and Randy Royster while at Albuquerque Community Foundation; Jean Coblentz, Ellen Otto, Steve Player, Chris Yates, Pat Boesch and John Ford at Stanford; Ann Haines Yaskowitz and Lynn Trojahn at ACCION; Lisa McCulloch, first at Amy Biehl High School and now at CNM; Pam Hurd-Knief at UNM; and Lori Peterkin from Senator Jeff Bingaman's campaign are but a few shining examples.

Service on the Stanford Board of Trustees kindled some wonderful relationships. President Gerhard Casper was a superb and visionary leader, and I will be ever-grateful that he cared to come to my father's memorial service. Condoleeza Rice was a study in competence and dedication. Peter Bing lurks behind every good thing done at Stanford. Isaac Stein, Bob Bass, John Friedenrich and Burt McMurtry demonstrated able and sensitive Board leadership. And it was a pleasure to see young talent flourish, such as Victor Arias, search firm executive and fellow Southwesterner, Cory Booker, the sensational Mayor of Newark, Chien Lee who faithfully makes the arduous trip from Hong Kong, and Bill Halter, the recently elected Lieutenant Governor of Arkansas.

When I joined the foundation board for the Anderson Schools of Management at UNM it was, in the words of Yogi Berra, "*déjà vu*, all over again." Their foundation did have a designated purpose, the funding of summer grants for junior faculty research projects, but it was a pass-through foundation with annual giving stuck at a paltry $70,000. When I became board chair, I insisted on an annual giving commitment from board members, plus the hiring of a "constituent development officer" dedicated to fundraising for the business school. When the school said they had no budget for such a position, several of us stepped up with "an offer they couldn't refuse," that we would guarantee to make up the difference if the new hire's productivity didn't more than justify the expenditure. With the capable leadership of Doris Rhodes, that next year annual giving rose tenfold to almost $700,000. I was pleased to be honored by the designation of a professorship in my name.

Money would help Anderson Schools, but the school was plagued with turnover at the deanship level – six deans during a ten-year period. Worse yet, most of the ex-deans remained on the faculty, often fomenting actions in opposition to their successors. Many senior faculty managed to avoid any teaching assignments on Mondays and Fridays. I got a taste of this behavior while serving as chair. The then Acting Dean surprised our board at our spring meeting by saying that summer grants for the faculty would not be necessary that year, that we could reinvest the income to build the endowment. Based on this advice we did so. Then at a social gathering in late spring, I was confronted by a junior faculty member, angry that there would be no allocations for research grants that summer. When I related the Dean's report that this support was unneeded, he said that it was typical of the Dean and his cohort that once the senior group had managed to find their own funding, they chose to ignore the needs of the rest of the faculty. We quickly reinstated the grants, and the duplicitous Acting Dean "retired" shortly thereafter.

Another start-up opportunity came at the university level at UNM. Having been exposed to a very successful "President's Club" at Stanford, I recommended that UNM give it a try. The staff indicated that such a giving club at the $2,500 level had sputtered and died a few years ago, having attracted only eight members, all of them previous loyal supporters anyway. We re-engineered the concept, establishing a $5,000 requirement with at least $2,500 to be designated to an unrestricted Presidential fund. The President then established a compelling initial purpose, the creation of small-scale freshman learning communities. It had been noted that students easily get lost among the 33,000 member student body, and their lack of engagement with the university contributed to a high drop-out rate. The revised President's Club quickly grew to over 100 members, and its annual funding of over $500,000 enabled the spread of the learning communities to most of the class and led to a subsequent material improvement in the freshman retention rate. A very satisfying post-script to this effort was to see that the state legislature subsequently agreed to provide mainstream funding for this activity, thus freeing up the President to allocate the funds to other promising initiatives. We feel especially good about serving the needs of the current UNM President, the able David Schmidly.

Service to the board at Stanford and later at UNM could hardly have been more different. Both institutions covered roughly the same ground in terms of curriculum, and while Stanford had campuses overseas, UNM had satellite branches around the state. Despite Stanford's edge in prestige, its budget was only about 25% larger.

Stanford runs so smoothly. It is the same age as UNM, but has had half the number of presidents. The changeover from President Casper to President Hennessy was a seamless internal passage from one brilliant leader to the next. The competence that is legendary among the faculty and students extends to the staff. In fact, most

Stanford staffers who I have encountered are themselves Stanford alums. Staff proposals to the Board were invariably thorough and well-presented. The Trustees were well-prepared, as nearly all of them had extensive backgrounds of previous involvement with Stanford. There were 34 trustees and five meetings per year. Occasionally, a new or controversial topic would arise, but most matters had been thoroughly pre-digested and went down easily. President Casper was present at all Board meetings, but he often turned over the gavel to Provost Condoleezza Rice. Condi was a superb leader, so intelligent and such a good communicator. It is a shame she has been dealt such a poor hand to play as Secretary of State.

Being a UNM Regent presented a crushing time burden (for the staff as well as the Regents). We met every month for 1 ½ days with substantial advance preparation required. With only seven Regents, there were only a few of us to share the work. I had served on two Stanford Trustee committees and chair of none. At UNM I served on six committees and subsidiary boards and as chair of four of them. The open meeting rules tended to make the meetings long ones, but I came to admire open meetings as a healthy practice. UNM Regent President, Jamie Koch, has been especially conscientious about strict observance of open meeting rules. As a result, UNM students are generally aware of the role of the Regents, while few Stanford students know what Stanford's Trustees do.

Stanford is sometimes accused of displaying a touch of arrogance. I remember a tee shirt for sale at the Stanford Bookstore reading, "~~Stamford, Standford, Stanferd~~, Cal." It is perhaps to be expected when one has elite credentials. As legendary St. Louis Cardinals pitcher Dizzy Dean said, "If you can do it, it ain't bragging." At least, Stanford isn't nearly as arrogant as its Ivy League peer institutions, remembering of course that Harvard regards itself to be without peer. That said, I've long admired former Harvard President Conant's self-deprecating remark that "when occasionally we uncover the spark of genius, we carefully water it."

Stanford's leadership is sensitive to avoiding a posture of superiority, but sometimes alums are less so. I was chagrined to hear this comment at the end of a business meeting in Seattle. This fellow turned to me and said, "I understand that you went to Stanford. You're the first Stanford alum I've met who hasn't worked that affiliation into the conversation in the first 30 minutes." Stanford people harbor a particular disdain for USC, dating back to alleged USC shenanigans on the football field. There is also an overlay of the dislike that many San Franciscans have for Los Angeles. At Stanford gatherings, Sarah was often asked what year she graduated from Stanford. When she would answer that she was a USC graduate, the usual jocular responses ranged from, "What are you doing here" to "and you seemed like such a nice person!" The frequent repetition of this needling became tedious for Sarah, or as she has said, "It's like I went to the University of Satan!" This dynamic has detracted from her enjoyment of Stanford events and has been troublesome to me, too.

The University of New Mexico has a daunting challenge in trying to provide quality educational and research opportunities while giving access to a horde of students with inadequate high school preparation. There is a substantial amount of remedial education required, and only 44% of entering freshmen graduate within six years. The main campus is in an urban setting with little on-campus housing. Most students split study time with work and/ or heavy family responsibilities. A majority of the student body are from minority families. UNM is one of America's leading Hispanic serving schools and a top Native American serving school. It also ranks among America's leaders in terms of percentage of students who are the first in their family's history to attend college. President Schmidly has undertaken a number of promising new initiatives to improve student success.

And these aren't the only challenges. A public university must go hat in hand to the state legislature for funding. Instead of approving an overall budget and letting Regents and administrators take it from there, the legislators get into line item approval with only the sketchiest of bases for such decisions. The state maintains full control despite the fact that as a source of university revenues, it has shrunk from a one-time majority to under 20% currently. In some states, public funding of public universities has shrunk to under 10% of the total school budgets. No wonder the wry comment that "We've gone from state-supported to state-located and now state-molested."

Serving as a UNM Regent was both satisfying and challenging. Led by Jamie Koch and Mel Eaves, fellow Regents were very conscientious, including excellent participation from Student Regent, Rosalyn Nguyen. There was a helpful Advisory Council consisting of the Student Body President, the Graduate School President, the Alumni head, the Foundation head, the head of UNM staff, and the president of the Faculty Senate.

UNM can be justly proud of many of its accomplishments. Led by the irrepressible Terry Yates, its research grants have grown to a respectable total of over $300 million annually. Terry's recent passing leaves a large void in our lives. The Law School, School of Engineering and Medical School are first-rate, especially Cheryl Willman's Cancer Center, which was recently accorded coveted "NCI" status (a year before Stanford's was!). The athletic program is well run, with decent student GPA's and graduation rates. We are proud of the women's sports program, especially with Don Flanagan's women's basketball team which has consistently been successful both on the court and in the classroom. The Steve Alford era in men's basketball is off to a promising start. The main campus is an attractive place, currently undergoing some dramatic improvements. A surprise to me was the constructive role played by UNM's four branch campuses around the state. They provide affordable local access and are an excellent feeder source for upper division students to the main campus. The role of the Gallup campus struck me as especially worthy. The 2,500 student body is about 90% Native Americans, most of whom would not otherwise have access to higher education.

As may be surmised from the tone of my comments, I am impressed by the constructive role UNM plays in our state. As loyal and devoted as I am to Stanford, UNM will continue to draw a substantial portion of my commitment to the community.

Academia is hierarchical. From my experience with hundreds of private colleges and universities in the Tuition Plan, all were aware of their rankings in various published surveys and strove mightily to move up. The ploys to do so were occasionally an ethical stretch. Some lower-ranking colleges would deny entry to students they felt were over-qualified because they feared they were being used as safety-net schools and that the likely turndowns would hurt their admissions yield ratios. One even set up a shell corporation run by the school to provide a haven of employment for unemployed graduates who would otherwise bring down that metric. Other ploys were not counting unlocated alumni to enrich gift participation rates or artificially stretching out gifts into multi-year pieces for the same purpose. Many colleges would post impressively high tuition rates and then routinely discount them by 40% or more as a marketing tactic. Speaking of college rankings, I've always wondered why the rating services ignore what I believe is probably the best measure of academic standing, especially at the graduate level. For those students accepted at several schools, where do they choose to go? There could be some distortion due to financial aid differences and personal factors, but a more valid pecking order should emerge.

Neither Stanford nor UNM engaged in unethical practices, but they were not uncommon among the mid-level and lower tiers of American academia. I found it ironic that academics regarded with great suspicion anyone from the corporate world as being ethically challenged. In my judgment, ethical practices in both fields are probably on a similar level.

A hierarchical mind-set extends to positions within the universities as well. Academically, physicists rank at the top, followed by other scientists, then engineers and mathematicians, on to liberal arts disciplines before bottoming out at physical education. As to the status of us business graduates, I believe there is significance to the color accorded business students on their hoods at graduation. Instead of the stately purple for law grads or the vivid green of medicine, business grads are relegated to a dusty brown color, whose official name is "drab." Richard Feynman tells the story of a colleague in Caltech's Physics Department whose wife ran off with another professor. A fellow physicist reacted with, "I can understand if she had run off with a bullfighter, but a chemist?" I have long subscribed to the philosophy espoused by John W. Gardner in his book *Excellence*, that it matters less what one does than how well one does it.

A longer term problem for American higher education is the trend of increases in tuition and fees that outpace growth in family incomes, year after year. The health care field recognizes this relationship as a grave national problem. Higher education generally has not. To be sure, there are periodic flurries of cost cutting and occasional salary freezes, but scant attention to an organized approach to improving productivity. Achieving productivity gains in the complex world of higher education is admittedly difficult. So, too, is it in many business settings. Yet all successful businesses establish productivity goals, appropriate metrics, and effective incentives. The incredible investment returns and fundraising success at the elite universities have enabled them to moderate their tuition growth and to offer generous financial aid packages to relieve the burdens for student families. However, without productivity gains, even these institutions may face financial pressures in times of economic downturn. And institutions without such endowment cushions are destined for financial calamity if productivity gains do not bring tuition expense growth in line with family income growth.

Sarah and I are pleased that we have been able to make significant financial contributions to our community, and in fact were recognized by the Association of Fundraising Professionals as "New Mexico's Outstanding Philanthropists of the Year." A few times, though, we have bumped into philanthropic ceilings, as described in the incidents below.

I've usually followed through on my volunteer commitments to the end, but there was one notable exception. My friend and Stanford classmate, Kay Sprinkel Grace, was the fundraising consultant for National Public Radio, and she recruited me to their board. I've long admired Kay and NPR and was pleased to accept. The Board was an impressive group, and the meetings exposed me to the inner workings of broadcast media. It also gave us the opportunity to

311

make an annual visit to the White House to meet the President. Part of the deal was an obligation to donate and/or raise $10,000 per year. Barely two years into my term on the board, one of the members from Wall Street suggested that the minimum should be raised to $15,000. Another wealthy New Yorker suggested at least $20,000. Like two rhinos rutting for a mate, these guys bid up the annual minimum to $60,000. I commented that they could probably raise that money on the way up in the elevator in their Park Avenue apartments, but that such a commitment from a New Mexican was an unrealistic expectation. When there was no retreat from their position, I and two other directors resigned from the Board.

Another exposure to what I term Manhattan's "Monopoly Money Mentality" came during Joe's graduation from NYU. We had been contributors to their annual fund at a moderate level, but decided to step up to the $5,000 bracket to honor Joe and to thank NYU for his great experience there. The dean of his school then invited us to breakfast during Joe's graduation weekend. How nice. However, our eggs suddenly cooled a bit when the dean suggested we increase our gift to $250,000!

Parenting

The disappointments of having a severely impaired child come in waves. One of the biggest of these waves came crashing down when I brought our autistic son, Kenny, to join the local Boy Scout troop in Castro Valley. My scouting experience with my brother, Kenny's namesake, had been such an enjoyable and broadening one. Upon learning of Kenny's limitations, the adult scout leadership rejected him for inclusion in the troop. I feel sure that the boys would have made the necessary allowances for Kenny, as his classmates in school always had. This decision was all about serving the convenience of the adults. I know Kenny would have treasured a scouting experience. I have tried not to let this incident turn my fond feelings towards scouting to bitterness, but I've never felt quite the same about the Boy Scouts since.

Both Elliott and Joe had brief flings with Indian Guides and Cub Scouts, but they and their friends were consumed with sports and school activities by the time they might have joined the Boy Scouts. I did enjoy a moment of Indian Guide glory with Elliott and later with Joe. The "Pinewood Derby" is an event where teams of fathers and sons build little wooden cars to be released at the top of a ramp of plywood. Cars are raced in pairs and endure successive eliminations. From the highly polished and professional look of many of the cars, it was apparent that they were entirely the creation of the dads. I felt it was important that our boys be the primary builders, so my role was restricted to making sure the wheels were round and well-lubricated. In both cases, we had the satisfaction of our ungainly kid-made cars winning. In watching the father-son teams, it was clear that the children's enthusiasm for the event was in direct proportion to the extent of their participation in building the car.

Parenting has been a joy. Also a bit of a frustration when a divorce is involved. For all practical purposes one divorces the kids, too. No matter how attentive a remote parent may be, one is not there to share the moments, good and bad. The fact that I got the chance to get it right the second time doesn't fill the gap from before. There is solace in that I feel my relationship with Becky is positive and the relationship with Kenny more distant, but positive. But I will forever feel an ache of regret.

As with any management practice, parenting is both an art and a skill. Modeling behaviors, consistency, good communication, and integrity are the pillars. Parenting is daily and it is relentless. There are few shortcuts to the expenditure of time. Always, respect should be expected from all family members. Perhaps the best measure of parenting success is in raising kids who become independent, responsible, and evolving, yet still welcome the continuing influence of their parents. Successful parenting can be one of life's most fulfilling experiences, perhaps the true consummation of a marriage.

Being a parent has a number of social benefits as well. In moving to a new community it is a source of instant rapport with new neighbors. Standing by the soccer field or baseball diamond with other parents forges an instant network, and nothing else bonds one as quickly to colleagues at work as talking about your respective families. I also feel that lessons learned in family management and in vocational management overlap and reinforce.

New Mexico Friends

The very best part of living in New Mexico has been the ability to share it with so many wonderful new friends. Steve and Beth Moise and their sons, Adam and Grant, have shared many special moments, as have Hal and Donna Hankinson and their kids, Todd and Sam.

The Moises are one of the pioneer families of New Mexico. From early days in general merchandising in Santa Rosa, their enterprise grew to be one of the state's premier cattle ranching operations. Although Steve grew up in Lubbock and then went to college and law school at the University of Colorado, he returned to New Mexico for his legal and merchant banking careers. The best legacy from Boulder was fellow Buffalo, beautiful Beth Maxwell Moise from the cornfields of Illinois. In addition to her high profile international telcom career, Beth has joined Steve in making great contributions to community leadership. Steve is the best friend I, or anyone, could ever have.

A tiny paperweight on Hal Hankinson's desk is the only indication that one is in the presence of the #1 graduate of Tulane Medical School. Nowhere in the office of this distinguished neurosurgeon is there an indication that he has served as the president of both international associations of neurosurgeons. From his intent, deliberate approach to his medical practice, one would not expect Hal to have set a new standard in the practice of courtship. While serving as a naval officer on a submarine stationed in Hawaii, he was introduced to pretty, vivacious Donna Cameron. Not content merely to sweep her off her feet, he swept her up in the air as he commandeered a private plane to fly her to a picnic at gorgeous, secluded Hana, Maui. Anybody want to compete with that?

A spectacular occasion involved Sam Hankinson. When Senator Jeff Bingaman called to ask if I could find a Cherry Blossom Princess to represent the State of New Mexico, I didn't have to look far. Who better than the lovely Samantha? After checking with Hal and Donna to make sure they were on board with the prospect of their daughter's vault into the world of semi-celebrity, I made a call to Sam at her dormitory at Vanderbilt. As usual, I hammed it up with something along the lines of, "How would you like to be a princess without having to kiss any more frogs?" Her reaction was tinged with a dash of the dubious, but she soon agreed.

A formidable assemblage of adult supervision gathered in the form of the senior Hankinsons, Moises, and Browns. When we checked into the J. W. Marriott Hotel in Washington, D.C., we found ourselves awash in a sea of satin sashes, each proclaiming the state of origin of its gorgeous bearer.

The pageant's main celebration was an elegant dinner at the Marriott Wardham Park. I don't usually remember meals as Sarah does, but the handmade sushi by top Japanese chefs was especially memorable. It soon became apparent that there was a strong linkage to the Japanese Cherry Blossom Festival and that the entire event was somewhat of a cultural exchange. The evening's showcase moment was a parade of the princesses, followed by the selection of a queen. Not surprisingly, Samantha was one of the two finalists and lost only by the spin of a wheel. Runner-up status, though, rated her a featured spot on the main float in the parade the next morning, thereby sparing her the humiliation of having to ride on "The Duck." The Duck was a hulking, gray Navy amphibious landing craft which served as the float for the rest of the princess contingent.

The weekend abounded with highlights, including a limo-driven visit to the Inn at Little Washington, one of the nation's premier dining experiences. But our fondest memory was seeing Sam aboard that float, beaming her lovely smile and waving away all the cares of the world.

I have intentionally refrained from attempting to list all our friends, as it is a risky undertaking and invariably produces egregious oversights. In addition to the many friends involved in the stories in this narrative, many others have made us feel so welcome and have so enriched our lives.

New Mexican women are strong, purposeful, and accomplished. With few exceptions they have enjoyed successful careers, often as entrepreneurs. Whether international cable and telcom executive Beth Moise, or development officers Donna Hankinson and Gale Doyel, or CEO Maria Griego Raby, or realtors Nancy Pierce, Susan Feil and Susan Anderson, or financial executive Louise Campbell, or community leader, Thelma Domenici, or nationally recognized water rights expert, Eileen Hillson, or communications consultant, Kyla Thompson, or famed designer Eleanor Brenner, they are leaders in their respective fields. Rosalind Roembke Hurley has become an accomplished artist, right alongside her late husband and New Mexico's leading landscape artist, Wilson. All of us are proud of Diane Denish, the State's first female Lieutenant Governor, Debbie Johnson, the first female chair of the international advertising agency group, and Roberta Ramo, the first female president of the American Bar Association..

We were referred to pediatrician Stan Stark even before moving to Albuquerque in 1986. Marilyn Stark practically adopted us, volunteering babysitters and calling frequently with helpful advice. Mary Ann Eaves, Kathy Pugh, Terri Salazar, Rosalie Sherman, and Malka Sutin were others who formed an instant support group for Sarah.

Stan is a world-class physician and was selected to be on the medical team from the U.S. that went to the Ukraine to assess the damage from radioactive fallout from the Chernobyl disaster. Fortunately, Stan found less health damage to children than had been feared. He also provided us with enlightenment as to the deplorable condition of medicine under the Soviet system, including his report that most of the hospitals there lacked even hot water! While shocking, that news was not entirely surprising to me, as on a visit to Russia in the 1960's, I had seen legions of women sweeping the streets with tree branches.

Stan also contributed a memorable moment to our family lore when examining our Joseph, then about eleven. Like all children,

Joseph was anxious about his eventual height. He asked Stan if he might get to be "as big as my brother." Stan grabbed the front of Joe's skivvies, peered in and said "You're getting there."

Harvey Yates delivered a classic wedding toast at his daughter's wedding. He related that at another daughter's wedding the year before, he had wished the bridal couple "all the children you can afford." Harvey said that his wife, Jan, and his daughters berated him later for having made a toast that was "much too Republican." Harvey went on to say that he was taking this opportunity to even the record by making a Democrat-oriented toast, "May you have all the children the government can afford."

An especially memorable occasion with Steve Moise was when we traveled to the Moise ranch in Eastern New Mexico. Steve's father, Joseph Moise, and two of his chums, plus Steve, Hal and I, and our three classmate sons, Grant Moise, Todd Hankinson, and Elliott all rode in a van rented for the occasion. The occasion was the annual round-up where the young male calves are branded, vaccinated and "cut." A rite of passage is for young boys to wrestle a calf into the chute that clamps them in place for these procedures. Grant, being strong and lanky, as well as experienced, quickly dispatched his calf. Todd was of slight build but managed to handle his animal after a bit of a struggle. Then came Elliott, the smallest of the three. To the surprise of all of us, he hugged the calf and gently led it to the chute. The weather bitten wranglers sitting on the fence were aghast. I heard one of them mutter, "Must have been a fag calf!" Another calf was summoned for Elliott. Another peaceful entry into the chute. The cowpokes concluded Elliott must be "some kind of calf whisperer." It never occurred to them that perhaps all their scrapes and strained muscles could have been avoided with a kinder, gentler approach. It is interesting to note that animal trainers have now found that positive reinforcement is a more effective training technique than brutal coercion.

Steve Moise and Doug at Lake Como – 2002

Sarah and Beth Moise at "Academy Awards" – 1999

Sarah's Surprises

Of course, my most enduring and best imaginable friend has been Sarah. Not only has she put up with my ventures and misadventures, she has had quite a few of her own. The surprises that continue to pop up have added so much zest to our lives. In her early fifties she announced one day that she was going out for senior women's basketball! For the next several years, she and the CanyonNets had a great run. What Sarah lacks in height she makes up in aggressiveness, especially on defense. And she is a darn good shot, which used to drive our boys crazy when she would sometimes beat them in games of "HORSE." A highlight of her basketball career was making two appearances in exhibition basketball games at halftime during UNM games at The Pit before 18,000 fans. Another was as captain of the state team that twice went to the nationals and one time reached the semi-finals. There they ran into a Chicago team with a Shaq-like center who was 6'3", almost that wide, and had a deft shooting touch.

When shoulder problems interrupted her basketball career, Sarah proposed that she and I take up marathon walking. For the next year, we trained with the "Team in Training" organization. Our long training walks on the roads and trails turned out to be a wonderful time of togetherness for us.

The climactic event was the San Diego Marathon. What a pageant it was! Twenty-one thousand runners, walkers, and wheelchair competitors gathered in groups according to their ability. To our surprise, the wheelchair contingent was released first, as they negotiate the course faster than even the elite runners. Next came the elites, a whippet-like group with a sprinkling of Kenyans, Ethiopians, and Somalis. Then the rest of us, wave on wave. Official times are recorded from a computer chip tied onto one's shoelace that measures the elapsed time between crossing the start line and the finish line. It also provides a defense against cheaters who might take shortcuts, as there are several electronic checkpoints along the way. This system was devised by Bill Bice, an Albuquerque native, when he was only 16. Subsequently, he has gone on to a very successful career in software company start-ups locally.

Officially, the race was the Rock'n Roll Marathon, and every mile or so a different rock band played. In between were squads of high school cheerleaders, plus all manner of volunteer well-wishers. An especially welcome one was a guy who offered a spray of mist from his hose at mile 18. It wasn't quite the wacky show of San Francisco's Bay to Breakers Race, but there were a number of colorful characters, such as a squad of Elvis impersonators. Our favorite, though, was a guy in a fisherman's outfit. He had fashioned a harness onto his shoulder that held a fishing rod extending several feet in front. Dangling from the line was a baggie, and inside the baggie was a Krispy Kreme doughnut. For 26 miles he chased that doughnut.

Our inspiration was Elliott. Although not a formal race competitor, he was very fit from running and hiking the steepest hills of San Francisco. As Sarah and I separated, he shuttled back and forth between us, offering encouragement and covering the better part of a marathon himself.

Proper hydration and nutrition are essential during a marathon, and mastering one's needs is an important part of marathon training. Forget your Atkins diet for the duration; you'll need carbs. Insufficient carbs may cause you to "splat," the inelegant term used to describe when a marathoner's nose suddenly becomes in close proximity to the pavement.

During a multi-hour race, there are the obvious needs for periodic relief. No one wants to stop for long, and the line at porta-potties can be frustrating. Where possible, the bushes are best. At about mile nine, I detoured into a dense clump along the roadside. Just as I was finishing, three young women appeared, and voop-voop-voop squatted naked right in front of me. Seeing me, one remarked acidly, "Don't get excited, buddy!" I responded that I was indeed excited to have three attractive women strip in front of me, and I didn't even have to take them to dinner. They enjoyed the comment to the point that one of them keeled over.

Finally, the finish line came into view. Both Sarah and I made it under the time maximum, and despite my being the oldest New Mexican competitor, my 6 hr. 37 minute time was tops among our 21-person walking team. We were greeted by Elliott and by the Gills and savored a hard-earned brew at Bryan and Becky Gill Walley's nearby home. We were also pleased to have the vicarious participation of our wonderful friends who collectively chipped in over $21,000 to benefit the Leukemia and Lymphoma Society in memory of our three siblings who have succumbed to those diseases.

Sarah's surprises extended to other family members as well. She had such a fond relationship with my dad and felt sorry for the neglect he experienced in his childhood. One day, Sarah presented him with a scrapbook of his baby pictures and news items from that era. Dad treasured this item, which Sarah titled, "Bobby's First Baby Book."

Sarah's greatest adventure (to date) has been the Gold Street Caffé. She has long been a "foodie." Foodies are folks who "live to eat," as opposed to dullards like me who "eat to live." Sarah can remember thousands of meals over the years at all kind of places. Her focus is reminiscent of a golf pro who may be a high school dropout, but can remember using a four iron from the left rough on the 14th at Sawgrass six years ago.

By the mid 1990's, none of the major coffee house chains had found Albuquerque yet, which Sarah saw as a great opportunity. Her biggest challenge was finding a suitable location. Albuquerque's commercial centers are widely scattered, and there is no cluster of upscale urban development. Sarah's friend, Patti Harrell Hoech, had an attractive gift/gallery downtown on Gold and convinced Sarah that the historic tree-lined block was the right place. Sarah chose the premises next door to Patti's which had been vacant for over five years and was in shambles. The transformation to a tony, inviting environment was remarkable. Among Sarah's inspirations was Sue

Campoy who created "Julienne's," the premier bistro in the Pasadena area. Architect Ed Fitzgerald and builder Stanley Mount did a great job. Seeing the financial commitment the build-out would take, we and the Hoechs decided first to buy the building.

After four years of study and preparation and over a year preparing the building and fixtures, Sarah opened Gold Street Caffé in September, 1996. It took a while for the enterprise and the location to get known. Meanwhile, the coffee house morphed into a full service restaurant. The downside of being Albuquerque's pioneering coffee house was that patrons expected more than biscotti and scones. Gradually, full breakfast and lunch fare came to be offered, and within a few years, dinner and wine service. Five days a week stretched into seven. A payroll of six employees grew to 26.

The business got a big boost from earning a coveted four star rating by the *Albuquerque Journal* food writer. Other awards included Best Bacon, Best Soup, and Best Place to Hang Out. Both U. S. Senators have been frequent visitors, and the Mayor held his weekly staff meetings there. Occasional celebrity sightings included Bill Murray and John Travolta. The place became a favored spot for shooting local TV commercials, and the film "Wild Hogs" had extensive footage shot there. It was also the usual venue for dating services such as "It's Just Lunch."

Staffing was ever a challenge. Beyond chefs and managers, few on the staffs of Albuquerque restaurants are professionals, committed to the restaurant business. For servers, bussers, and dishwashers it's a means of support while going to school or seeking a star turn as an actor. We were fortunate that most of the service staff did quite well, but frequent turnover was inevitable, as the staff's young lives are so unpredictable. One young male server came to Sarah just before the "lunch crunch," handed her his apron, and said "I'm leaving." She asked if he could return quickly as the lunch crowd was just building. He said "Oh no, I'm getting on the bus to San Diego now." Sarah asked if this was his idea of notice. With apparent sincerity, he said, "Yes, I'm giving you notice." He was a charter member of what we came to call the "Whatever Generation," for whom "You're welcome" has disappeared in favor of "No problem."

Another inelegant expression is when the server comes by as you are finishing your meal and asks, "Are you still working on that?" I feel like responding, "Yes, but would you please bring me a hammer and chisel so I can finish my work."

Sarah's first two chef/managers were talented, but erratic. Things settled down under the leadership of David Smidt, the former Academy classmate of Elliott's. When Dave joined me to start up SeniorDiscounts.com, Sarah attracted another excellent leader in Joaquin Garofalo. When Joaquin finally left to start his own restaurant, the talented Matt Nichols took over. All this while, Sarah spent upwards of 60 hours per week at Gold Street, working on menus, promotions, catering, bills, greeting and seating, bussing tables, laundry duty, and whatever else needed doing. With the inevitable turnover, training was constant. Also, if Sarah didn't hover, the wrong music or wrong napkins or wrong food presentation would inevitably occur. After ten years of relentless demands, and with the prospect of my retirement, Sarah sold the business in March, 2006 to Matt Nichols. This sale in many ways provided relief, but Sarah has at least one more round to go on her career.

Party Time

Sarah throws wonderful parties. In fact, one of the reasons we bought a bigger house as the boys were going off to college was so we could entertain community groups better. Large groups have gathered at our place several times a year. We were pleased to host high school graduation night parties for both boys, annual symphony recitals, and countless charitable and milestone events.

My favorite such events were her imaginative birthday parties for me. Usually, I was kept in the dark as to the details. Among memorable parties was a Boy Scout celebration where everyone showed up in neckerchiefs commissioned for the occasion. Another time, I was ushered out onto the lawn at 7 a.m. on a Sunday morning to find a group of friends awaiting in workout clothes for group calisthenics guided by a fitness instructor.

Sarah's benign deception reached new heights on the occasion of my 50th birthday. I knew there was going to be a big gathering, but I didn't know any of the specifics. As my big day drew near, I asked, "Shouldn't the carpet be cleaned?" Sarah said something vague, so I found myself cleaning the carpet. Just a few days to go and the windows hadn't been washed, so I spent hours on them. When the day finally came, several buddies met me at my office that evening and took me across the street for a drink. Emerging from the bar, I was confronted by a large bus filled with friends. Off we went for a glorious dinner at the Old House in Santa Fe. About halfway there, I realized Sarah had duped me into cleaning the house from stem to stern.

It wasn't the only surprise for me that day. When I had gone out to get the paper in the morning, there was a 4' x 8' billboard across the street. For all the neighborhood to see, it read, "Over the hill and rolling down. Today you're 50, Douglas Brown" – courtesy of Paul

Bardacke, Mel Eaves, and John Porter. Later that day, the offending billboard was transported to the front of my office building.

I haven't quite come down from the splendid celebration Sarah arranged for my recent 70th birthday. It was held at historic Los Poblanos Cultural Center, beautifully restored by Armin and Penny Rembe. For dinner we were ushered into the soaring ballroom, where three majestic refectory tables spanned the length of the room. The table settings, flowers, cuisine – all were perfection. The toasts and roasts by friends and family were touching, especially those from "the kids," Becky, Elliott, Deborah, and Joseph. It was such a joy to share the occasion with friends from the Bay Area and Southern California, as well as favorite local friends.

Among so many other special occasions, the parties surrounding Elliott's wedding to Deborah Kelson stand alone. The weekend began with a "K-Mart" party in San Francisco's Mission District, recalling Elliott's unique choice of a proposal site. We all wore outfits from K-Mart, and hosts Steve Hall and Danny Della Lana, along with the New Mexico host contingent of Eaves, Hankinsons, Moises, Pierces, Reidys, Starks, and Sutins, celebrated the occasion with K-Mart paraphernalia, Bounty paper towels, etc. Sarah's Rehearsal Dinner at the Ferry Building the following night was a spectacular Southwestern fiesta, complete with mariachis, luminarias, and all the New Mexican touches.

It was hard to top these occasions, but Laurie and Paul Kelson managed to do so with their wedding and reception at the Bohemian Club. The wedding officiant, Jed Verity, presided over a moving ceremony which fused beautifully elements of Christian and Jewish tradition. The arrangements were perfect and ever so gracious, but livened with delightful personal elements, such as the place cards being displayed with little Pez dispensers, reflecting Deb's extensive collection of these whimsical pieces. Guests entering the reception were greeted by a curtained photo booth which produced a hilarious array of poses. The music, the toasts by Paul and Laurie Kelson and by Amanda Kelson and Joseph Brown, all were perfection. Of course, the main attraction of this occasion was the incomparably lovely bride in her elegant gown. Forever, we will treasure these memories and the photos and video recordings that the Kelsons thoughtfully provided.

A warm afterglow came the following morning with a brunch hosted by Pam and Terry Elliott at their beautiful Pacific Heights home, along with Mike and Penny Gill and Richard and Susan Olness. There we were pampered by tuxedoed servers plying us with Ramos Fizzes to the accompaniment of a New Orleans jazz trio. The bridal couple then embarked on a weeklong jaunt down the California coast, through the Santa Maria wine country to Pozo and on to Los Angeles. There the Kelsons held another elegant reception at the L.A. Farm for guests who were unable to make the trip north, especially Laurie's mother, Helen "Penny" Coleman. This elegant and accomplished woman who meant so much to the family was lost to us just a few months later.

Elliott Brown and Deborah Kelson
October 28, 2006

Paul and Laurie Kelson – 2006

Best Man, Joseph

Sarah Belle Shelton and Sarah

Lucy Ross, Travis Parsons, Peggy Kappler,
Goddaughter Kate Parsons, Frank Kappler

Penny Gill with Pam and Terry Elliott

"Marathoner Sarah"

Doug Brown as Treasurer

Doug and Sarah as penguins- 2007

Doug and Pastry Chef Sarah in Manhattan – 2007

Traditions

As our society becomes increasingly cyber-connected, nomadic, and multicultural, horizons broaden and opportunities increase. But in the process, our traditions tend to fade. My parents lived in the same home for fifty-five years. Sarah's parents lived in three, but all in the same community. In my adult life I've lived in sixteen widely scattered homes, and Sarah has lived in eight.

Growing up, the holidays were celebrated in the same places and in the same way. Now, each holiday occasion is up for negotiation. Weddings and funerals have followed very traditional practices in cultures throughout the world. Until now. These days we are treated to much more customized ceremonies, which I enjoy as it affords a more personal connection with the families involved. But we do sacrifice a bit of the sanctity that traditional observances bring.

Another tradition that seems to be unraveling is the family vacation. With near-universal cell phone and email access, it is difficult to resist the temptation to stay in touch. Which means, of course, that one is never out of touch, the principal idea of a vacation. Fortunately, our families grew up in the era of true vacations, and we were able to maintain that tradition with Becky and Kenny and then with our boys. Sarah and I and the boys enjoyed vacations to various U.S. destinations, Europe, Mexico, Hawaii, and Australia. An especially memorable trip was when Mother's health took a bad turn, and she and Dad had to abandon a pending Alaskan cruise with their grandsons. As Sarah couldn't get away on short notice, the boys and I had a glorious two weeks together, cruising the Inland Passage, seeing Glacier Bay, rafting down the Kenai River, and just having a ball on the ship.

It was perhaps the loosening of traditions that led to such a tepid celebration of our nation's bi-centennial. I had anticipated a nationwide surge of enthusiasm as July 4, 1976 approached. Philadelphia was chosen to act as a focal point for our nation's festival, but they couldn't seem to get it together and the whole occasion fizzled. One would think there would be a lasting legacy from such an occasion, an inspiring monument perhaps. All I've seen are a few bi-centennial streets, none major.

We did a little better in the celebration of the Millennium. Sarah and I enjoyed the occasion as guests of the Moises at the splendid Las Campanas Country Club in Santa Fe with fireworks visible at towns across the horizon. The occasion prompted the following reflection:

The Millennium

Most of what we hear about this remarkable milestone seems to be in the nature of commercial messages ("We want to be your dry cleaners for the new Millennium!") or about the Y2K problems caused by lack of foresight of computer software creators. When the significance of the calendar event arises, most discussion centers on the turning of the century. A century turn is itself a very significant event. Fewer than one person in a thousand of us will ever experience more than one. But a Millennium is more, much more.

A Millennium is an event of such significance it strains our ability to grasp it. Probably none of us can trace our relatives back as far as 1000 A.D. Few of us have a manmade object in our possession that is a thousand years old. If we did have a letter from that era, we would have great difficulty deciphering it. Among Western languages, only Icelandic remains largely unchanged.

What was life like for our ancestors forty generations ago? Providing for the necessities of life occupied nearly every waking hour. The movement of the sun regulated their day. Entertainment, like almost everything else, was homemade. Except for a few merchants, seafarers and soldiers, people lived their entire lives near their home villages. Feudal lords dominated society, and upward mobility was almost unknown.

If we were suddenly transported back to those times, we would probably miss most the sense of control over our lives. Plague and famine were common, and a family was indeed fortunate if all children survived into adulthood. Average life expectancy was barely 30 years. Learning and scholarship were confined largely to the church, and luxuries were the stuff of rulers only. There had been very little improvement in the quality of life since Biblical times.

At 1000 A.D. a number of non-European cultures were flourishing. The Anasazi culture was at its peak, as were some Asian, African, and South American societies. The Moors spread learning and culture across the Mediterranean crescent.

While we may think of those times in Europe as the "Dark Ages," it is unlikely that they did. With dangers abounding and little mobility, strong bonds of family and community were forged. Folks knew each other so well that surnames were uncommon. Limited opportunities and limited expectations can limit anxieties, too. Our forebearers' lives ebbed and flowed in harmony with nature. Today we go to great lengths to find vacation spots as quiet as their daily life must have been. Medieval beliefs were shared widely, and religious faith was strong. Dozens of saints' days enlivened their calendar, each providing lessons and occasions for reflection. Valentine's Day is one of the few survivors to modern times.

So, as we celebrate the second Millennium with pyrotechnics, televised laser shows, and imported champagne, let us think also about our ancestors who celebrated the first one with songs, dances and mead by torchlight. We owe a great debt of thanks to those hardy, resourceful, brave souls who persevered and kept the faith that better times would greet the next Millennium.

D. M Brown
12-13-99

Corruption[*]

> "I have my principles. And if you don't like them,
> --- I have others"
> Groucho Marx

I'd done several corporate turnarounds, but nothing to prepare me for this experience. After launching Tuition Plan's Independent 529 Plan, I was ready for retirement. Sarah had sold her business, and we were planning an eight-month sabbatical in Manhattan. Then Bill Richardson's advisor, Paul Bardacke called, asking me to meet with the Governor. The New Mexico State Treasurer's Office had just erupted in scandal. Four former employees would eventually be indicted for various crimes ranging from extortion to conspiracy. The two previous State Treasurers were both destined to spend time in a "gated community" run by the Feds. Would I please be willing to fix it? Partly out of a sense of duty, and partly for the intrigue of the challenge, I agreed to do it.

My epiphany that this job would be different came early. After being sworn in to duty, Chief Justice Dick Bosson and I signed the oath of office. A notary acknowledged the document and then turned to me and said, "That will be $3." Clearly, I wasn't in the corporate world anymore.

Fact finding was made easy thanks to a thorough investigation by Deloitte & Touche begun months before. The facts they found were anything but easy. The state's checkbook was out of balance by $160 million, and unreconciled items stretched back over five years. The officer in charge of the banking department had no banking experience. His previous job was as a baggage handler for America

---

[*]   A variation of this chapter was published in *Stanford Business*, August, 2008.

West. Only one of my staff of 42 had any previous investment industry experience, and we were running a $5 billion portfolio. There were few controls, little disclosure, and no effective oversight. Investment guidelines, purchasing policies, and personnel policies were routinely ignored. All efforts had been directed to overpaying on commissions and purchases to generate the wherewithal for "campaign contributions." The agency's outside auditor was a small firm from the southern part of the state and had for years given the Treasurer's Office clean opinions with no material weaknesses. That relationship was so cozy that other CPA firms had stopped bothering to bid. I came to appreciate Warren Buffett's observation that there is seldom just one cockroach in the kitchen.

Now for the scary part. Document shredders had been working overtime. The alarm contacts on doors and windows had been super-glued together to enable after-hours entry. Video cameras had been redirected and videotapes erased. Staff members who were reluctant to go along with these schemes had their personnel evaluations downgraded retroactively. One had her car vandalized. Alerted to this pattern of criminality, I had a detective agency check the premises for telephone bugs. They found five, including one on my phone.

The most chilling moment came after I immediately had the alarm system repaired. The very next morning, an early-arriving employee went to her desk and then realized she had forgotten to turn off the alarm. Her panic turned to puzzlement when there was no police response. The alarm was not working. Later that day, the alarm company revisited and informed us that someone had tampered with the system that very night by inserting a sophisticated lens to divert the electric beam.

From the Deloitte findings and my extensive interviews with staff members, it became clear that all roads led to a cohort of nine staff members. Several of them were related to the former State Treasurer. Fortunately, all but two of them were patronage appointments who could be summarily replaced.

At the staff meeting I assembled to announce the departures, I had expected some regrets – after all, there are always lunch groups, car pools, friendships. Instead, the news was greeted with a standing ovation. Clearly, I had gotten it right, and clearly the remaining staff was with the new program. There were two other surprises. An agency veteran said that this was the first staff meeting that the agency had held during her ten-year career there. The other surprise was that there was no extra burden of work despite a reduction of over 20% of the workforce. That rogue group had been doing nothing but making mischief.

Progress came swiftly, in large measure due to several key executives from other state agencies who were willing to join the team, and in no small part due to a dedicated existing staff. I will forever be grateful for the contributions and leadership provided by Scott Stovall, Mark Valdes, Joelle Mevi, Mark Canavan, Janie Tabor, Jodi Porter, Laura Montoya and Judy Espinosa. Help from other government agencies was indispensable, notably from David Abbey, Amy Chavez, Jan Goodwin, Olivia Padilla-Jackson, Roy Soto, Stephanie Schardin, and Hilary Tompkins. For the first time, we included professionals from the securities industry on our investment committee. I am grateful for the invaluable guidance provided by Steve Bohlin from Thornburg and Paul Cassidy from RBC Dain Rauscher.

Accounts were balanced; all transactions were posted on the web site; oversight was created; electronic trading platforms eliminated commissions; four investment specialists were hired; 300 revisions were made to the investment policy; personnel, purchasing, and security policies were created; and the head count was reduced by 20%. The payoff was earning an AAA rating from Standard and Poor's for our principal fund, a first for the State of New Mexico. The fund's yield climbed from 46th among the states to 7th. We got a clean audit that meant something. I am pleased that my elected successor, James Lewis, is committed to integrity and to building on the foundation that our team built.

As I exited in favor of James, I did so with several regrets:

1. Try as we did with counseling resources and morale-boosting events, there remained significant trauma from the abuses of the previous administration.

2. Several of the employees I fired were quickly rehired by other state agencies. One had previously been fired by two state agencies before landing at my agency, and subsequent to my firing her, she was hired and than fired for the fourth time before again being re-hired by yet another state agency. Continuing on this trajectory may rate her mention in the *Guinness Book of Records*.

3. Despite strong advocacy by Bill Richardson, to date there has been little appetite for ethics reform at the New Mexico State Legislature. Proposals by the Ethics Reform Task Force appointed by the Governor (on which I serve) were largely ignored. Campaign contribution laws are very weak and loosely enforced. There remain no limits on the size of contributions for state office, even on cash contributions. We will continue to plug away to work with the Governor on getting reforms enacted.

A few observations about corruption. I have come to regard it as a fairly natural state of affairs. While some people have a moral compass that will lead them to do the right things when no one is looking, many don't. If there is a group that is in a position of power, who have been in place long enough to set up mechanisms to exercise that power, and if there is inadequate oversight and a lack of checks and balances, stir well and you will have corruption. I would venture to say that this vulnerability can be anticipated in any type of organization, corporate as well as government.

Then there's what I call the "Myth of the Lovable Rogue," the public official who may be on the take, but the city or whatever runs like a top anyway. Don't believe it. In my experience, a truly corrupt outfit diverts, distracts, and demoralizes. When the wrong things are being done, the right things don't get done.

Taken to a larger context, corruption is a significant impediment to economic and social progress throughout the Developing Nations. If a society mistrusts its institutions and cannot rely on the protection of laws, it will not attract the capital resources or the human resources to be competitive on the world stage. Thomas Friedman coined a very apt term for such nations - "kleptocracies".

The Press

You now know more about the turnaround at Treasury than most New Mexicans. The local papers and other media which had for months reported daily on the scandal, voting it "the news story of the year" in New Mexico, showed no interest in carrying the story of our turnaround. We thought it would be in the public interest, but apparently they were stuck on the "if it bleeds, it leads" mentality.

Actually, I was not entirely surprised by this lack of coverage of good news. A few months before, the national state treasurers group and I finally won a long-fought battle to get permanent favorable tax treatment for Section 529 college savings accounts. Beverlee McClure, the New Mexico Higher Education Secretary, and I held a widely advertised press conference at the University. Not one reporter bothered to appear. Perhaps we would have had better attendance if we had reported in urgent tones that "a 529 was in progress at the University."

The press is addicted to alarmist stories. The flames of alarm are further fanned by parties who stand to gain from the issue of concern – businesses trying to profit, universities seeking research dollars, and politicians seeking problems to address. Y2K was a classic non-event. So much time and capital resources were siphoned off to deal with this largely phantom problem that capital spending on productive projects sagged nationally for a year or two. This folly came home to me when all the employees in our building were required to replace their garage access cards with ones that were "Y2K compliant." And all these cards did was make the gate go up and down!

There is one area of media coverage that should be reformed, weblogs sponsored by newspapers. If someone wants to spew trash by posting anonymous inflammatory or false entries on a self-sponsored "blog," I support their right to do so. But if a newspaper will not publish a letter to the editor or an op-ed piece without attribution, why should they be able to sponsor a blog that does so? All during my time as Treasurer, a blog sponsored by the *Santa Fe New Mexican* published untrue, vile, and salacious items about our staff members – entries allegedly posted under pseudonyms by the group fired for misconduct.

New York

For several years, Sarah had been promoting a "sabbatical" in New York while both boys were still in Manhattan. She could go to culinary school while I finally got around to writing these family memoirs. At last, in March, 2007, a window opened upon eight of the most enjoyable months of our lives.

The best part of this adventure was the opportunity to reconnect so actively with our sons and daughter-in-law as young adults. Elliott, Deb and Joe were great navigators, guides, and sherpas. They found us lodging, restaurants and entertainment and were just great company.

Sarah enrolled in the Pastry Arts program at the Institute of Culinary Education, where she graduated with "high honors." The program was very challenging, but she produced an endless array of sumptuous treats. My challenge was trying to offset the tastings with two-hour workouts at the Chelsea Piers Gym. Her classwork was followed by a two-month internship at Del Posto, Mario Batali's and Lydia Bastianich's celebrated restaurant, where she trained under award-winning chef, Nicole Kaplan.

Just as most clichés are true, New York is brash, busy, and rushed. And noisy. Outside our window was endless noise from traffic and construction. It truly is a 24-hour city where one can get almost anything delivered at any time. It is dense and intense and sometimes rude. Not all people are rude, but where else would one encounter a response such as I received at a New York doctor's office? The doctor asked me to fax a form to my doctor in Albuquerque. I completed the form and then turned to the receptionist to ask if she would please fax it for me. She replied, "That's not on my agenda." I then gathered myself and asked politely what was on her agenda, and if service to her patients was not on today's agenda, might it be there tomorrow so I could return then? To the amusement of others in the waiting room, she then snatched my form and faxed it for me.

Greetings of "Hello" and "Good morning" are rare. If a passerby nods, it is probably in response to the rhythm on an iPod, not you. One reason for this attitude may simply be that one encounters so many people on the street that greetings would be constant. I am reminded of the practice in the halls of the Pentagon where one encounters so many officers of rank that all saluting is suspended.

Perhaps the New York attitude was best exemplified by a taxi driver taking me to the airport. As we drove north on Roosevelt Parkway, we could see miles of cars backed up on the lanes coming south. When I asked the driver if it was his practice to alert the taxi dispatcher to direct colleagues away from traffic congestion, he said "Are you kidding? I hope all our other cabs get caught up in that mess, so I can get more fares." It reminded me of the time when Tiger Woods was a rookie. Upon returning to the locker room, he confided to another pro that he was embarrassed to have taken an 8 on a hole. The veteran pro responded, "Son, the rest of the guys were elated, only we wish you'd taken a 9."

The edgy, scrappy New York attitude appears everywhere. The scales in the deli start at minus an ounce or two with a sign above reading, "The weight of your take-out container has already been deducted from your purchase." One can infer that constant complaints against being charged for the featherweight containers led to this practice. A telling event occurred to us shortly after our arrival that underscored the universality of the New York attitude. After taking our order, the server asked, "You're not from here, are you?" We admitted we weren't and asked what led her to believe so. She said, "Because you're nice." At the end of the meal, she brought us a free drink.

Actually, I had a foretaste of the New York attitude some years earlier when a very bright (and very civil) young man joined our team at Wells Fargo. He was Frank Newman who had come from an elite group of Citibankers headed by John Reed, who eventually became Citi's CEO. Our boss brought Frank by for me to brief him on our unit's activities. After a thorough briefing, Frank thanked me and left. Then a few moments later, he popped back in the door and asked, "Why were you willing to tell me all that?" Puzzled, I responded that I thought that was what my boss requested and that it would help Frank acclimate. Frank again expressed his gratitude, but then said that such candor and sharing never happened at Citi, where "we competed as hard against rivals across the hall as we did with Chase across the street."

There is probably lots of learned research as to the source of the New York attitude. Being crowded and rushed surely plays a part, and negative attitudes can be contagious. I also wonder if both the disparity and the abundance of wealth are factors. In Jane Goodall's experiments with chimps, she found that when the banana supply was insufficient, fighting broke out. When there became enough bananas to go around, peace ensued. She then introduced a considerable surplus of bananas, which stimulated the most fighting of all, as the stronger chimps engaged in hoarding behavior.

In fairness, one seldom encounters greetings from strangers in other bustling urban centers, such as Boston or San Francisco. Also, my reflections should be considered in the context of one who is from New Mexico, a place of compulsive friendliness, where some folks even wave at strangers in passing cars.

Our stay in New York was brightened by the friendship shown by Don and Ilona Quest, Mary Carroll Scott, Laurie Sanderson and Sarah's incomparable pastry buddies, Aimee Graham and Melissa Gorris and their warm circle of friends. Visits from my daughter Becky, the Brodys, Diane Callahan and Dawn Friend, Gills, Hankinsons, Josses, Moises, Terri Salazar, Richard and Laurie Shelton, Randy and Nathan Talbot, the Tolber/Campbell family, and the VanDevenders gave us welcome opportunities to go out on the town. Delightful side trips took us up the Hudson River Valley, to the Berkshires, all up the New England coast and to Nantucket. We enjoyed wonderful hospitality from Hank Smeal and Aimee, the Reidys and the Albuquerque "ex-pats," Tom and Cindy Bonafair and Ian and Sonnet McKinnon, plus Barbara Goodbody.

New York truly has become a great deal safer – kudos to Giuliani. When I was in the Army in the late 1950's, we occasionally spent weekends in Manhattan at the apartment of a buddy's family. One morning I decided to jog up the length of Central Park West. At about 95th Street, I was hailed by two policemen who asked where I was going. They then said, "Well, son, you should know that above 95th, we go in pairs – with a dog, but you can proceed up there in your short pants if you wish." A round-trip suddenly seemed like a good idea.

For all its convenience, there are gaps and anomalies in Manhattan. The Kinko's service that is 24 hours in Albuquerque is closed for the evening in New York. Cell telephone service is spotty due to the shielding of tall buildings. There are no neighborhood urgent care centers. Garbage is picked up daily from bags delivered to the curb. That's the good news. The rest of the news is that there are always garbage bags lining the sidewalk.

In Manhattan, everything seems to be in miniature. Apartments average less than 700 square feet, so there is very little room for anything. Consequently, local grocers sell small sizes of everything. As there are few supermarkets, one visits several small stores almost daily to keep stocked on life's essentials. Instead of walk-in closets, here you have "shove-in" closets. As with any new environment, there were intriguing cultural and linguistic discoveries, such as "stoop sales" and "Juliet balconies."

Jaywalking is constant in New York. Actually, our Joe maintains that jaywalking is safer than crossing in the crosswalk. His reasoning is that jaywalkers are more attentive to oncoming traffic than cross walkers who may take for granted that cars will stop at the red light. Also, crossing in mid-block avoids cars turning left and right. Perhaps the greatest pedestrian hazard is the one-way street frequented by two-way cyclists, hurtling by at top speed. Speaking of traffic patterns, I am reminded of Woody Allen's comment that the only cultural contribution of California was to permit right turns on red. I now understand why right turns on red are not permitted in New York. It is because in so doing, one might mow down scores of pedestrians, anytime day or night.

I experienced first-hand being mown down by a taxi – while in a crosswalk, walking with the green light in broad daylight. It was probably fortunate that the car struck me from slightly behind, as I had no opportunity to brace myself. Like someone who is drunk, I was relaxed upon impact, and while airborne was able to turn to land fully on my side. A few scrapes and bruises were accepted as a very lucky outcome.

Native New Yorkers for the most part seem to take all this in stride. One can adjust to a different social dynamic. When Sarah was involved in the San Francisco Chinatown project, we would attend some unbelievably crowded street fairs. As I kept bumping into people and muttering "excuse me's," I noticed that the Chinese throng just accepted mild bumping. It was like a giant arena of little bumper cars gently careening off each other. It took me a while to reach a new comfort zone, but I eventually was able to join in the practice.

Then there are the dogs. Nearly everyone in lower Manhattan has a dog, generally a small one. I'm not sure whether it is for companionship or for protection or because they can't afford to have children. Evidence of dogs is everywhere, especially on the sidewalks. I'm told that the architecture in our neighborhood is magnificent, but I didn't dare look up.

Shortly after our Joseph came to New York, he got a lesson in New York street smarts. He and a roommate were moving, and not wanting to take their ratty sofa, they left it on the sidewalk. When no one took it after several days, the landlord complained. Upon learning that the boys were trying to get someone to take it, the landlord said, "Boys, here's how to do it." He posted a sign reading: "For Sale, $45." Within hours the sofa was gone.

9/11 still hangs in the air. Nearly everyone who was here then knows someone who was directly affected. New York still swaggers, but with a bit of wariness in its step.

Yet all the challenges were worth it – to be a part of the vibrant throbbing scene and to have languished a while in this cradle of creativity. When we surveyed *New York Magazine* for events and activities we might enjoy, our heads ached from the array of choices. The food was superb. Within three blocks of our apartment were more excellent restaurants than can be found in most entire American cities. Like most lower Manhattan apartments, our unit was barely 600 square feet, but we found it cozy. Instead of thinking of it as a tiny apartment, it helped to think of it as a spacious hotel suite. Or as Sarah put it, "married student housing." Our "dining room" was the superb Cookshop Restaurant right downstairs, where Manager Todd McMullen and Debra Foley always made us feel welcome, and a world-class hairdresser, Brian Meehan, often brightened Sarah's day.

The weather in New York? At times it is cold and blustery and for long spells, it's hot and steamy. But it is such a great walking city that one can largely ignore the discomfort of the weather. Each block seems to have its own character, and the neighborhoods are distinctive. The parks are beautifully maintained, and daily walks down the Hudson River Parkway are to be remembered. History reaches out to grab you. A plaque by the Trinity Church announces that George Washington was inaugurated here. Right here! Perhaps our friend Kathy Reidy expressed it best when she observed that, "After one gets to know New York, all other American cities are just towns."

Corporate Board Service

I have found corporate board service to be a very satisfying late career activity. At this point I believe I have a fair amount of knowledge, experience, and perspective to lend. After eight years of service on the Servo Products Board, over the years at various times I have served on twelve other corporate boards including the mortgage banking, insurance agency, commercial banking (5), Internet, and utility fields. In serving on the boards of community foundations, private foundations, universities, state investment organizations, and public pension funds, I have been involved in managing investments in excess of $60 billion.

Service on the Board of California Water Service has been an especially rewarding experience. I have long admired fellow director Linda Meier in connection with her Stanford leadership, and I have come to admire the other members equally. CEO Pete Nelson is a very competent, diligent, effective executive and teams perfectly with Chairman Bob Foy, who has great judgment and a very high order of decency. I was honored to be named as lead director of this New York Stock Exchange company. I look forward to adding a few more directorships to my schedule.

Board service in the public arena is an entirely different manner. While ISS corporate governance guidelines sensibly limit outside directors to five boards, public officials are eager to pad their resumes with an indigestible number of board positions. Most major government agencies have associated boards or commissions. By statute the State Treasurer is a member of ten public boards. All meet monthly with reams of preparation material. Most have two-day retreats added to the schedule. This system was designed to maximize exposure for elected officials whose careers depend upon visibility, while their deputies really run the show back home. A few elected officials, such as Lt. Governor Diane Denish, have the competence to handle it well, but neglect of important initiatives is a common by-product of this system. That these boards are able to function is due in large part to excellent contributions from volunteer directors such as Lou Hoffman, Ike Kalangis, Bruce Malott, Maria Griego-Raby, Roberta Ramo, and Kim Sanchez-Rael.

Dribs And Drabs

There is a common human tendency to overcompensate. I was reminded of this behavior while on a bumpy flight. As the turbulence increased, I lifted my coffee cup off the tray table and tried to offset the motion of the plane. Just then, a flight attendant came by and asked if I would please put it down and just cover it with the napkin. She said "Invariably, you will zig when the plane zags, and I will have to clean it up." I wonder whether that pattern isn't true of a lot of the activities we engage in to little avail. Changing lanes on the freeway and trading stocks may be two examples.

A top executive at Wells Fargo, Ward Krebs, told an illuminating story about stress on the job. Ward commuted daily to the city by train. As the train proceeded toward San Francisco, a train worker named Howard would come through the cars periodically, collecting items left in the racks above the seats and then taking them to the Lost and Found Dept. at the San Francisco station. That was the extent of his job responsibilities. One day Ward spotted Howard and realized that he hadn't seen Howard for a month or two. Howard explained that he had been off for a couple of months due to a heart attack. "Too much job stress," Howard said. The incident reinforced Ward's belief that stress is a condition one brings to the job as much as it is a condition of the job.

I believe it was Mark Twain who observed that "Forecasting is difficult to do, especially with respect to the future." My favorite futuristic comment came from a sign I noted in a customer's office, "There is an alarming rate of increase in things I know nothing about."

I have had invaluable help from mentors at every turn in my life – teachers, coaches, Dick Rosenberg, Ernie Arbuckle, Bill Barkan and other bosses, Don Kennedy at Stanford, and always, my father. In the New Mexico community, Jack Rust, Bob Stamm and Bob Taichert have paved the way for me. At Bohemia, Marty Anderson fulfills this role. In turn, I hope to have been helpful to some rising stars such as Sean Clifford, Joaquin Garofolo, Gary Gordon, Tom Growney, Bill Halter, Fred Nathan, Rosalyn Nguyen, Ryan Scott, David Smidt, Sam Stark, and Deke Willard. It will be a joy to follow their journeys through life.

Not only is it enjoyable to witness the flourishing lives of the next generation, it helps one maintain a positive attitude as one grows older. Often, elderly people sink further into depression with the loss of each lifelong friend. Brick and Ruth Elliott cultivated a coterie of young friends who spanned several generations. Restocking one's treasury of friendships can provide a welcome lifting of one's spirits.

Some people quest for fame. I've enjoyed a little time in the spotlight and have relished its glow, but I quickly return to a conclusion I reached sometime ago – of a definition of fame as "being well-regarded by a great many people who don't know you very well." The only opinions that truly matter are from those persons who do know you well.

The transitory nature of fame and glory became jarringly apparent upon leaving Crocker Bank for Albuquerque. At Crocker, I could survey my kingdom from the top floor of a 54-story building. My palatial office was over 800 square feet and had a full private bath. Upon phoning back on some matter just two weeks after leaving for New Mexico and announcing my name to the new receptionist, I was greeted with a languid "who?"

Perhaps my favorite incident of this type was told by Dick Rosenberg. His storied banking career was crowned by a highly successful reign as CEO of Bank of America. About two years into retirement, he was wandering through a grocery store when another shopper approached him and asked, "Didn't you used to be Dick Rosenberg?"

Epilogue

As you may have noted, I have left out stories of the kids as adults. They can write their own stories better than I could hope to do. All have developed good, productive lives. Becky, after an early career at Macy's, became manager of a home for disabled and retarded adults for ten years. She then decided to return to college for her certification as a medical assistant (and was on the Dean's List). Becky lives in a lovely condo she bought in San Mateo. Kenny has moved to a house on Orcas Island in the San Juans where his mother and stepfather have retired. He has grown into a loving and productive adult. Elliott got a law degree from USF and was admitted to the California Bar, but wasn't excited about the practice of law and was excited about writing fiction. He just graduated (4.0 GPA) from NYU with an MFA in creative writing, and he and Deb have returned to San Francisco. They both have good jobs in Internet companies, and they just bought a home in the Noe Valley area of the city. Deborah is such a welcome addition to our lives – lovely, bright, capable (Stanford Phi Beta Kappa) – and a rabid Stanford basketball fan to boot. We are so proud of Joseph. He graduated from NYU with an excellent record and then signed on with the College Board where he has been for five years and served on their editorial staff. With a steady girlfriend, a co-op apartment purchase, and the required French bulldog, Joe became the complete New Yorker. We are pleased with the news just received that Joe has been accepted into Stanford's MBA program and will be attending in the fall.

Upon our return to New Mexico, Sarah is employing her bakery skills, and I will work on my retirement skills. After 45 years without missing a paycheck, this transition will take a while to smooth out.

I do not envision a life of leisure, but I do relish seldom needing an alarm clock and the luxury of scheduling drive time away from rush hour traffic. I hope not to sink into the torpor that a friend in Hillsborough seems to enjoy. He claims that he knows it's Sunday when the paper is thicker. For me, several corporate boards, plus some non-profit boards should allow time for a reasonable amount of golf, entertainment and travel, as well as seeing through the potential of SeniorDiscounts and "Chilly Chips," a promising new food product idea. However, I am still open to periodic work assignments if interesting and hitched to worthwhile endeavors.

One Thousand Places to See Before you Die. One of my kids bought me this book. I know it was intended to be uplifting, to give me a "bucket list" of fascinating experiences to anticipate and to savor. Visit the Pyramids! But it had the opposite effect on me. I felt being directed on a mission to use up life's best experiences, and that doing each one would bring me closer to the end.

In fact, I have been a little reluctant to complete this book as I anticipate that exciting new chapters lie ahead. I have resolved to pursue only one goal before I die: To keep adding to my list of things I'd like to do and places I'd like to see and people I'd like to meet.